Reconsidering
Difference

Reconsidering Difference

Nancy, Derrida,
Levinas, and Deleuze

Todd May

The Pennsylvania State University Press
University Park, Pennsylvania

Library of Congress Cataloging-in-Publication Data

May, Todd, 1955–
    Reconsidering difference : Nancy, Derrida, Levinas, and Deleuze /
by Todd May.

        p.   cm.
    Includes bibliographical references and index.
    ISBN 0-271-01657-4 (cloth : alk. paper)
    ISBN 0-271-01658-2 (paper : alk. paper)
    1. Difference (Philosophy)—History—20th century.   2. Nancy, Jean-
Luc.   3. Derrida, Jacques.   4. Lévinas, Emmanuel.   5. Deleuze,
Gilles.   I. Title.
    B105.D5M38   1997
    194—dc20   96-42210
                                                                    CIP

Copyright © 1997 The Pennsylvania State University
All rights reserved
Printed in the United States of America
Published by The Pennsylvania State University Press,
University Park, PA 16802-1003

It is the policy of The Pennsylvania State University Press to use acid-free paper
for the first printing of all clothbound books. Publications on uncoated stock
satisfy the minimum requirements of American National Standard for Information
Sciences—Permanence of Paper for Printed Library Materials, ANSI Z39.48-1992.

*For Kathleen, David,
Rachel, and Joel*

Contents

Preface

In my first three books with Penn State Press, I tried to develop a philosophical perspective that arose from within the broad parameters of French poststructuralism. Readers of those books are aware that I also appealed to recent Anglo-American philosophy in answering some of the questions that arose. The current work is more critical. It addresses what I see as a number of wrong turns taken in some dominant strains of French philosophy. As I try to make clear, I am sympathetic with the aims of those I criticize, just not with their chosen paths.

Several people were instrumental in reading and commenting on earlier drafts of this work. Patrick Hayden read the first, third, and fourth chapters; Mark Webb, the third chapter; and Dorothea Olkowski, the fourth chapter. All offered helpful comments. Constantin Boundas read the entire manuscript and, as always, made incisive comments that made me rethink several formulations. An anonymous reader for Penn State Press offered detailed commentary and suggested several important revisions. Keith Monley's copyediting forced an additional level of precision upon the work.

A portion of the chapter on Derrida appeared initially in an article co-authored with Mark Lance, with whom I have had ongoing discussions over the years regarding many of the issues that appear here.

Regarding Penn State Press, I am beginning to run out of words. I know of nobody in the philosophical profession who can boast of a more cooperative and engaged publishing house than the one I have had the good fortune to be associated with over the past five years.

At several points in this work I have incorporated revisions of previously published articles. Thus, grateful acknowledgment is due to the following:

Kluwer Academic Publishers, for permission to reprint parts of "Gilles De-
leuze and the Politics of Time," *Man and World* 29, no. 3 (1996): 293–304;
Penn State Press, for permission to reprint parts of "The Limits of the Men-
tal and the Limits of Philosophy: From Burge to Foucault and Beyond,"
Journal of Speculative Philosophy 9, no. 1 (1995): 36–47; Philosophical
Forum, for permission to reprint parts of "Two Dogmas of Post-Empiricism:
Anti-Theoretical Strains in Derrida and Rorty" (coauthored with Mark
Lance), *Philosophical Forum* 25, no. 4 (1994): 273–309; and Routledge,
for permission to reprint parts of "Difference and Unity in Gilles Deleuze,"
in *Gilles Deleuze and the Theater of Philosophy,* ed. Constantin V. Boundas
and Dorothea Olkowski (New York, 1994).

Finally, I am grateful to the Lemon Fund for a Lemon Summer Stipend
during the summer of 1996.

Introduction

The philosophical problems that occupy a generation are often difficult to discern until that occupation is well under way. Philosophers, like most folks, work primarily from within their milieu rather than upon it. A problem here, an inconsistency there, a perspective on a particular issue to be worked out: this is the stuff of the daily life of most philosophers. If there is a theme or an overarching problem upon which many philosophical works converge, the recognition of this theme or problem rarely arises until much of the work is already under way. A pattern emerges from the individual threads. It is a pattern that might not have been guessed beforehand, but now makes sense. Moreover, what that pattern is might be reinterpreted by later generations.

A pattern has emerged in the French philosophy of this generation, of the generation running roughly from the mid to late sixties up to the present. It is the generation associated with the terms "poststructuralism" and "postmodernism" and the names Gilles Deleuze, Jacques Derrida, Michel Foucault, Luce Irigary, Julia Kristeva, Emmanuel Levinas, Jean-François Lyotard, and, more recently, Phillipe Lacoue-Labarthe, Michelle LeDoeuff, and Jean-Luc Nancy. The pattern concerns difference and its valorization. It has become clear that the articulation of an adequate concept of difference, and as well a proper sense of how to valorize it, is the overriding problem that occupies recent French thought. To cast the issue in terms common to many Continentalists, the problem is how to avoid reducing difference to the logic of the same.

Although the problem is singular, its manifestations in various writings are diverse. Difference has been thought to be a constitutive factor in community, in language, in ethics, and in ontology. It is part, at least, of the sharing of others, the *differance* of meaning, the obsession with the other, or the singularities that subtend the phenomenal world. Corresponding to each manifestation is a unique conception of difference, and corresponding to each a unique way of valorizing it. The philosophers discussed in this book can be seen to disagree as often as, and perhaps more often than, they agree. What binds them first of all is not a convergence upon a single viewpoint, but rather a convergence upon a single problem. The problem is that of how to conceive difference and how to valorize it.

In addition to this convergence, there is a second one. The second convergence operates at a deeper level than the first one, and binds the thinkers I discuss here more tightly to one another than their convergence on a problem. This second convergence also distinguishes the thinkers that are my concern—Nancy, Derrida, Levinas, and Deleuze—from other thinkers who want to privilege difference, both within and apart from the French tradition. The philosophical operation common to the four thinkers I treat here concerns a privileging of difference as a constitutive element in some part of our experience. This privileging is not necessarily a privileging of difference over identity—for Nancy and Derrida it is not, while for Deleuze (and perhaps Levinas) it is—but a view that difference plays a more fundamental constitutive role than has previously been recognized in the history of philosophy. Moreover, with three of the thinkers discussed—Nancy, Levinas, and Deleuze—it is on the basis of the constitutive privileging of difference that the valorization of difference occurs. (The argument can be made that Derrida also proceeds this way, although I only consider Derrida's valorization of difference briefly, spending more time on his analysis of it as constitutive.)

Not all French thinkers in recent memory have privileged difference in this way. Michel Foucault did not, and even Deleuze is ambivalent about it. Although the protection and perhaps even valorization of alternative practices and ways of being may be an essential part of any decent philosophical outlook, there is no need for that protection or valorization to proceed by way of privileging difference as a constitutive part of some aspect or aspects of our experience. Whether some forms of difference ought to be privileged is separate from the issue of their constitutivity. I return to this point below, and in the chapters that follow.

For philosophers outside the French tradition, there may be some puzzlement as to why one should be so concerned about difference. Let me indicate first why there has been such concern, and then say a bit about why there should be.

There are a couple of important reasons the philosophers I discuss have sought to privilege difference. One reason is that they link the marginalization or neglect of difference with philosophical foundationalism. By "foundationalism" I mean the project of giving an account (of some object of study) that is exhaustive and indubitable. An exhaustive account is one that says all that needs to be said on the issue. There may be more details to add, but the essence of the matter is captured. An indubitable account is one that cannot be surpassed; it is the final say on the matter. There are, of course, many different ways in which an account may be said to be indubitable. It may be said, for instance, that all competing accounts would necessarily run into self-contradiction. This is a strong form of indubitability. Alternatively, it may be said that this account is founded on a bedrock of truisms and with derived inferences so solid that it is inconceivable that a better account could arise. This, I think, is a more standard type of foundationalism, one that we might associate with the work of Descartes or Husserl.[1]

The worry that occupies the thinkers of difference I am concerned with is that by putting difference to the side, the philosophical tradition, inasmuch as it has also been a foundationalist tradition, has allowed itself to function under the illusion that the world and our experience of it can be brought under absolute or indubitable conceptual categories, categories that do not allow for conceptual slippage. Exposure of the connections these philosophers draw between the marginalization of difference and foundationalism will have to await the consideration of specific treatments. Suffice it to say, for the moment, that foundationalism has been one of their targets.

This first reason is connected to a second one, which looms large across the landscape of contemporary French thought. Thought, for these philoso-

---

1. This way of defining foundationalism shows it to have much in common with the epistemic foundationalism of twentieth-century Anglo-American philosophy. For Continentalists, the idea of foundationalism tends to cover a bit more ground—not only epistemology, but areas such as ethics and views of language. The basic idea is the same, however. (And even in Anglo-American philosophy, there are foundationalists outside the realm of epistemology, for instance, thinkers like Alan Gewirth or Stephen Darwall, who attempt to found ethical thought on an indubitable and exhaustive basis.)

Totalitarianism

phers, is perpetually haunted by the specter of what we might call (and what Nancy and Levinas have called) "totalitarianism." Although I discuss the idea of totalitarianism more in the next chapter, I can offer a few orienting remarks right off. In thinking about the totalitarianism these thinkers seek to combat, we should not rely too heavily on intuitions about repressive political regimes. Although there is a relationship to such regimes, the totalitarianism they conceive is of much wider scope and is more deeply rooted in our own conceptual approach to the world. We might think of totalitarianism at a first go as the project of constraining people's lives and identities within narrowly defined parameters. We will see that for many of the thinkers discussed here, that project is inseparable from the attempt to capture all of reality within a narrow conceptual framework. The idea here is that the scope of different possible lives and identities is often unacceptably narrowed by the pretension of specific conceptual approaches or philosophical viewpoints to give exhaustive accounts of the phenomena in their domains.

Totalitarianism, on this view, is related to foundationalism, the philosophical project of giving an absolute or unsurpassable account of whatever the philosophical phenomena at issue are. The thinkers I discuss in the following chapters are often at pains to show how their approaches avoid foundationalism. But the deep problem with totalitarianism is not merely that it is false; it is also insidious. It is not merely mistaken to be totalitarian in one's conceptual approach to the world; it is also evil. And the reason it *Evil* is evil is that it marginalizes or eliminates that which is different. Thinking of community in terms of a common substance that we all must participate in marginalizes those who are different from the participants in that common substance; thinking of language in terms of presence masks the difference that subtends it; thinking of ethics in terms of the likenesses or analogies of others to oneself refuses the insight that what is ethically relevant is often the difference of others from oneself; thinking of ontology in terms of identity precludes consideration of ontological possibilities that are irreducible to any identity. In all these cases, the different—although in each case it is a different "different"—is lost, distorted, repressed, or reduced. Each thinker we consider attempts to recover this difference and thus to avoid the totalitarianism that has characterized the philosophical tradition.

Although this way of thinking of totalitarianism is more conceptual than political, its links with political totalitarianism are not far to seek. Both Nazism in Germany and fascism in Italy, for instance, proclaimed the superiority of their respective peoples and attempted to marginalize or eliminate those who were different. In Nazism, particularly, the project of elimination took on gruesome proportions. This rejection of the different occurred in the name of an identity, a sameness, that was said to exhaust what was worth preserving, relegating everything that did not conform to the camps. Thus, according to these thinkers, the philosophical project of foundationalism and the political project of totalitarianism are not so far apart. It is not that foundationalism leads to political totalitarianism; rather, they drink from the same well.

One might ask here, why the concern with totalitarianism? Why the need to save the different? One answer—and certainly an adequate one—would be that if that which is different is being unfairly marginalized, efforts need to be expended to rectify that unfairness. This is a justification that lies behind much of the discussion of difference in recent French thought. In addition to *justification*, one can point to two particular events that go some distance toward an *explanation* of why this particular concern has preoccupied French philosophers in this particular historical period. Let me take a quick moment to flag these events. Since the bulk of this book is philosophical, rather than historical, in nature, it will not hurt to have in mind the context within which the approaches treated here have taken place.

The first and most obvious factor is Europe's recent history of fascism. No European philosopher has been untouched by this history, and those in Germany and France have felt its horrors particularly keenly. In particular, philosophy in the wake of the holocaust has felt the need to grapple with the questions of how such a thing could come about and what can be done to ensure that it does not come about again. Not only the thinkers I treat here, but others, most notably the Critical Theorists from Germany, have considered themselves duty-bound to understand the holocaust and to prepare thought against its return. Had not the other explanation I discuss below been operative, this alone would have been enough to spur the investigations discussed here.

To see the continuing importance of the holocaust in contemporary French thought, one needs only to glance at the reaction of French philosophers to the appearance of Victor Farias's *Heidegger and Nazism* in 1987. For many, especially Derrida and Nancy, Heidegger's later thought offered the clues to a new, nontotalitarian approach to philosophy. The appearance of a book whose purpose was to link Heidegger as closely as possible with the holocaust had to be considered—and was considered—a deep intellectual affront. In the wake of the controversy stirred by Farias's book, no less than three major French thinkers published books of their own attempting to show that Heidegger's thinking, although flawed, presented at least some

Heidegger

of the resources necessary to overcome the political commitments he made to the Nazis.[2] A discussion of "the Heidegger affair," or of the much larger issue of Heidegger's influence on recent French philosophy, is clearly beyond the scope of the present study. However, the fact of his profound influence, particularly in the area of thinking about difference (which for Heidegger was the ontological difference between Being and beings), and the use to which this influence has been put in trying to resist totalitarianism are not matters of controversy. It is natural, then, that a linking of Heidegger and the holocaust would elicit the magnitude of reaction that it did in French philosophical circles.[3]

The importance of the holocaust in refashioning French thought can also be seen in the development of that thought over the past fifty years. The immediate post–World War II years in France were, of course, the years of existentialism. With its emphasis on and even valorization of human free will, existentialism was ill prepared to account for the ravages of the Second World War. How was one to square the tragic but noble struggle of a human being in a world without meaning with the everyday evils that were the stuff of people's lives? The conclusion seemed inevitable: people are not nearly as free or as noble as the existentialists would have it. The rise of structuralism must be seen, in part, against this background of the disaffection of French intellectuals with the picture of humanity drawn by existentialism.

Structuralism seemed to cure the twofold problem of freedom and nobility by situating people as moments of determining structures that are largely inaccessible to the consciousness of those who are determined by them. Theorists disagreed, of course, about what those structures were. For Louis

Structuralism

Althusser, the pertinent structure was the economic structure of society, for Claude Lévi-Strauss the kinship structure, for Jacques Lacan the structure of the unconscious, while for Jean Piaget the structure of cognitive and so-

2. These were Derrida's *Of Spirit: Heidegger and the Question*, trans. Geoffrey Bennington and Rachel Bowlby (Chicago: University of Chicago Press, 1989; or. pub. 1987), Lyotard's *Heidegger and "the Jews,"* trans. Andreas Michel and Mark Roberts (Minneapolis: University of Minnesota Press, 1990; or. pub. 1988), and Lacoue-Labarthe's *Heidegger, Art, and Politics,* trans. Chris Turner (Oxford: Basil Blackwell, 1990).

3. Not all recent French thinkers are so positive about the possibilities of Heidegger's thought in articulating difference. The obvious dissenter here is Levinas, for whom Heidegger's thought of Being was a continuation of a totalitarian philosophical position. Thus, Levinas is less surprised with the "revelations" (in fact, most of Farias's historical claims were a matter of public record before the publication of his book) about Heidegger's involvement with the Nazis. Cf. Levinas's "As If Consenting to Horror," trans. Paula Wissing, *Critical Inquiry* 15, no. 2 (1989): 485–88. (This entire issue of *Critical Inquiry* is dedicated to reactions, particularly among recent French thinkers, to Heidegger's involvement in Nazism.)

Levinas & Heidegger

cial maturation. But for all of these thinkers, people's experience needed to be seen as a product of forces of which they were largely out of control. Structuralists thus substituted a picture of people as products of their world rather than its masters. It was a picture that possessed, among its virtues, that of according better with holocaustal practices than the tragic picture existentialism offered.

Structuralism's advance, however, was not had without a cost, a cost that could lead thinking back down the paths of totalitarianism. Structuralism is reductionist; it attempts to reduce experience to a theoretically manageable size by citing a single founding structure by which experience is to be explained. As such, it falls into the foundationalism that poststructuralism has sought to overturn. There is no room for an irreducible difference in structuralism, and for that reason structuralism in all its forms threatens the marginalization or elimination of difference that has been the central concern of more recent French thought. One of the lights in which to view poststructuralist French thought, then, is that of a sympathy with the antihumanism of structuralism coupled with an aversion to its reductionism. Seen in this light, the term "poststructuralism" is not a misnomer; it indicates a revision of the structuralist program.

The preceding sketch is not intended to be either an exclusive or a comprehensive take on the context of the thinkers to be discussed here. Rather, it is intended to place the concern with difference into a broader historical context. Important to this context, in addition to the holocaust, are the events of May 1968 in France. Although these events came after some of the central texts of the thinkers who are my concern (for instance, Derrida's three 1967 texts and Levinas's *Totality and Infinity*), the "events of May" have reinforced the concern with difference that has characterized French thought to this day.

What transpired during May and June of 1968 has become the stuff of folklore in France, and particularly in French intellectual circles. It has no exact equivalent in the United States during the sixties (the "turbulent sixties," as the cliché goes, so as to be sure that by categorizing it that way we can distance ourselves from it). However, many will recall that during that time both intellectuals and activists conceived the hope that oppressive Western social arrangements and political practices could be radically transformed into something more equitable. In France, there are two distinguishing characteristics of the explosion of this hope worth calling attention to. First, the central period of the action was more compressed. While "the sixties" in the United States can be said to begin with the Montgomery bus boycott of 1955 and to run at least until the pullout of U.S. troops from Vietnam in 1972, much of the energy of the French equivalent was concentrated into those two months of 1968.

Second, and more relevant to my purposes, were the characteristics of those who engaged in the "events of May." They were, as in the United States, not only workers but students, professionals, intellectuals, feminists, and generally marginalized elements of society. Now, this fact will come as no surprise to U.S. readers, but it was of great significance to the French. Unlike here in the States, France at that time had a large, well-organized, and active Communist party—the Parti Française Communiste (PFC). The PFC, moreover, saw with alarm that the events unfolding in Paris in the spring of 1968 were led neither by workers nor, more to the point, by the PFC itself. In fact, those events were not "led." And, in the end, the PFC collaborated with the DeGaulle government to put down the uprising in which some of its own workers participated.[4]

There is a dual lesson that many intellectuals have drawn from the way these events unfolded and from the PFC's response to them. The first lesson is that political and social demands that people have regarding how their lives are governed by the institutions that surround them are not reducible to a single analysis, for example, Marxist analysis. Those demands are irreducibly various; they cannot be held under one umbrella. The second lesson is that the attempt to reduce these different demands to a single analysis often ends in totalitarianism. Here the evidence of totalitarianism was the betrayal of the uprising by the very party whose mission it was to envision an alternative, more nearly just society. Because the uprising was different, because it did not conform to the analysis offered by party functionaries, those functionaries thought it acceptable to participate in destroying it.

The "events of May" reinforced the idea, first drawn from the holocaust, that that which is different must be recognized and protected. Such a recognition has been formative for recent French philosophy, although it would be a mistake to claim that the perspectives to be discussed can be understood solely by reference to these events. The holocaust and the uprising in May 1968 should be seen as important aspects of the background—neither the whole of the background nor any of the foreground—for the concerns that have driven the philosophical approaches I treat here.

4. For an in-depth account of the events of May and especially the role of the PFC, see Richard Johnson's *French Communist Party Versus the Students: Revolutionary Politics in May–June 1968* (New Haven: Yale University Press, 1972).

Having discussed what motivated recent French thought to engage in the project of protecting or valorizing difference, I hope also to have revealed some reasonable motivation for *anyone* to be concerned about this project. The holocaust requires of us that we engage in forms of thinking and living that do not reduce others who may be unlike us to the status of mere things. The events of the last generation should convince those who are political progressives that reducing political struggle to a single set of stakes is at best misguided and more often insidious. And those of us who are philosophers ought to ask ourselves whether there is anything in our tradition that contributes to events like the holocaust or to political structures of totalitarianism. In addition to these motivations, there are others that should move us to think about difference. Racism, for instance, is on the rise rather than on the decline. Religious fundamentalisms—in Bosnia, in Israel and Palestine, in the southeastern United States—threaten to marginalize and even to destroy those who do not conform. The rejection of multiculturalism is often, if not always, an excuse for the valorization of one culture at the expense of others. In a fragmented world, people are finding it difficult to respect the differences of others, and this, ironically, at a time in which technology brings what is different closer to them. Whether or not we accept, in the end, the specific projects of difference that are treated here, the question of difference and of differences, of how to understand them and of how to respect them, needs to occupy us much more than it has.

So far, I have mostly engaged in describing both the object of the present study and the historical conditions in which that object unfolded. I want now to state my thesis: the attempts to articulate and valorize difference offered by the objects of this study are a failure. In particular, the attempt to introduce difference as a constitutive element of our world and our lives has failed. Having said this, I should be clear right away about what kind of failure I believe it is. The failure is not one of persuasion. It is not that many of the philosophers discussed here—Derrida in particular—have failed to convince anyone that they are right. On the contrary, one of the factors that has occasioned the writing of this book is that these thinkers have in fact been found quite persuasive. Neither is the failure I am interested in one that concerns whether in fact differences have been protected or valorized. The question whether, among the community of those who read and are influenced by the philosophers discussed here, there has been a movement toward greater openness or respect for difference, or otherness, is a sociological question that is wide of my own purposes. (For the record, I have not witnessed an embrace of divergent viewpoints among the philosophical part of that community.)

The failure that interests me is a specifically philosophical failure. What fails in the philosophers I discuss here are their arguments; those arguments are either self-refuting or unconvincing. This is not to claim that they say nothing of interest, or that their concerns ought not to be ours. Rather, it is to claim that they have not articulated those concerns in ways that should cause us to embrace their philosophical approaches. Nor should we mourn the failure, since there is at least one other approach that captures many of the concerns of these philosophers without having to absorb their failures. That approach, which will be developed as I proceed, is holistic as much as it is differential.

The failures of these philosophical programs are not all of a piece. Each philosophical approach has its own weaknesses that need to be addressed. Corresponding to this, the more holistic approach I advocate as a way to articulate each philosopher's concerns more adequately needs to have a new dimension added in order to address each new concern. The bulk of this work as it appears in the following chapters tries to cope with these tasks. In the rest of my introductory remarks, I would like to call attention to several problematic themes that run through all—or most—of the philosophical approaches I discuss here, and then to turn briefly to a discussion of the holistic approach I propose as an alternative to them.

The most prominent theme that pervades the approaches discussed here is, as already mentioned, the pride of place that difference receives. I want to emphasize here that in giving pride of place to difference, not all of these philosophers privilege difference *over* identity. Derrida surely does not. His concept of *differance* involves a play of identity and difference, a play he characterizes as between presence and absence. The same is true of Nancy's concept of sharing. Like *differance,* the concept of sharing is an economic concept, in a sense of "economic" to be elucidated in the chapter devoted to his thought. Sharing involves a play of the identity of the individual and the difference of the other in which the other is partially constitutive of the identity of the individual, but in resonance with, rather than founding for, that identity. Levinas can be read, as can Nancy, as claiming that difference in the form of the other is partially constitutive of selfhood; on the other hand, some of his statements about the precedence of the ethical over the ontological might be read as endorsing a view of the primacy of difference. (I tend toward the former view as a more sympathetic reading.) Alternatively, Deleuze's ontology attempts to give the nod to difference as primary, although

I argue that even here an ambivalence appears in his writings that is lacking in his pronouncements about difference.

Entwined with the role difference plays in the writings of these philosophers is another commonality binding all four philosophical approaches. Inasmuch as difference is given pride of place, theoretical articulation of the domains they treat can be had only in ambivalent and roundabout ways. The reason for this is not difficult to see, even without entering into specific analyses. Their point is not simply that foundationalism is false. I share the view that foundationalism is false, although I embrace none of the types of privileging of difference for which these philosophers argue. Rather, the idea is that inasmuch as difference is constitutive of the domain of inquiry, what can be said about that domain must be said in ways that (at least partially) cancel their content even as it is spoken. The reason for this has to do with the bond these thinkers assume exists between theoretical articulation—giving an account of something—and foundationalism. For them, a theoretical account of a domain of inquiry is a bringing of that domain under the conceptual categories to which one is committed. Those categories are categories that by their very nature attempt to preclude difference. Bringing a domain under my conceptual categories is reducing it—theoretically at least—to what I have to say about it. It is to claim, in the very act of accounting, that the account exhausts the domain and that there is nothing more to be said about the domain aside from what the account has said. Otherwise put, giving an accounting, in the straightforward sense of accounting, is shining a Cartesian light upon the phenomena under study. If the light is a truly Cartesian one, then the phenomena are exhausted—they have been frozen into categories and cannot escape from them. This is foundationalism. Thus, if foundationalism, and with it the threat of totalitarianism, is to be avoided, accounts that are given of the domains under study must be given in such a way that those accounts undercut their own pretensions to exhaustiveness in the very gesture by which they proclaim themselves.

This attitude toward theoretical articulation, toward the giving of accounts of a domain of inquiry, appears everywhere in the thought of the philosophers discussed here. It defines for them not only what can be said in the areas they discuss, but also how it can be said. Many of the statements proffered by these philosophers about community, linguistic meaning, ethics, and ontology cannot be taken as making claims in any straightforwardly traditional sense. This is not to say that all of the claims or concepts they use must undercut themselves even as they state themselves. Rather, it is to say that at crucial moments—those moments when difference is making an "appearance"—the philosophical articulation must change into something that possesses a more nearly self-negating status. Thus, concepts go "under erasure"; paradox or metaphor is introduced; claims are inverted or their traditional meanings suspended even as they are introduced.

All of this suspicion of theoretical articulation banks on a view of language that holds the giving of accounts and philosophical foundationalism to be inseparable. This, of course, is a view of the status of philosophical language, and shows the centrality of Derrida to the whole discussion of difference. In the chapter on Derrida, I reject the assumption of the inseparability of theoretical articulation and foundationalism. I argue there that the giving of accounts, and even of philosophical accounts, does not necessarily land one in the embrace of foundationalism. If I am right on this point, then theoretical articulation can at least be imagined in a way that does not point toward philosophical totalitarianism. This imagining is given more substance in the chapter on Levinas, in which I argue for a position of respecting differences that does not commit itself to effacing itself at the moment of articulation. The differences I discuss respecting are not the differences cited by the philosophers considered here. The differences I am concerned with are, in fact, much more pedestrian than the ones offered by Nancy, Derrida, Levinas, or Deleuze. But the point of my proposal in the Levinas chapter is that philosophical totalitarianism can be avoided without introducing a notion of difference that defies articulation. Otherwise put, one can at the same time offer straightforward philosophical accounts, avoid foundationalism, and respect difference.

The last overall convergence to which I want to call attention concerns the philosophical status of the claims these philosophers put forward when they articulate their approach to difference. This convergence is distinct from the previous one, although that convergence also concerned the status of these philosophers' discourse. This third convergence concerns the issue of whether to read these philosophers normatively or constitutively. Otherwise put, there is an ambivalence in these philosophers (Derrida excepted, as we shall see) as to whether they are offering constitutive claims about their domains of inquiry or views of how we should conceive those domains regardless of how in fact those domains are actually constituted.

This ambivalence reveals an unresolved conflict in the entire approach to difference characteristic of much of French poststructuralism. At the outset of this introduction, I said that the overriding problem of much of contemporary French philosophy concerns how properly to conceive and valorize difference. But, as I argue at length in the next chapter, proper conceptions can come in different varieties, depending on the goal one has in view in articulating a conception in the first place. To pick a simple example, a proper conception of the universe would seem to have to involve relativity theory, if one's goal is to conceive it accurately. However, if one's goal is to induce wonder in one's younger children, a conception of the universe involving relativity might be counterproductive. In the former case, one ought to think of the universe as finite but unbounded; in the latter case, perhaps one ought to think of the universe as going on forever.

Applied to the issue of thinking about difference, there can be a distinction between what might constitute an accurate theory of how difference operates in a certain domain (although, given the second convergence on the limits of theoretical articulation, the notion of accuracy cannot be taken to be straightforward) and a normatively acceptable way of thinking about how difference operates. It might be the case that an accurate view of community or ethics or ontology does not valorize difference in a way we would like to see it valorized. Putting the issue broadly and a bit simplistically, it could be that the facts do not mesh with our intuitions about what the facts should be, in which case we are left with the question whether our theory should account for the facts or should give us a way of conceiving the domain of inquiry that is otherwise normatively defensible.

This ambivalence between constitutive and normative readings appears when we approach the texts of Nancy, Levinas, and Deleuze. For Nancy, the question is whether he is offering an account of what it is to be in community or an account of how we should think about community in order to avoid totalitarianism. For Levinas, the question is whether he is offering a view of how we are constituted by the other or how we should think of ourselves relative to the other. For Deleuze, the question is whether he is making ontological claims about difference or constructing an ontological perspective that allows difference an important role to play. Regarding Derrida, I believe the case is more straightforward. In his theorizing about language, he is offering a view of how language works—a constitutive view. There is a tendency to "normativize" that view, which I address briefly at the beginning of the Levinas chapter, but there is nothing in Derrida's views about language (although there are things in some of his more political works) that invite that reading.

Before turning to my readings of this ambivalence, let me clear up a possible confusion. I claimed above that each of the thinkers considered here offers a constitutive view of difference, a view of difference as somehow constitutive of their domain of inquiry. Am I now backing away from that claim and saying that in fact they offer some sort of normative view instead? No. The ambivalence to which I am calling attention does not concern the place of difference in the thought of these philosophers, but instead the status of their thought about difference. Constitutive approaches to difference can be taken constitutively, as making claims about what difference really is and how it really constitutes some domain, or normatively, as telling us how we ought to think about a certain domain regardless of how it is actually constituted. There is nothing incoherent in saying that there are normative reasons for thinking that difference is (partially) constitutive of a certain domain, even though it might not in fact be. Thus, the ambivalence I am remarking here concerns how to take the philosophical positions articulated, not how to understand difference.

I have dealt with this ambivalence in the following fashion. Regarding Deleuze, I read him normatively. I offer an argument at the outset of the chapter on his work to justify that reading, in part by recalling Deleuze's own conception of philosophy. In addition to that self-conception, I believe that the normative reading is the most appealing one, for reasons I offer there. Regarding Levinas, I read him as offering both a constitutive and normative analysis at the same time. For Levinas, the ethicist, this ambivalence is at once most central and most damaging to his project. A good part of Levinas's position rests on the idea that because we are constituted a certain way, we have ethical claims already placed upon us. I argue that Levinas's particular derivation of the normative from the constitutive is untenable. Regarding Nancy, I read him both ways. It is difficult to know what to make of Nancy's view of community, because there are contradictory indications in his own work in this regard. My strategy in evaluating Nancy, then, is to consider him first as offering a normative approach and then as offering a constitutive one.

I am aware that even raising the normative/constitutive distinction in the way I have is controversial. I do not pretend to have made a case for this distinction in my introductory remarks. I make a fuller case in the next chapter for this distinction, and throughout the text try to be sensitive to the particular nuances of each philosopher's particular ambivalence about the issue.

These three themes—the privileging of difference, the distrust of signification, and the ambivalent status of their writings—are pervasive in the work of the philosophers discussed here, with the exception of Derrida on the last theme. Calling attention to these themes may help, as does calling attention to the historical context within which they work, to offer a framework within which to view their philosophical approaches. There is a danger to constructing such a framework, however, which requires immediate recognition. It is tempting to see the thinkers I discuss here as doing "the same thing," and therefore as all subject to "the same problems." That temptation would lead us into false belief. Although there is a convergence of several important thematic preoccupations in their work, in no sense do they do "the same thing," or even "the same thing" applied to different fields. The work of these thinkers, although they are lumped into the general categories of "postmodernism" or "poststructuralism," is not of a piece. It would, for instance, be difficult, if not impossible, to reconcile, on the one hand, Deleuzian ontology and the Deleuzian view of language to which Deleuze ties that ontology, with, on the other hand, the Derridean approach to language.

There is no substitute for individualized treatments of the philosophers under consideration. That is why I discuss each thinker separately. In the course of those discussions I point to some of the more specific convergences in their approaches that have not found their way into the Introduction. But those convergences should not be read as claiming any similarities beyond those explicitly acknowledged. In short, although there is a theme and some general commonalities of approach that have occupied much of recent French thinking, that theme has been instantiated in ways that are divergent and at moments irreconcilable. I believe that all of the instantiations I discuss here are philosophical failures, and that the general approach of a constitutive privileging of difference is unpromising. Those failures, however, are played out in distinct ways.

One of the upshots of my own approach, then, is that, even if I am correct in my specific arguments, I have not constructed a case against the general project of constitutive privileging of difference. Cast doubt on the project, perhaps. But I have not, and have not tried, to make the case that such an approach is bound to fail.

It may seem at this point that the goal of the following chapters is wholly negative, to refute certain approaches to difference characteristic of recent French philosophy. There is another goal I have in mind, however, that occupies about the last third of each chapter. In addition to critique, I sketch an alternative way to conceive the phenomena treated by each thinker. This alternative is in each case an attempt to show how the concerns that have occupied that thinker can be conceptualized to preserve the goals of their

Positive Rearticulation

commitments while often jettisoning the commitments themselves. I call these alternative frameworks "positive rearticulations," in order to show that I am trying to solve similar problems in a different fashion.

Unlike the critical portions of each chapter, the succeeding positive rearticulations are not meant to be exhaustive accounts of the domains of inquiry they treat. I do intend the critical work to be, if not in each case a knockdown refutation, then enough to motivate abandoning the approaches I criticize in these philosophers. However, I make no such claims for the positive rearticulations. Criticizing a philosopher is often both a shorter and cleaner affair than saying more adequately what should be said in that philosopher's area of concern. That certainly holds in the present case. It is far beyond both the scope of this text and the capabilities of its author to offer full and defensible accounts of community, language, ethics, and ontology.

Contingent holism

Nevertheless, I hope that the positive rearticulations, taken together, offer a coherent framework within which philosophical thinking on the matters of concern to recent French philosophy can proceed. I call the framework a "contingent holism," in the hope of capturing a couple of its significant features. One of these stems from a philosophical commitment that I share with the philosophers I criticize: antifoundationalism. Philosophical foundationalism has a bad name in Western philosophical circles these days, as I believe it should. This bad name derives in part from the belief that foundationalism is a mistaken approach in any philosophical field, and in part from the belief, noted above, that foundationalism can easily be tied to exclusionary practices.

The problem facing philosophers who want to reject foundationalism is how to do philosophy as something other than a search for foundations. This is the point at which I diverge from those I criticize in the following pages. Instead of giving some sort of privilege to a difference that disrupts the discourse of foundationalism, I believe that we need to turn toward a view of philosophy committed both to holism and to contingency. That holism, of course, has a slightly different appearance depending on what domain of inquiry is at issue. Its general features, however, run throughout.

The most salient fact to which contingent holism wants to call attention is that we humans are primarily members of communities that comprise specific practices. Those practices are many and diverse. There are, for instance, sporting practices, ethical practices, various kinds of friendship practices, epistemic practices, business practices, and church practices, to name but a few. To be a member of a community is to be a participant in the rele-

Practice

vant practice or practices of that community. And to be in a practice is, as I discuss in the next chapter, to be a participant in a behavioral regularity, one that is usually goal directed, and that is socially normatively governed. In the view I sketch, the concept of practices is central, and allows for a nonfoundationalist philosophical viewpoint that accomplishes the goals of the thinkers I treat, without running into the problems they face.

discursivity

One of the key aspects of a practice is its discursiveness. Practices involve what Wittgenstein called "language games," and thus to understand practices we need to know something about language. But conversely, in order to know something about language we need to understand discursivity as a practical matter, a matter of practices. In the chapter on Derrida, I outline a view of language that ties its semantic view—its view of linguistic meaningfulness—to its pragmatic approach. The meaningfulness of language stems from the role that language plays in our practices. Thus, language is treated *in practice*—or, better, *in practices*—in order to give an account of linguistic meaningfulness that allows the Derridean claim that we can never give an exhaustive or indubitable account of linguistic meaningfulness while it does not embrace the Derridean strategy of rejecting semantic accounting altogether.

This view of community and discursivity, which I articulate in the positive rearticulations in the chapters on Nancy and Derrida respectively, is both holistic and nonfoundationalist. It is holistic in that participating in a practice and its discursivity involves knowing how to do several things at once. One does not, for instance, learn baseball one rule at a time. Instead,

holistic

one gets a sense of the game and then of the rules as structuring aspects of that game. As Wittgenstein says, "Light gradually dawns over the whole."[5] The view is nonfoundationalist in that our practices come down to us not— *Non-* or not solely—as products of the way the world is, but also, and perhaps *fundat.* primarily, from the vagaries and contingencies of our history. These vagaries and contingencies (whence the term "contingent" in contingent holism) affect not only our nonepistemic practices but our epistemic ones as well— a fact to which Foucault often calls our attention. I reinforce a recognition of that fact, and attempt to stem some of its seemingly untoward consequences, in my discussions of moral practice in the chapter on Levinas and of ontology in the chapter on Deleuze.

In the Levinas chapter, I offer a moral principle of respect for differences

5. Ludwig Wittgenstein, *On Certainty*, ed. G.E.M. Anscombe and G. H. von Wright, trans. Denis Paul and G.E.M. Anscombe (New York: Harper & Row, 1969), 21e.

that tries to accomplish what Levinas seeks in his discussion of the infinite other but that, or so I argue, he cannot achieve. The principle of respect for differences is an action-guiding principle that is part of the practice of morality. To be a principle in this practice does not imply that everyone recognizes it as such, but rather that, given the fundamental commitments that our morality holds, this principle is a logical consequence of them. Now, one might wonder here whose morality is being discussed; to that, the answer is, inevitably, *our* morality, the morality of you (dear reader) and me and folks we can talk morality with. It is a morality that cannot itself be founded on something else, but that, to the extent that one is committed to it, involves a commitment to a host of principles, including the principle of respect for differences.

Finally, in discussing ontology, I propose that the ontological entities to which a person ought to be held to be committed are just those that the discursive practices to which that person is committed are themselves committed. Rather than take Deleuze's (periodic) tack of positing Being as difference, I suggest that we can have all the ontological differences we need if we are more austere in our ontology. Instead of seeking Being itself and requiring of it that it contain all the differences that we would like to see instantiated in our world, we can turn directly to the practices in which people are engaged. Practices are a rich source of ontological posits; differences abound in different practices. Thus, by jettisoning the project of *a* philosophical ontology, we open the way to the kinds of ontological differences Deleuze commends to us.

The framework for a contingent holism that I construct here owes much to recent work both in contemporary French and Anglo-American philosophy. Although references to more specific works will be given as the positive rearticulations unfold, let me now call attention to two specific strands of thought that have been crucial to the formulation of the framework I propose. The first is a movement of what might loosely be called "neopragmatism" in Anglo-American philosophy. It stems from the work of Ludwig Wittgenstein, and is perhaps best articulated in the works of Wilfrid Sellars and, more recently, Robert Brandom. The positive rearticulation of language offered in the chapter on Derrida derives much of its impetus from their approach. In fact, it was cowritten with a student of Brandom's, Mark Lance.

Neopragmatism has, unfortunately in my view, been too closely associated with the views of Richard Rorty. What is unfortunate about this has nothing to do with Rorty's own work, but rather to do with the fact that

Rorty gives a particular gloss to pragmatism that is not the only gloss that can be given. To put the matter schematically, there are at least two ways of reading pragmatism and neopragmatism, one opening up the possibility of a more radical politics than the other. Rorty's view, the more conservative one, is to take pragmatism in its pragmatic connotation—what we ought to believe or do is what works for us. (One obvious question that arises here is, Who is the we that is "us"?) The potentially more radical view understands the lesson of pragmatism to be that the proper level of analysis—epistemically, linguistically, and politically—is the level of practices. If we want to comprehend our knowledge, our language, our political and social life, we need to comprehend the practices in which those appear. This type of pragmatism is (at least initially) agnostic on the question of whether or in what ways or for whom those practices *work,* and so leaves open the possibility of their critique.

The other strand of influence on the contingent holism I develop here lies [Foucault] in the thought of Michel Foucault. My own reading of Foucault sees his work as having deep affinities with the neopragmatism of recent Anglo-American thought. However, he has added a political dimension to that thought that renders the Rortian assumption that social structures can be understood solely "pragmatically," that is, by reference to how they help us navigate the world, seem naive. Foucault, like neopragmatists such as Brandom and Sellars, situates his analysis at the level of practices. But rather than seek to understand their constitution, as Anglo-American neopragmatists do, he seeks to understand—and at points to criticize—their effects. In other words, Foucault can be seen as taking the radical possibility opened up by the neopragmatists and developing it into a true radical politics.

Before turning to the specific treatments that form the heart of this work, let me conclude these introductory remarks by emphasizing a point that I remarked earlier, but that may be easily lost amid the twists and turns of the discussion. Although I believe that the philosophers I criticize here are mistaken and that their common privileging of difference is misguided, I do not believe that they are onto nothing worth thinking about. In fact, the effort expended in the positive rearticulations in each chapter assumes that in fact these thinkers *are* onto interesting issues. The problem is not with the issues but with the approaches. In the end, then, the service their writings have performed—and this is not a small service—is to awaken us to the need to address more adequately important issues in philosophy that have gotten neither the attention nor the articulation they deserve.

1

From Communal Difference to Communal Holism

Jean-Luc Nancy

Why is it that we are so concerned with the idea of community these days? We are asking ourselves what constitutes a community, what it means to be in one, how the community or communities in which a person lives play a role in the constitution of that person's identity. These concerns are particularly evident in philosophy, and not only in the debate in political philosophy between communitarians of both the Left (Charles Taylor) and Right (Alisdair MacIntyre) and liberal theorists (John Rawls). Philosophers of language, following either Habermas's or Wittgenstein's lead, have invoked the idea of community for explanations of linguistic use and meaning.[1] Philosophers of mind have turned toward the community in seeking explanations of mental content.[2] Since the appearance of Thomas Kuhn's seminal *Structure of Scientific Revolutions*,[3] philosophers of science have pondered the role of the scientific community in the formation of scientific theories.

The concern with community, however, is not limited to philosophy. In an age of increasing individual isolation, people feel the need to belong to

---

1. I, too, following Wittgenstein, invoke the idea in my positive reinterpretation of Derridean concerns in the next chapter.
2. Tyler Burge, whom I discuss below, is an important figure in this turn.
3. Chicago: University of Chicago Press, 1962.

some kind of community with which they can identify. Politicians of both the Right and Left have responded by promoting different visions of community. For the Right, the community is one of traditional values that may be imposed upon those unwilling—and in some cases even unable—to abide by them. For the Left, the community is one of obligation to those who find themselves in a less fortunate situation than others. For both, but for very different reasons, the ideology of rampant individualism that has characterized the traditional liberal approach to politics has shorn us of a resource that is central in sustaining not only our lives but our very identities.

On the Left, however, this concern to reintroduce the notion of community into political thinking has been tempered by the history of Communist experiments in the twentieth century. (It is puzzling that the Right has not been nearly as concerned with the results of its own communal experiments.) In the name of community and community obligation, individual freedoms and lives have been sacrificed without seeming concern and to no appreciable gain. The step from community to totalitarianism has seemed, in practice at least, to be all too short. And so the question arises, If the concept of community is central to any viable approach to understanding what makes people's lives worthwhile, then how shall we conceive community?

It is here that the recent thought of Jean-Luc Nancy becomes relevant. In his most extended reflection on the concept of community, *The Inoperative Community*,[4] Nancy takes it as his task to reconceive community in a way that articulates its place in our lives without its lapsing into totalitarianism. He sees this articulation as one that finds its home on the political Left. "In order to speak of the site that we are dealing with, I might venture the following thought: 'left' means, *at the very least,* that the political, as such, is receptive to what is at stake in community." [5] If the Left is to end its romance with totalitarianism, it must provide a conception of community that combines both the obligation proper to a fully communal spirit and the respect for others that has often been overridden in the name of obligation. Nancy sets it as his task to provide just such a conception.

---

4. Jean-Luc Nancy, *The Inoperative Community*, ed. Peter Connor, trans. Peter Connor, Lisa Garbus, Michael Holland, and Simona Sawhney (Minneapolis: University of Minnesota Press, 1991; or. pub. 1986).

5. Ibid., xxxvi. The alternative to the Left that Nancy sees seems to be not the Right that I have alluded to but a more traditional liberal laissez-faire Right. He follows the quote I have just cited with this parenthetical remark: "(On the other hand, 'right' means, at least, that the political is merely in charge of order and administration)." This conception of the Right, however, particularly with its ambiguous word "order," can be interpreted in both communal and individualist ways.

I should note at the outset that the sense of the term "totalitarianism" as I use it here is often wider than—although related to—the sense of the term when it is used to categorize a type of state governance. Traditionally, "totalitarianism" means something like a government in which the state has a near monopoly not only on the means of violence but also on the means of communication, education, and expression. However, a product of this state totalitarianism—and here Nazism serves as the most striking example—is that people are forced to define themselves and their communities within narrowly defined parameters (e.g., Aryan or Christian or Muslim or Serb or some small combination of these or others). This self-definition within narrowly defined parameters can itself be called, and willed be called here, "totalitarianism."

Totalitarianism, then, in the sense that I am using it, refers to narrow constraints placed upon individual and social identity and behavior rather than just to a type of state. Having said this, I should also note that totalitarianism in that sense need not be a product of state totalitarianism. Although almost all state totalitarianisms, if at all successful, will foster totalitarianism in the sense I mean it, there can be totalitarianisms that are not state fostered. (Before the rise of the Christian Right in politics, the influence of certain forms of Christianity in the Bible Belt could be cited as an instance of nonstate totalitarianism.)

Returning to Nancy, then, among the questions motivating Nancy's approach to community, two emerge as central. At the outset, I want merely to cite them. Later, I discuss a tension between them that has not been fully resolved in Nancy's writings to date. The citing of that tension leads to two alternative readings of the status of Nancy's writings, neither of which is satisfactory. But for the moment, let me just pose the questions that preoccupy him: (1) What is it to be in a community? (2) How can we conceive community in a nontotalitarian manner?

The first question is a constitutive one. It asks about being-in-community and what that is. I have posed the question that way rather than asking, for instance, What is it to be a member of a community? The latter question, unlike the former, seems to assume (or at least inclines one to assume) that before entering into a community, one is preconstituted, that one enters the community as somehow already constituted.[6] Since Nancy denies precisely

6. This is an idea that the communitarian Michael Sandel attributes to—and criticizes in— John Rawls. Cf. *Liberalism and the Limits of Justice* (Cambridge: Cambridge University Press, 1982), esp. chap. 4.

such preconstitution, the question must be posed in a more neutral manner. Thus the articulation I have given it.

The second question is normative. Rather than ask about how things are, it asks about how things should be. It is a question not about correct and incorrect conceptions of what it is like to be in a community, but about more and less valuable conceptions. In order to see the distinction at work here, the second question could be formulated like this: Regardless of what being in a community is really like, how might we conceive it in ways that avoid the problem of totalitarianism? Nancy does not formulate matters this way, and indeed does not distinguish between the two questions I have posed. Instead, he addresses them indifferently in the course of his discussion, to which I want now to turn.

For Nancy, the being of individuals is, above all, an exposure to what has traditionally been considered outside the provenance of individuality. "'To be exposed' means to be 'posed' in exteriority, according to an exteriority, having to do with an outside *in the very intimacy* of an inside."[7] Rather than view individuals as self-enclosed beings, Cartesian style, to which is added the outside world, Nancy views individuals as always already constituted by what is outside of them. "[W]e are brought into the world, each and every one of us, according to a dimension of 'in-common' that is in no way 'added onto' the dimension of 'being-self,' but that is rather co-originary and coextensive with it."[8] Thus Nancy denies at the outset any conception of individuality that would lend itself to the traditional liberal view of a community as an interaction of preconstituted individuals. A view of that type would be mistaken both about individuals and communities, since not only are individuals not preconstituted, but communities are something other than the sum or the relations among individuals.[9]

Nancy offers something of a "proof" against the view of an individual self-enclosed, a proof that, by its language, seems directed mostly against Hegelian notions of the absolute as a self-enclosure. It is worth quoting in full.

> An inconsequential atomism, individualism tends to forget that the atom is a world. This is why the question of community is so markedly absent from the metaphysics of the subject, that is to say,

7. *Inoperative Community*, xxxvii.
8. Ibid., xxxvi.
9. There is, of course, a disagreement within liberal circles about whether to consider the idea of a preconstituted individuality an ontological commitment or a methodological starting point. The former view is more constitutive and the latter more normative. Since Nancy does not make the constitutive-normative distinction, it is difficult to make out which of the two interpretations he would set himself against.

from the metaphysics of the absolute for-itself. . . . A simple and redoubtable logic will always imply that within its very separation the
absolutely separate encloses, if we can say this, more than what is
simply separated. Which is to say that the separation itself must be
enclosed, that the closure must not only close around a territory
(while still remaining exposed, at its outer edge, to another territory,
with which it thereby communicates), but also, in order to complete
the absoluteness of its separation, around the enclosure itself. The
absolute must be the absolute of its own absoluteness, or not be at
all. In other words: to be absolutely alone, it is not enough that I be
so; I must also be alone being alone—and this of course is contradictory. The logic of the absolute violates the absolute.[10]

Nancy is arguing here that exposure is a necessarily constitutive aspect of
individuals (and also, as he notes, of states, art, science, history, and ideas)
because the idea of an individual absolutely separated from others is self-
contradictory. It is self-contradictory because, in order for the separation to
be an absolute separation—one that excludes exposure to the other—the
closure that performs the separation would have to double itself as a closure, being not only a closure but a closure of a closure. A closure must
close around something else; it cannot close around itself without losing its
characteristic as a closure. Thus, if a closure must, in order to perform its
role as closure, close around itself, it thereby loses its ability to be a closure,
and the idea of it as a closure is self-contradictory.

The argument here might seem a bit elusive, but perhaps it will become

10. *Inoperative Community*, 4. Because of the importance of this argument to Nancy's overall position, it is also worth citing the French original (including the part of the quote I deleted
from the translation, which I put in brackets): "L'individualisme est un atomisme inconsé-
quent, qui oublie que l'enjeu de l'atome est celui d'un monde. C'est bien pourquoi la question
de la communauté est la grande absente de la métaphysique du sujet, c'est-à-dire—individu
ou Etat total—de la métaphysique du pour-soi absolu [: ce qui veut dire aussi bien la métaphysique de l'*absolu* en général, de l'être comme ab-solu, parfaitement détaché, distinct et clos,
sans rapport. Cet ab-solu peut se présenter sous les espèces de l'Idée, de l'Histoire, de l'Individu, de l'Etat, de la Science, de l'Oeuvre d'art, etc. Sa logique sera toujours la même, pour au-
tant qu'il est sans rapport.] Elle sera cette logique simple et redoubtable qui implie que ce qui
est absolument séparé renferme, si on peut dire, dans sa séparation plus que le simple separe.
C'est-à-dire que la séparation elle-même doit etre enfermée, que la clôture ne doit pas seule-
ment se clore sur un territoire (tout en restant exposée, par son bord externe, à l'autre territoire, avec lequel elle communique ainsi), mais sur la clôture elle-même, pour accomplir l'absoluité de la séparation. L'absolut doit être l'absolu de sa propre absoluité, sous peine de n'être
pas. Ou bien: pour être absolument seul, il ne suffit pas que je le sois, il faut encore que je sois
seul à être seul. Ce qui précisément est contradictoire. La logique de l'absolu fait violence à
l'absolu" (*La communauté désoeuvrée* [Paris: Bourgois, 1986], 17–18).

clearer if we see it against a Hegelian background. One of the lessons of Hegel is that things often harbor within themselves their own opposites, so that in their unfolding they themselves become the opposite of (or at least in some way opposed to) what they were before. This, of course, is the movement of the Hegelian dialectic. Nancy is making a dialectical move here concerning the possibility of self-enclosure. Self-enclosure, in order to be true self-enclosure, would have to immure itself against all contact with the outside. But in order to do that, its own enclosure would itself have to be enclosed. That cannot be, however, because enclosures do not enclose themselves; they enclose that which is within their enclosure. Thus enclosures are, by their very nature, exposed to the outside. But if that which encloses me is exposed to the outside, then I cannot be completely separated from the outside. There is always commerce along the enclosure, and a wholly separate individuality is impossible.

If Nancy is right here, then not only is exposure a necessary aspect of individuality, but the denial that it is, is logically impossible. Although I believe there is much merit in the idea that individuals are exposed to communities (if in a way different from the one Nancy articulates), I am not convinced that the denial of that exposure is self-contradictory. Wrong, but not self-contradictory. In order for Nancy to make his case here, he would have to offer a convincing argument that the closure of individuality must enclose its own enclosure. He states that this is so, but does not give any reason to believe it. Moreover, I think it is at least conceptually possible (and, after all, it is conceptual possibility that is at issue here) to deny it.

Hobbesian-inspired forms of social contract theory, for instance, create the scenario of self-enclosed individuals engaging in negotiations in order to realize the maximum of self-interest for each negotiating individual. If Nancy is right, such a scenario must be self-contradictory, because the enclosure of (communicating) individuals must have to enclose itself. But why must that be? Cannot it not be said that the individuals, while communicating, do so only for strategic reasons, and thus retain a strong form of "personal self-enclosure" while doing so? Now, one might argue that this scenario is impossible because in order to communicate one must, for instance, learn a language, and that cannot be done without exposure to others. While this is true, it does not reinforce Nancy's case, because the necessity of learning a language from others is a factual necessity, not a conceptual one. I can imagine beings, preformed in such a way that they are ready to speak, engaging in such communication for the sake of self-interest. If one argues here that that is a bit far-fetched, I would agree. The point is not to defend the idea of self-enclosure—in fact I attack it below—but to resist Nancy's argument that it is conceptually impossible. In resisting that argument, however, I hope, by the implausible nature of my counterexamples, to have begun to motivate at a more concrete level the idea that there may be something to his positive view. Let us return to pick up the thread of that view.

To be an individual, then, is to be constituted by what is "outside" one as well as what is "inside" one. The terms "outside" and "inside" are misleading, however, since once it is recognized that individual being is always already exposure, then the outside is no longer outside of one, nor the inside inside of one. What is outside of the individual on more traditional views is actually constitutive of him or her, and what is inside is part of the outside that is constitutive of the "inside" of others. When Nancy speaks of the relation of sharing, a concept I return to below, he says that "the relation is not one between human beings, as we might speak of a relation established between two subjects constituted as subjects and as 'securing,' secondarily, this relation. In this relation, 'human beings' are not given—but it is relation alone that can give them 'humanity.' " [11]

Before deepening the analysis any further, it is worth calling attention to the influence of Heidegger's thought on Nancy here. Although others, most notably Derrida, have developed Heidegger's thought in other directions, Nancy has been particularly concerned to show how a Heideggerian view of personhood can be developed in such a way as to offer a viable conception of community and of the obligations that flow from that conception. Unlike many who have followed Heidegger, however, Nancy's borrowings are from themes that are continuous between the "early" and "late" Heidegger. From the latter, he uses the Derridean theme of presence and absence in a way we will come to see further on. But in his view of individuality as exposure, he relies on earlier Heideggerian writings. For instance, in *Being and Time,* Heidegger writes, "When Dasein directs itself towards something and grasps it, it does not somehow first get out of an inner sphere in which it has been proximally encapsulated, but its primary kind of Being is such that it is always 'outside' alongside entities which it encounters and which belong to a world already discovered." [12] In Nancy's view, however, Heidegger did not

11. Jean-Luc Nancy, *The Experience of Freedom,* trans. Bridget McDonald (Stanford: Stanford University Press, 1993; or. pub. 1988), 73.

12. Martin Heidegger, *Being and Time,* trans. John Macquarrie and Edward Robinson (New York: Harper & Row, 1962; or. pub. 1927), 89. Cf. idem, *Basic Problems of Phenomenology,* trans. Albert Hofstadter (Bloomington: Indiana University Press, 1982; or. pub. 1975), 65: "Transcendence, transcending, belongs to the essential nature of the being that exists (on the basis of transcendence) as intentional, that is, exists in the manner of dwelling among the extant. Intentionality is the ratio cognoscendi of transcendence. Transcendence is the ratio essendi of intentionality in its diverse modes."

fully understand the implications of his own insight, and kept regressing to
a concept of a preconstituted individuality.

> I will not undertake here the dense and meticulous explication that
> Heidegger's text would demand. I will be content to propose dryly
> this double hypothesis: in approaching more closely than we ever
> have the *altered* (crossed by the other) constitution of Being in its sin-
> gularity, Heidegger (1) determined the essence of the *Dasein* outside
> of subjectivity (and a fortiori outside of inter-subjectivity) in a being-
> exposed or in a being-offered to others, of which philosophy (since
> Plato? despite Plato?) has been, despite everything, the denial, and
> (2) kept (despite himself?) the assignation of this *Dasein* in the ap-
> parent form of a distinct individuality, as much opposed as exposed
> to other individualities and thus irremediably kept in a sphere of au-
> tonomic, if not subjective, allure.[13]

Returning to the analysis, if individual being is constituted by what is
"outside" one, then it is constituted as well by the community in which one
exists. And indeed, for Nancy, the interesting aspect of exposure to the
"outside" is the exposure to the community of others, rather than to nonhuman beings or inanimate objects. But if to be is to be already in community, this being-in-community should not be seen—and Nancy is most em-
phatic about this—as an immersion in some sort of common or communal
substance. If I am exposed to others in my being, if who I am consists at
least in good measure in my exposure to others, this exposure is not an exposure to a thing, an otherness, which would then come to constitute me. In
seeing why this exposure is not exposure to a something, we will come to
recognize two important themes in Nancy's view of community: how it is an
attempt to avoid the totalitarian temptation I referred to above and how it
resists all attempts to give it articulation.

If exposure were exposure to a common substance, if the community in
which one is exposed were a thing that everybody had in common, then there
would be a single characteristic, or at least a group of them, that everyone
possessed. In order, then, to restore community where it is lost, one would
only have to retrieve this characteristic or group of characteristics and impose them upon the individuals in the community. Or, if those characteristics were already instantiated in everyone, one would only have to force a

13. *Inoperative Community,* 104.

recognition of them upon those who refuse to do so. Nancy is leery of the idea that these characteristics exist and particularly of the history of attempts to impose some recognition that a certain characteristic or group of characteristics is definitive of a community.

Nancy's argument against the idea that there are specific characteristics that form the common substance of a community concerns the relationship between the immanence of such characteristics and death. For Nancy, the idea of a common substance that forms the glue of the community is interchangeable with the idea that there is a primal bond between individuals in that community that binds them together in immanence. "Distinct from society (which is a simple association and division of forces and needs) and opposed to emprise (which dissolves community by submitting its peoples to its arms and to its glory), community is not only intimate communication between its members, but also its organic communion with its own essence." [14] This is the Rousseauian picture of community—an intimacy or immanence that binds individuals into a common substance and that is lost with the development of modern society.

This picture of community as an organic communion cannot be realized except in death, for it is only in death that full immanence is attained. The reason for this is that individuals, while alive, can never completely close themselves off—either by themselves or as a community—from exposure to what is outside of them. Otherwise put, a community can never become a community of immanence. Recall here Nancy's argument that the logic of complete separation is self-contradictory. If this argument is sound—which I have argued it is not—then the separation from others required for complete immanence is impossible, and thus the idea of an organic community is also impossible. Only with death, when exposure to the outside ends, can immanence be achieved.

Now, one can raise the question here to Nancy, which I will do when turning from the expository to the critical, whether Nancy is justified in thinking of a common substance solely in terms of immanence. Is it not possible to consider a common substance in terms other than those of a bond that encloses the community in upon itself? If, for instance, the language of a community is part of its common substance, then the community is bound together by something that is itself exposed to the contingencies of history and contact with the outside. (Of course, if one thinks of language in a Derridean way—which Nancy surely does—then language itself cannot be con-

14. Ibid., 9.

sidered a common substance. That is an issue that will have to wait until the next chapter.) In any case, I want to flag a concern here that I will linger over later.

For Nancy, any project that has as its goal the formation of a community of immanence is a project of death. "Immanence, communal fusion, contains no other logic than that of the suicide of the community that is governed by it." [15] And with this recognition we can begin to see Nancy's second suspicion regarding the idea of a common substance. Not only is the idea of a common substance illusory, it is also dangerous. It underwrites projects that are suicidal and detrimental to the community it is their seeming goal to construct. For Nancy, the suicidal project of forming an organic community is the character of all totalitarianisms. "[C]ommunity does not consist in the transcendence (nor in the transcendental) of a being supposedly immanent to community. It consists on the contrary in the immanence of a 'transcendence'—of finite existence as such, which is to say, of its 'exposition.' . . . By inverting the 'principle' stated a moment ago, we get totalitarianism." [16]

The exemplar of totalitarianism *par excellence* is Nazism. In a coauthored article, Nancy and his colleague Phillipe Lacoue-Labarthe argue that the logic of Nazism—and indeed of fascism generally—is that of trying to form an identity by means of the contradictory attempt to imitate, and at the same time distinguish oneself from, a model that mythically preexists one. For the Germans, this model was that of the Greeks. Thus the task for Nazism was to imitate the Greeks in such a way as to become *themselves*—not Greeks but Germans. The logic here is one of what Nancy and Lacoue-Labarthe call a "double-bind." "Why a logic of the *double-bind*? Because the appropriation of the means of identification must both take place, and not take place, through the imitation of the ancients, especially the Greeks." [17]

The Nazi resolution to this double-bind was to try to discover beneath the classicism of the Greeks a darker Greece, one of blood and sacrifice. Thus, Nazism created a myth—a fictioning of reality—that both was and was not Greek, so that it could become German. The problem is that this mimetism can only be complete, can only achieve immanence, in death. Thus the Nazis tried to exterminate everyone who was not immanent in the

15. Ibid., 12.
16. Ibid., xxxix.
17. Jean-Luc Nancy and Phillipe Lacoue-Labarthe, "The Nazi Myth," trans. Brian Holmes, *Critical Inquiry* 16, no. 2 (1990): 300.

organic community they were fictioning. But since there is no immanence, such an extermination could be applied to everyone: Nazism was suicidal.[18]

To conceive community, then, in terms of a common substance is both misguided and dangerous: it fails to recognize that such a conception can be realized only in death, and thus it promotes death—including its own death—in trying to realize it. Inasmuch as community cannot be a matter of common substance, however, there is another implication for the attempt to articulate a conception of community, an implication that cannot be avoided: a community's nature cannot be straightforwardly signified. That is to say, one cannot say what the communal nature of the community is. To say what the communal nature of a community is, to signify it, would be to ascribe to it a common substance, which is exactly what Nancy seeks to avoid. Community, then, must lie either beneath, beyond, or in the interstices of signification, but it is not susceptible to a straightforward accounting. "This *us* of sense, which is sense, this sense that is 'our' being before all anthropology, before all humanism and all antihumanism, requires an ontology that is still to come, that does not mean that it will come, but perhaps that it is in itself, as thought, ordered in the dimension of a 'coming' or of an 'overcoming': that of our compearance [*comparution*], which is our presentation in the element of sense. This presentation does not itself have signification; it has only place [*lieu*], ceaselessly, traversing innumerable significations."[19]

18. For more on mimetism and its relationship to Nazism, see Lacoue-Labarthe's *Heidegger, Art, and Politics,* trans. Chris Turner (Oxford: Basil Blackwell, 1990), esp. chap. 8. It is worth noting that this melding of mimetism and community is not, in Nancy's and Lacoue-Labarthe's eyes, confined to the Nazi project. "We wish only to underline just how much this logic, with its double trait of the mimetic will-to-identity and the self-fulfillment of form, belongs profoundly to the mood or character of the West in general, and more precisely, to the fundamental tendency of the *subject,* in the metaphysical sense of the word" ("Nazi Myth," 312.) Here we can get a good glimpse of the normative character of Nancy's project: to try to articulate a conception of community that is no longer totalitarian. More on this below.

19. Jean-Luc Nancy, *L'oubli de la philosophie* (Paris: Editions Galilee, 1986), 95. Translations from this work are my own. I use the term "compearance" to translate *comparution* in conformity with existing translations of Nancy's work. Although a full discussion of this would be beyond the scope of the present chapter, it is worth noting the internal coherence Nancy sees between what he calls "sense" (which is not to be confused with linguistic signification, but rather is, like *differance,* the "ground" of its possibility), being, and community. In his introductory essay to *Une pensée finie,* Nancy writes, speaking of being, that "[i]t is a matter of a diaresis or a dissection of the 'self' that precedes all relationship with the other, as well as all identity of the self. In this diaresis, the other *is* already the same, but this 'being' is not a confusion, and still less a fusion: it is the being-other of the self insofar as neither 'self' nor 'other,' nor some relationship of the two can be given to it as an origin. It is less and more than an origin: the to-self [*a-soi*] as appropriation of the inappropriable of to-being [*a-être*]—of its sense" ("Une pensée finie," in *Une pensée finie* [Paris: Editions Galilee, 1990], 17; my translation).

The idea that community cannot be straightforwardly signified may strike readers as odd and self-defeating. After all, is Nancy's project not an addressing of community in order to offer an account of it? Is he then telling us that no account can be given, and that therefore he cannot realize his own aims? Actually, no; he is not saying that. The situation with Nancy regarding community is very close to that with Derrida regarding linguistic meaning. Although the treatment of Derrida's specific view will have to await the next chapter, it can be said here that for Derrida linguistic meaning is not something one can give a straightforward account of, but that does not preclude one from giving an account of why one cannot give a straightforward account of it, and it does not preclude one from denouncing attempts to give a straightforward account of it.

The situation with Nancy closely parallels the Derridean position. The fact that one cannot give a straightforward account of what community is does not prevent one either from giving an account of what is going on in community that resists straightforward signification or from criticizing attempts to give a straightforward signification of community. We have already had a glimpse of the latter in Nancy's treatment of Nazism. I want to turn momentarily, by way of discussing Nancy's concept of "sharing" (*partage*), to the former. What needs to be emphasized here, however, is that for Nancy the lack of a common substance that characterizes community precludes giving an account—in the traditional sense of an account as that which says what the accounted is, that which signifies the accounted—without precluding discussion of community and while still articulating important aspects of it.

This articulation will involve, as do Derrida's articulations of that which gives rise to linguistic meaning, terms that do not themselves have a straightforward linguistic meaning. Some of Derrida's terms are well-known: *differance*, trace, supplement. Nancy also employs such multivalenced terms, perhaps the most illustrative among them being that of "sharing." In English as in French, the idea of sharing (*partage*) can be read as indicating two opposed movements at the same time. First, to share is to divide something up among the participants in the sharing; it is an act of division. Second, and in an important way opposed to this, to share something is for the participants themselves to take part in that something which itself may remain undivided. In the first movement, that which is shared is divided among participants who themselves remain undivided. In the second movement, that which is shared remains undivided and the participants, as it were, divide themselves into it. Taken together, sharing indicates a movement in which division and undivision are in an economic relation, an unstable mutual engendering in which neither shared nor participant retains its boundaries.

For Nancy, this idea of sharing indicates the relationship among the members of a community. In a community, individuals are both the participants and the shared of the sharing: they both share of themselves and share in the sharing of others. Nancy claims that Georges Bataille captured this idea of sharing when he stopped thinking of subjectivity as self-enclosed but rather as exposure to others.

> [Bataille] gave up thinking the *sharing* of community and the sovereignty in the sharing or *shared sovereignty,* shared *between Daseins,* between singular existences that are not subjects and whose relation—the sharing itself—it not a communion, nor the appropriation of an object, nor a self-recognition, nor even a communication as this is understood to exist between subjects. But these singular beings are themselves constituted by sharing, they are distributed and placed, or rather *spaced,* by the sharing that makes them *others:* other for one another, and other, infinitely other for the Subject of their fusion, which is engulfed in the sharing.[20]

In another context, discussing hermeneutics and the hermeneutic circle, Nancy makes much the same point: "If we are in motion always already 'in the everyday understanding of being,' it is not that we have in an ordinary fashion—nor extraordinary!—*the* meaning of being, nor *a* meaning of being, nor *the* meaning in order to be. It is that we are, we exist, in multiplying voices, and that this sharing is what we *are:* we give it, we share it, we announce it. 'To be' already in the understanding of being is not to be already in the circulation, not in the circularity of meaning: it is 'to be,' and it is to be abandoned in this sharing, and to its difficult community."[21]

To be in a community—and to exist (at least as Dasein exists) is to be in a community—is a matter of exposure to others who are similarly exposed, a sharing of exposure in which the borders of the individual are neither clearly drawn nor completely effaced. If the borders were clearly drawn, there would be no exposure, and thus no community; if the borders were completely effaced, there would be a common substance in which all were

20. *Inoperative Community,* 25.
21. Jean-Luc Nancy, "Sharing Voices," in *Transforming the Hermeneutic Context: From Nietzsche to Nancy,* ed. Gayle Ormiston and Alan Schrift (Albany: State University of New York Press, 1990; essay or. pub. 1982), 244.

immersed. Thus the sharing that constitutes a community involves an economy of limits and borders that cannot be fixed—and consequently signified—any more than the economy of *differance* can be brought to presence.
"Community is the community of *others,* which does not mean that several
individuals possess some common nature in spite of their differences, but
rather that they partake only of their otherness. . . . All the selves are related
through their otherness, which means that they are not 'related'; in any
case, not in any determinable sense of relationship. They are together, but
togetherness is otherness." [22]

The term Nancy uses for this communal nature is "being-in-common." [23]
Being-in-common clearly does not mean having something in particular in
common; rather, it means being exposed to the others in a relationship of
sharing in which the limits of the individual exposed are neither stable nor
destroyed. "Being-*in*-common means that being is nothing that we would
have as common property, even though we *are,* or even though being is not
common to us except in the mode of *being shared.*" [24] For Nancy, only such
a conception of community can articulate what the "Left" needs without
falling into the temptation of subordinating all individuality to real or perceived communal needs. Otherwise put, only this conception of community
avoids the twin dangers of liberal individualism and (left- or right-wing) totalitarianism. It avoids the former danger by refusing to countenance the
idea of an individual as preconstituted before his or her immersion in the
community. (In fact, Nancy even avoids using the term "individual," prefer-
ring "singularity" [*singularité*] instead.) It avoids the latter danger by refusing to countenance the idea of a common substance by which the community is identified and its communal nature articulated.

If community resists articulation in terms of a common substance that
can be signified or a closure that can circumscribe it, it resists as well and
for much the same reason articulation in terms of what it produces or works
on. "Community necessarily takes place in what [Maurice] Blanchot has
called 'unworking,' referring to that which, before or beyond work, with-
draws from the work, and which, no longer having to do either with pro-

22. Jean-Luc Nancy, "Finite History," in *The Birth to Presence,* trans. Brian Holmes et al.
(Stanford: Stanford University Press, 1993; essay or. pub. 1990), 155.
23. Cf., e.g., Jean-Luc Nancy, "Of Being-in-Common," trans. James Creech, in *Community
at Loose Ends,* ed. the Miami Theory Collective (Minneapolis: University of Minnesota Press,
1991).
24. *Experience of Freedom,* 69.

duction or with completion, encounters interruption, fragmentation, sus-
pension."[25] This resistance, which Nancy derives (with acknowledgment)
from Bataille as well as Blanchot, follows from what has already been said.
For if a community is not to be defined by a common substance, surely it
cannot be defined by those substances that are the objects made or worked
on by the community. Moreover, the situation does not change even if one
defines what is produced by the community as "justice" or "a common division of basic necessities." These, too, are common substances that Nancy
is at pains to resist as threatening to lead us down the road to totalitarianism. Why? Because, as defining principles for a community's identity, they
risk being imposed on everyone in a way that once again subordinates individuals to the perceived needs of the community. If community is to be
thought, it must be thought at a level beneath or beyond or in the interstices
of what can be signified or produced as a recognizable common identity.

With this turn, Nancy diverges profoundly from the mainstream of the
Marxist tradition, which defines community in terms of communal labor. I
believe that Nancy intends this divergence. For many who have witnessed
the abuses of "existing socialisms"—as well as those no longer existing—
the question arises, Where did it all go wrong? For Nancy, the place it went
wrong was in the thought that there could be a defining communal identity
that would subsume all individualities within it. Forced collectivization, the
abuses of basic human rights, the marginalization and often institutional-
ization of those deemed unworthy or threatening—all this occurred in the
name of the communal identity of productivity to satisfy the needs of all.
Once productivity is deemed to be the defining characteristic of a community, the delicate balance of interpersonal relationships and recognition is already threatened. "[I]t was the very basis of the communist ideal that ended
up appearing most problematic: namely, human beings defined as producers
(one might even add: human beings *defined* at all), and fundamentally as the
producers of their own essence in the form of their labor or their work."[26]

We can see here also why Nancy believes that the nature of community
resists signification altogether. "We are the community of sense, and this
community does not have signification. . . . This means very precisely that it
is the community *of* not having signification and *because* it does not have

25. *Inoperative Community*, 31. The original French title for *The Inoperative Community* is
La communauté désoeuvrée, which might also be translated as "the unworked community."
26. Ibid., 2.

signification." [27] Just as productivity or the possession of a common substance threatens to lead to totalitarianism, so does any signification that the
community holds over itself as its defining identity. Communal significations are, in the end, significations of common substances that, in defining
who "we" are, also define who "we" are not and cannot be on pain of marginalization, exclusion, or even extermination. It is in the nature of signification—at least the nonindexical signification with which Nancy is concerned—to create generalities out of specificities. Linguistic meaning cannot
be bound to a time and place: a point Derrida has exploited in his deconstructions. Therefore, insofar as a community gives itself a signification—a
linguistic account of itself—it runs the totalitarian risk that Nancy discovers
in Nazism and the experiments in "existing socialism." Nancy's term "sharing," in being an economic concept that cannot be reduced to a single meaning, resists the signification that would make it a candidate for the totalitarian temptation he seeks to avoid in addressing communal "structure." [28]

In more recent writings, Nancy has also used the term "freedom" (liberté)
to articulate this communal structure. By "freedom," Nancy does not mean
either freedom from determinism or political freedom as it is traditionally
understood. Rather, he means "ungrounded" or "lacking a determining
principle." Thus, a free being is a pure gratuity, a gift that exists, "is there,"
without a reason for being there. "To be sure, here there is no longer even
'freedom,' as a defined substance. There is, so to speak, only the 'freely' or
the 'generously' with which things in general are given and give themselves
to be thought about." [29] This freedom is, in turn, intimately connected to
the being-in-common of a community. "The community shares freedom's
excess. Because this excess consists in nothing other than the fact or gesture
of measuring itself against nothing, against the nothing, the community's
sharing is itself the common excessive measure of freedom. Thus, it has a
common measure, but not in the sense of a given measure to which everything is referred: it is common in the sense that it is the excess of the sharing
of existence." [30] The link between freedom, thus understood, and community runs (unsurprising for a student of Derrida's) precisely through signifi-

27. L'oubli de la philosophie, 101.
28. For that reason, I think we should read as among the totalitarians Nancy wants to
struggle against those who Nancy cites (without naming them) at the beginning of L'oubli de
la philosophie, decry the current "crisis" in philosophy, and want to return to sense, "sense intended as signification . . . [which] consists in the establishment or in the assignation of presence" (30–31).
29. Experience of Freedom, 55.
30. Ibid., 72.

cation. Freedom is not a definable characteristic that people possess; instead, it is the inability to reduce people to a defining (set of) characteristic(s), to a signification. The community, then, is the sharing of that inability to be reduced to a signification, which is the nature (shall I put this word under erasure?) of freedom. In community, an individual's—or, in Nancy's terms, a "singularity's"—freedom is exposed to the freedom of other individuals, and in that mutual exposure exists the relationship that, resisting signification, forms the communal bond. This does not mean that freedom is then the common substance that defines the nature of the community. Freedom is instead the opposite of a common substance; it is precisely the resistance to the kinds of identities of which common substances are made.[31]

Before turning to a critical appraisal of Nancy's conception of community, I want to deal with an objection, mentioned above, that many may want to raise to him. For Nancy, community cannot be signified; the being of community—being-in-common—cannot be given a straightforward articulation. But has Nancy, in his entire treatment of community, not sought to give us nothing other than such an articulation? Is not Nancy's approach to community another in the series of offerings of communal identities that he sees as leading down the road to totalitarianism?

I do not believe that it is. In order to understand why not, we must understand what Nancy means by signification. Although a full treatment of the Derridean view of linguistic meaning is discussed in the next chapter, I can here give enough of a sketch of that view to shed light on how Nancy would defend himself against this charge. For Nancy, signification is a matter of stable identities. It is bound up with the general philosophical project of foundationalism, of giving answers to philosophical questions that are either unsurpassable or indubitable. If, for instance, we can signify who we are as a community, then we can, at least in principle, answer the question, Who are we? in such a way that we have exhausted the phenomenon of our communal being, that we have captured it completely and therefore left nothing more to be said about it.

Whatever else Nancy has done, he has surely not given an account of some sort of stable identity that constitutes the nature of community. If he is giving something like what we might want to call an "account," it is only partially an account of community—a community that itself admits of only partial accounting. In addition to the partial account of community, however,

---

31. We should also be clear here that it is not individuals who, in their freedom, resist signification. Rather, it is freedom as constitutive of an individual that is this resistance itself.

Nancy offers another account, an account of what it is about community that resists giving an account of it. That both the partial account of community and the account of why any such account is necessarily partial rely on a term—namely, "sharing"—that does not have a stable or determinable meaning is exactly to the point of what Nancy is saying. There is something that happens in the being of community, in being-in-common, that, while constitutive of both community and of individuals, resists articulation in a straightforward manner, articulation by means of a determinable linguistic meaning or an ascription of a stable identity. Therefore, it is false to say that Nancy is offering more of the same, since the status of his "account" is not that of wholly accounting for the phenomena but only partially that and partially accounting for a particular nonaccountability that inhabits the phenomena.

Given this, there are at least two further challenges one may want to raise to Nancy here. First, one might query whether language has to be signifying in the sense of forming stable identities. For Nancy, as for Derrida, it does not and indeed cannot. People may use language in an attempt to signify in this way—and, as we will see, for Derrida this attempt is precisely what characterizes the philosophical project. However, language, resting as it does on an unsignifiable "ground" of *differance,* cannot do so. Signification (i.e., full signification), then, is not even one aspect of language; one would be most accurate in calling it one of language's false temptations. For Nancy, however, it is the temptation that is dangerous, because it is what motivates the totalitarian project.[32] Thus, even if signification is an illusory temptation, we must avoid engaging in it, especially in our reflections upon community, because of the damage subscribing to this illusion leads to.

The second challenge one might raise is in the connection between signification and foundationalism. Is signifying—again, in the sense of giving a stable identity—necessarily bound to foundationalism? Is giving an account (of something) that one can defend against all comers necessarily the same thing as giving an account that is unsurpassable, an account that one can be assured (presumably through some sort of transcendental guarantee) exhausts the phenomena it attempts to account for? Otherwise put, is the ascription of a common substance to a community necessarily a project of signification?[33] This is a question I return to both in this chapter and in the

32. We might recall here that the impossibility of realizing the totalitarian project parallels the impossibility of realizing the project of signification.

33. It is clear that, for Nancy, the idea of a common substance and the project of signification must be internally linked. Otherwise, the critique of the idea of a common substance as totalitarian would be unmotivated. For Nancy, there is an either-or here: either a totalitarianism of common substance (a project of immanence) or sharing. This either-or is structurally the same as Derrida's either-or I discuss in the next chapter: either foundationalism or *differance.*

next one, since it assumes a connection, between the giving of accounts and foundationalism, that is spurious.

Before turning to that second challenge, however, we must first return to a question, posed at the outset of this discussion, regarding the ambiguity of the question Nancy is attempting to answer in his treatment of community. There I noted that Nancy attempts to answer two questions that he does not distinguish, the question of what it is to be in community and the question of how we can conceive a community in a nontotalitarian fashion. The first question is a constitutive one, the second a normative one. It is time now to confront this ambiguity, because on it depends the status of Nancy's own discourse and, consequently, the issue of how he is to be evaluated.

Is Nancy attempting to answer the constitutive question, the normative one, or both at a stroke? In order to approach this issue, we need to see how separable these questions are. And in order to do that, we must recognize that a satisfactory answer to one question may not be a satisfactory answer to the other. Let us suppose, for instance, contra Nancy, that there were a constitutive answer to the question of community that involved a common substance. And let us further suppose that recognition of that common substance would indeed lead to some form of totalitarianism. Let us suppose, for instance, that the United States really is a Christian country and that what forms the essence of a community here is its adherence to Christian principles of the kind advocated by one of our current televangelical luminaries. Or, if that is too much to stomach, suppose that we were really Hobbesian agents that formed and stayed in communities in order to realize our own self-interests. Even if this were constitutive of community, discovering it to be so would not give us a satisfying answer to the normative question. In fact, what it would mean is that community possesses a totalitarian nature. A satisfying answer to the constitutive question, then, is not necessarily a satisfying answer to the normative one.

The same thing happens if we go the other way around. It may be a normatively good idea to believe that what constitutes community is a sharing of the kind Nancy proposes. And this may be good to believe even if that is not what constitutes community. If community were really constituted by some sort of implicit social contract among Hobbesian agents, we would be wrong in thinking it to be constituted by sharing. But nevertheless, it still might be a normatively good thing to think so. Why? Because it might dull some of the sharper edges of our nature if we possessed certain mistaken beliefs about who we were. Of course, if we really were Hobbesian, this dulling could only go so far; but normatively, that would be better than the cynicism that a recognition of our true natures would, in all likelihood, promote.

Thus the constitutive and normative questions are separable. They might have answers that diverge, and even diverge profoundly. The answer to the question of what it is to be in community is not necessarily the answer to the question of how to conceive community in a nontotalitarian fashion. This does not mean that the answers to the two questions *cannot* converge. They very well might. But it does mean that we must ask the two questions separately, and cannot presume that, having answered one, we have answered the other.

Although it is clear that the two questions are separable, it is equally clear that Nancy did not separate them. At moments, his approach to community seems constitutive; he seems to be telling us what it is to be in community, and in doing so tells us what it is to be an individual or "singularity." A particularly important moment in this orientation is his argument that complete separation is inconceivable. Alternatively, at other moments he seems much preoccupied with avoiding the totalitarian implications of certain conceptions of community. Among these moments, the argument against a common substance is prominent. Now, it may be that he believes that we are in the fortunate situation in which what constitutes community is also what can save us from totalitarian conceptions of community, if only we could come to realize it. However, since he does not separate the questions, we cannot tell whether he believes this.

In offering a critical evaluation, then, the most effective way to move would be to approach each question separately, asking whether he has convincingly made his case, and then, should the answer to each be in the affirmative, ask about the relation between the two. As it turns out, we will not get to the issue about the relation. I believe that Nancy does not answer either the constitutive or the normative question adequately, and thus does not present us with the possibility of a happy convergence. Instead, Nancy presents us with a self-defeating answer to the normative question and an unconvincing answer to the constitutive one.

I want to turn first to Nancy's normative answer, or, more precisely, to the status of Nancy's conception of community as a response to the question of how to conceive community in a nontotalitarian fashion. I turn here first because the criticism of his conception construed normatively is straightforward, while the criticism of his conception of community construed constitutively is more involved. Has Nancy, then, offered us a conception of community adequate to the task of avoiding totalitarianism?

The answer to this question is in the negative, but not because his answer still permits totalitarianism a hold on community. Rather, it is because his conception of community, if it is to be understood as an answer to a normative question, presumes a prior commitment to a type of community bond that the conception itself excludes as totalitarian. Otherwise put, his conception of community proves too much against totalitarianism, eliminating in the same gesture not only totalitarianism but any grounds one could have to oppose it.

To see how this is so, we must bear in mind that, on the normative interpretation, the question Nancy is answering is that of how to conceive community in a nontotalitarian fashion. One must assume that the answer he offers is one that a community that opposes totalitarianism might consider embracing. Otherwise put, the conception he promotes cannot just hang out there as a way to conceive community nontotalitarianly (pardon the expression), but, in order to have normative force, must be a conception that a community can consider as a reasonable possibility for itself to adopt.

Unfortunately, no community can coherently embrace Nancy's conception of community as an antidote to totalitarianism, because in order to do so such a community would have to deny its own ratification of the value for which it would embrace the conception. How so? Whatever else a community that rejects totalitarianism would hold to (and, as I argue in Chapter 3, it must hold to much else), it would have to hold to a value something like "Totalitarianism is morally bad." Or, if we prefer to put the matter as a principle for action rather than as a value, "Communities should not choose totalitarian modes of self-constitution." In either case, the community is defining itself in terms of who it is or wants to be. And it is precisely that kind of self-definition that Nancy's conception of community precludes.

Let us recall that, for Nancy, community cannot be signified: "it is the community *of* not having a signification and *because* it does not have signification." But to hold a value or a principle like the ones discussed in the last paragraph is to have, if not full signification, at least a common substance, that substance being a value or principle by which the community defines itself. And it is precisely that which Nancy precludes as a possibility for a conception of community, because self-definition in terms of a common substance is a project of signification. To be precise, he precludes it not because actually giving such a signification is totalitarian or at least runs the risk of totalitarianism. In fact, he thinks that such an attempt is impossible to realize, because the project of signification is, for Derridean reasons, impossible to realize. Rather, he precludes it because the very project of such a signification, even though it always results ultimately in failure—that is, death—is precisely the totalitarian project, since the totalitarian project is a project of death. Thus, embracing Nancy's nontotalitarian conception of community cannot be done for the reason that it avoids totalitarianism, because a community cannot *at the same time* give itself that reason and hold to Nancy's conception.

The argument I have made does not entail that Nancy has not given a coherent answer to the question of how to conceive a community in an nontotalitarian fashion. I take it that he has done so. Rather, the argument is that it is a conception that no community can hold without denying the basis upon which it would hold it. Having seen this, it is important also to recognize that a community can hold to Nancy's conception if it decides to do so *for no reason whatsoever*. Otherwise put, if a community decides to conceive itself in a nontotalitarian fashion, it can do so according to Nancy's conception; but it cannot do so for the reason that it is a nontotalitarian conception or, for that matter, for any other reason. This is because any reason that one might adduce for embracing Nancy's conception would have to have reference to a value or a principle, which is precisely what Nancy's conception precludes. Why must a reason in this neighborhood have reference to a value or a principle? Because at issue is why a community would want to conceive itself one way rather than another, and reasons to do that refer to what is or should be valued or done.[34]

If all this is right, another conclusion follows as well. For Nancy, any common substance by which the community identifies itself runs the risk of totalitarianism. But it seems that we have isolated a common substance—a communal self-identification—that may be crucial in avoiding running this risk. That communal self-identification is in terms of a value or principle of nontotalitarianism. The situation is a bit complex here, so we need to move carefully in understanding this. I have argued that if a community were coherently to embrace Nancy's conception of community, it would have to do so for no reason at all. Such an embrace would be irrational, in the mundane sense of being done for no reason. But if the embrace of a communal nature is done for no reason, then any communal nature is as good as any other. There is no more reason to embrace Nancy's conception of commu-

---

34. It might be objected that I am begging the question against Nancy. After all, has he not offered a conception of community that does not refer to values and principles? And do I not, by stipulating that community must refer to values and principles, just define Nancy out rather than argue against him? In fact, I do not stipulate that community must refer to values and principles. If I stipulate anything, it is the more uncontroversial idea that *reasons for conceiving community one way or another must refer to values or principles*. Thus, I am arguing, not against Nancy's conception of community, but against a community's holding his conception for a reason.

nity than to embrace a totalitarian one. And if this is true, then it is the requirements that Nancy's conception of community places upon a community that might embrace it that run the risk of totalitarianism. The risk is run because no reasons are offered in favor of Nancy's conception, and thus no justification in favor of it as opposed to any other communal conception.

Now, this does not entail that the alternative of communal self-identification in terms of a value or principle of nontotalitarianism *guarantees* that a community will not become totalitarian. One can imagine a community that, in the name of nontotalitarianism, begins prohibiting all sorts of practices that it feels might pose a risk to full acceptance of other people. This would be a paradoxical situation, to be sure, but stranger things have happened. In the end, the idea that there may be a conceptual or philosophical guarantee against totalitarianism is suspect. Rather than claim that embracing a value or principle of nontotalitarianism guarantees—as opposed to Nancy's conception—that the risk of totalitarianism is avoided, I want to claim that it is a crucial condition for self-consciously avoiding that risk. A community cannot coherently embrace Nancy's conception of community as a means of avoiding totalitarianism except by accident. It would have to do so for no reason. But a community that wants to avoid totalitarianism— and not by accident—would seem forced to subscribe to a value or principle of nontotalitarianism. That route (or one like it) may be the only way to go to avoid totalitarianism by more than chance.

I want to emphasize here that the argumentative strand I have been following here does not claim that Nancy's conception of community is mistaken. Nor does it claim that Nancy's conception of community is self-contradictory. The question of the plausibility of his conception of community will be investigated shortly. Regarding self-contradiction, the claim is that a community cannot embrace his conception of community without either engaging in self-contradiction or irrationality. Thus it is not the conception itself that issues out in contradiction (or irrationality), but the attempt to embrace it that does so, for the reasons I have detailed.

So far, I have been investigating Nancy's conception of community as a normative conception, a conception intended to answer the question of how to think of a community in a nontotalitarian way. Some who either have read the previous summary of his thought or are familiar with Nancy may feel a bit uncomfortable, however, with the terms in which this discussion has been taking place. I have talked about a community's "embracing" Nancy's conception as though it were something a community had a choice to do. But Nancy often speaks of community as something that happens without a choice, as something any individual always already is. That way of speaking, to which I now want to turn, is the constitutive side of Nancy's conception of community. It tries to answer the question, What is it to be in a community? In the critical discussion so far, I have been reading Nancy as engaged in the normative project of offering a community a way to conceive itself in a nontotalitarian fashion. Another way to read Nancy, however, is as offering a constitutive account of community. This account is not, as mentioned above, a signification of what a community is, but instead an account of what it is in community that avoids the project of signification. Nancy does not separate the two issues, although I have argued that they must be considered separately. Let us turn, then, to a consideration of the merits of Nancy's constitutive account of community.

In a constitutive reading of Nancy, no clear self-defeating problem haunts it. I want to discuss four weaknesses to Nancy's position considered constitutively, but, unlike the case with the normative reading, these weaknesses do not rule Nancy's conception out of court. There is no knockdown argument here. Taken together, however, and moreover in combination with an alternative constitutive conception of community that I will outline, I believe these weaknesses render Nancy's conception of community an unattractive one to pursue. Although there may be lines of development that would allow one to come to terms with these weaknesses, those lines, if my arguments are right, are going to be long ones to reel in.

The first weakness concerns Nancy's justification for the constitutive case he offers. In fact, he offers no argument for the analysis of community in terms of sharing, and the one argument he offers for the necessary exposure of individuals is more limited in scope than Nancy believes. That argument, which we saw earlier, contends that to believe in complete enclosure or immanence is self-contradictory. I, on the other hand, have argued that while it may be that the idea of complete enclosure is wrong, it is not self-contradictory. Moreover, having failed to establish that enclosure is self-contradictory, Nancy's argument—since it was an argument concerned solely with self-contradiction—fails to show anything at all. In a bit, I will try to show that there are indeed arguments that complete enclosure is impossible (but not self-contradictory); these arguments, however, lead in a very different direction from the conception of sharing Nancy wants to promote.

Moreover, even if Nancy's argument were right, it would not go very far in buttressing his case for community as sharing. All that argument purports to show is that complete immanence, complete self-enclosure, is a conceptual contradiction. But that tells us nothing about what the nature of the opening to community must be. Even if there is a constitutive exposure to others—and I believe that there is—what is its nature? And if it does not have a nature, why not? The argument against enclosure, which is the only argument Nancy provides for a constitutive reading of his conception of community, does not tell us. And thus we have a controversial conception of community, one that claims that individuals are at least partially constituted by community, but does not offer any justification for itself as an account of that partial constitution.

Part of the reason for this lack of justification lies, I believe, in Nancy's failure to distinguish the normative from the constitutive interpretations of his conception of community. Much of the force of the argument for his conception carries normative, rather than constitutive, force. It is the urgency of avoiding totalitarian conceptions of community that preoccupies him: "In order to speak of the site that we are dealing with, I might venture the following thought: 'left' means, *at the very least,* that the political, as such, is receptive to what is stake in community." Rethinking the political approach of the Left, worrying about Stalinist and Nazi totalitarianism, trying to preserve difference without reducing it to identity: these are the concerns that drive Nancy's analysis. Thus the justifications he gives for his analysis, as we have seen, are largely normative. If the normative reading fails, however, then much of the justificatory force behind his approach is lost. Thus it is not entirely surprising that he offers little in the way of a constitutive interpretation of community—an interpretation of sharing as an answer to the question of what it is to be in a community—but it leaves this aspect of his view undeveloped.

This first weakness is related to a second one. Not only does Nancy not offer much in the way of defense for his conception of community considered constitutively; it is not clear that he is in a position to assert that much more could be said in defense of it. This is because of his Derridean view of language and signification, and of the role the term "sharing" plays vis-à-vis this view. Now, there is a separate problem that arises for Nancy inasmuch as he depends on Derrida: to the extent that he depends upon Derrida his own position stands or falls with Derrida. I argue in the next chapter that Derrida does fall—or at least that he fails to convince. I do not want to treat that issue here, however, since it may be possible to hold Nancy's position independent of a commitment to the specificities of Derridean views about language. Nancy's case is parallel to, but perhaps not founded upon, Derrida's own. However, there *is* a problem that haunts Nancy concerning signification and sharing, and it is to that question I want now to turn.

The problem is that, if Nancy's Derridean reading of signification is right, then it is unclear how far his conception of community actually admits of defense. Recall that the project of signification, the project of articulating linguistic entities with more or less stable meanings, is necessarily a failure. It is a failure because beneath (or within) signification is "sense," which is an undeterminable that generates (always partial) determinability. For Nancy, the term "sharing" is one of these undeterminables, as is *differance* for Derrida. It points to (one wants to say, although the terminology under consideration forbids it, "signifies") a constitutive feature of community, that not only does community resist signification or full determinability, but in addition it is this very resistance itself. "Sharing" is an economic concept; it designates the movement of double exposure that is constitutive of community (and of individuality). As such, it does not even admit of the partial signification that other, more pedestrian terms admit of. This, by the same stroke, also severely limits what can be said in justifying its use in a constitutive "account" of community.

The problem Nancy faces here is analogous to the one faced by Derrida. Many people are familiar with the fact that the practice of deconstruction occurs by means of operations on a given text. Deconstructive claims, on the other hand (as opposed to deconstructive practice), are of wider scope than those texts, which is what makes them philosophically interesting. Since, however, *differance* (arch-writing, trace, etc.) is discovered in a single text, the task of generalization is a difficult one. This is because the internal limits that deconstruction discovers are text-bound, and in that way deconstruction is always parasitic upon specific texts. Its findings do not readily generalize. Derrida attempted to get around this problem by providing deconstructive readings of many texts and finding analogous internal limits within them. But, as I argue in the next chapter, the limits he found are not as generalizable as he believes they are.

This issue of generalization is even more urgent for Nancy than it is for Derrida, because Nancy does not even offer any treatments of specific communities from which he can launch the term "sharing" in the first place. While Derrida can point to a number of specific texts and say, "Look, the same kind of internal limits are approached in each; something like *differance* is happening in each," Nancy has neglected his homework in this area. He moves directly to the construction of a perspective, without offering evidence for it. But, and this is the crucial problem, even if he did offer evidence in the form of treatments of specific communities, he would still face the problem Derrida does: How does one generalize a term that is used precisely to demarcate an undeterminability? How does one move from the communities upon which a term or analysis is parasitical to those communities that have not been treated? It is precisely in the nature of such parasitical terms that they do not readily generalize. How, then, would we even begin to understand the generalization of a term or a perspective from analyses of specific communities, assuming Nancy had given us any?

Thus the approach to signification that Nancy relies upon—and specifically the role he sees the term "sharing" playing in that approach—makes it difficult for him to construct an adequate defense of his conception of community as an answer to the general question, What is it to be in a community? Having said this much, though, I should say just a bit more in order to allay any fears that I have just argued that without a foundationalist philosophical approach one cannot give an adequate defense of a conception of community. My argument is not that there has to be something like an absolute, foundational signification in order for a concept to be useful in accounting for some phenomenon. In the positive rearticulations of each of the substantive chapters of this book, I sketch accounts of things like community, language, morality, and ontology that (I hope) do not require such signification. Moreover, as mentioned, the immediate connection that Nancy assumes between foundationalism and some sort of stability in identity is spurious. The argument here, rather, is that the specific linguistic role that the term "sharing" plays in this Derridean-oriented view of language renders the generalization of that term as an approach to community a difficult one to defend, for the same reasons that other terms occupying that role, for example, *differance,* are difficult to defend.[35]

The third weakness of the constitutive reading is that, in characterizing community in terms of a bond that does not occur by means of any shared normative principles, it fails to explain what we might call the phenomenology of community. People experience themselves as bound to others at least in part through their commonly held commitments, which are instances of Nancy's common substances. Communities of political activists are bound by the ideals they believe need to be instantiated or by revulsion at the oppression that others face. Familial communities are bound by the projects of contributing to one another's lives or by common passions or interests.

---

35. In the next chapter, I do not say much about this particular difficulty in generalizing Derrida's analyses of specific texts, in part because I have just said it, and in part because the kinds of texts he does treat (at least the way he reads them) have a constricted enough approach to linguistic meaning that Derrida runs into deep problems before one might even be tempted to worry about generalization.

Friendships are also bound by common interests, and often by an articulable common past that allows them to know one another better than others know them, and—in the case of deep friendships—in some ways better than they know themselves. These experiences, experiences of community in the pedestrian sense of "experience," not only do not find their way into Nancy's conception of community; they seem to be betrayed by it.

My claim here is not that an adequate constitutive conception of community must preserve the phenomenology of community intact. That would be an absurd requirement to place on any conception of community, or of anything else for that matter. Rather, my claim is that Nancy's conception fails to explain, and may be precluded from explaining, this experience as having anything to do with community. Before seeing why that is so, let me offer an analogy so that the claim is clear. In explaining my experience of a chair as brown, physics does not preserve the phenomenology of my experience intact. On the contrary, there are certain aspects of my experience that are called illusory, for instance, that there is something that is brown out there in the world, independent of my sensory apparatus. An explanation must, however—if it is to be an adequate explanation—explain why it is that I experience that chair as brown. What is it that gives rise to brown-experiencing where in reality there are only atoms in the void? Merely to say the experience is illusory, that the chair is not *really* brown, is not enough, because it does not address how this illusion can arise and yet seem real enough.

Nancy does not do this for the phenomenology of community, and it is not clear that he can do it without betraying that experience in a way that appears to me to be far too costly to his account. If he were to explain the phenomenology of community on the basis of sharing, he might offer an account of how common normative commitments arise from the bedrock of sharing—or, if we want to view sharing as woven into, rather than beneath, those commitments, how sharing is woven into them. Nancy does not do that. Now, the mere fact of his not doing it is hardly enough to constitute a weakness in the account. Philosophers do what they can; they do not do everything. After all, we philosophers have lives to lead. We cannot always be thinking of how to extend our analyses into whatever directions catch someone's fancy. The problem for Nancy lies not in the fact that he does not draw the explanatory connection between the phenomenology of community and sharing, but in the fact that he may not be able to even if he so desired it.

Recall that for Nancy the idea of a common substance is, rather than an extension of or a relation to sharing, an other to it—specifically, a totalitar-

ian other. On the one hand, there is sharing, and on the other, totalitarianism. Given this alternative, there seems little doubt on which side common
normative commitments would fall. Thus, rather than relating common normative commitments to sharing, they would seem to be betraying those commitments. Otherwise put, a conception of community in terms of sharing
would require that the phenomenology of community be read as totalitarian. This seems to me to be a betrayal of that phenomenology, rendering evil
not only many of the bonds through which people see themselves as related
to one another, but *any* common normative commitment that might act as
such a bond. That seems to me to be too high a price to pay for any conception of community, particularly if there are equally good constitutive conceptions of community available to us, as I argue momentarily that there are.

One might want to object at this point that I have misread Nancy here.
Nancy does not see the idea of a common normative commitment as a
straightforward betrayal of community, because he does not see in straightforward terms the sharing/totalitarian dichotomy I have outlined. We can
no more avoid common normative projects than we can avoid the project of
signification in speaking. What creates totalitarianism is not the mere fact of
having common normative commitments, but failing to recognize the sharing that must subtend or be woven into them. Therefore, the objection runs,
there is no strict division between sharing and common normative commitments, but rather a weaving in which sharing is primary but not exclusive.[36]

In dealing with this objection, we need to distinguish it from any normative reading we might be tempted to offer. What is at issue is not whether
a conception of community as sharing *ought to* allow a place for common

36. This reading sees Nancy's view of community as directly modeled on the Derridean view
of *différance*. One might want to ask, at this point, why I do not consider this interweaving between sharing and common normative commitments in my consideration of the normative
reading of Nancy's conception of community. There, I put the matter starkly as a choice between sharing and common substances. The reason I do not raise it there is that what is at issue at that point is not whether there is in fact a relationship between the two, but which way
of thinking about community we should appeal to in order to avoid totalitarianism. For Nancy,
this is clearly the normative issue, and his opting for sharing is clearly the only viable answer to
be given to that issue. To read Nancy as saying that we ought to give pride of place to both
sharing and common substances is, I think, not to be reading Nancy. Nevertheless, one might
want to ask, independent of the interpretation of Nancy, whether that is a viable position. To
that query, I think my positive rearticulation of community in terms of contingent holism provides a response: namely, that we can appeal to something like common substances—but nonfoundationally conceived—drop sharing, and get a good nontotalitarian conception of community. Otherwise put, sharing, as Nancy articulates it, need not even be introduced to achieve
a nontotalitarian view of community. (This does not mean that it *cannot* be introduced or that
it *should not* be introduced. Rather, it means something like, why bother?)

normative commitments, but whether it does. Once that distinction is made,
it seems clear that it does not. Sharing may be woven into common normative commitments, but it is woven in as two different pieces of cloth may be
woven together. These two different pieces of cloth may not be wholly different in kind. After all, the relationship between signification and sense is
not that between stable identities and what resists them, but the more subtle
relationship between the always only partially realized project of forming
stable identities and the resistance that internally destabilizes that project.
So it is with sharing and common normative commitments. The latter seek
the common substance to which the former is the resistance. The latter cannot achieve it, because of the former. It may be the case that the latter require the former, but even if they do, they do so in the form of a totalitarian
risk that the former acts to defuse in constituting what is really community.
Thus the latter, the common normative commitments that appear in the
phenomenology of community, can only be viewed, inasmuch as they are
common normative commitments, as a threat to community rather than a
constitutive part of it. Those commitments may be constitutive of community in the everyday sense, but not in the sense of what really binds us to one
another.

Now, an objection may be raised from another quarter here, complaining
that with this objection I have just betrayed my own distinction between the
normative and the constitutive. Is this third alleged weakness not a normative complaint against a constitutive analysis? Am I not saying that we ought
not to think of community this way, because of the normative price imposed
by such thinking—that is, its cost in terms of denying the constitutive value
of common normative commitments? That is in good part what I am saying.
My claim can be seen as having two parts: first, a part that says it is unclear
how Nancy could account for the phenomenology of community at all by
appeal to the notion of sharing; and second, a part that suggests that any av-
enue open to offer such an account would skate on normatively thin ice. The
first part of the claim is constitutive, the second normative.

Now the second part of the claim cannot, it is true, be raised by itself as
a reason to reject the constitutive reading of Nancy. It cannot be offered as a
claim that Nancy is mistaken in his answer to the question of what it is to be
in a community. However, it does have a place. If there is another conception of community that is at least as good as the one Nancy offers, and, in
addition to its power as a constitutive view of community, has the additional advantage that it can explain what I have been calling "the phenomenology of community" without making it look like a totalitarian moment in

the communal structure, then we have a reason to embrace that alternative conception. A normative reason, I grant, but a reason nonetheless. Otherwise put, its standing as a reason against Nancy is parasitical upon its being in favor of an account that is at least constitutively as strong as Nancy's.

Which brings me to the fourth weakness. There is at least one competitor analysis, which I shall sketch, that has the strengths but not the weaknesses of Nancy's account, and that does not make normative hash of our common normative commitments. To put the claim broadly, the fourth weakness is that Nancy's conception just is not as good as another conception of community. We are not stuck with the alternatives of Nancy's conception or totalitarianism, but can articulate another view, a view I have called "contingent holism," that can capture the insights that Nancy's approach yields without at the same time having to swallow its undue side effects.

The account I want to promote has roots in both contemporary Continental and Anglo-American traditions. On the Continental side, Michel Foucault can be seen to have articulated this view. It also has roots in the thought of Gilles Deleuze and Jean-François Lyotard, although their embrace of it is more ambivalent. In the fourth chapter, I criticize the side of Deleuze's ambivalence that tells against this account, while in this chapter I use him to bolster my arguments. At a more distant remove, one can cite this conception's affinities with Jürgen Habermas, although in order for those affinities to become identities, Habermas would have to jettison many of the transcendental or "quasi-transcendental" moves he makes. On the Anglo-American side, the clearest forerunner is Ludwig Wittgenstein. The debt of this conception to Wittgenstein's thought will become clear immediately. Also of note on the Anglo-American side are Wilfrid Sellars and Robert Brandom. In fact, when I turn in the next chapter to a positive rearticulation of the Derridean approach to language and linguistic meaning, I rely heavily on their own views.

Before turning directly to the account itself—or at least to a sketch of what such an account would look like—I want to list what I see as the requirements such an account must meet in order to be a viable competitor analysis to the one Nancy has offered. The best candidate for competitor would be able to embrace both the normative and constitutive claims to which Nancy lays claim. Fundamentally, the requirements upon such an account are two: that community be analyzed in a way that avoids totalitarian conceptualizations and that it do so while still recognizing that individuality is in good part constituted by community. The first requirement corresponds to Nancy's normative task, the second to his constitutive one. In approaching this account, we must bear in mind, as I have argued above, that these requirements are separable and answer to two separate questions. In order to keep that idea in view, I approach this sketch in three parts. First, I offer an answer to the constitutive question, What is it to be in a community? Second, I indicate how it is that being in a community means that community is partially constitutive of individuality. My view of that partial constitution diverges radically from Nancy's, although it shares with Nancy the idea that a community is not merely partially causally responsible for who one is, but is in addition conceptually a part of who one is. Finally, I show how the view of being in a community as I have sketched it is nontotalitarian in its implications.

The central claim about which this sketch revolves is this: that a community is defined by the practices that constitute it. In order to understand what a community is, we must understand both what practices are and how a community comprises them. From there, it is only a short step to answering the question of what it is to be in a community.

I want to define a practice as a regularity or regularities of behavior, usually goal directed, that are socially normatively governed.[37] Let me expand a bit on the three aspects of that definition. Most practices have some aim in view. Teaching, for instance, is a practice that has as its goal the imparting of knowledge to students. Cleaning is a practice that has as its goal the removal of dirt. Children playing baseball are engaged in a practice, although children running aimlessly around a playground are not. However, there can be instances of a practice that do not have an end in view. While staring off into space is not a practice, sitting Zen, which (at least according to its proponents) has no aim in view, is a practice. Such goal-less practices, I believe, are the exception rather than the rule. They do exist, however.

A practice must, in order to be a practice, be socially and normatively governed. I hesitate to say "rule governed," since there need not be explicit rules governing all the behaviors engaged in. However, although there may not be explicit rules, there will at least be "know-how" about how the practice is engaged in. There are right ways and wrong ways of engaging in the

---

37. There is another account of the concept of practices that, while developed independently, is similar to—and more detailed than—the one presented here. It appears in chapter 6 of Joseph Rouse's *Engaging Science* (Ithaca: Cornell University Press, 1995). (As this book was going to press, a fuller treatment of the concept of practices appeared, Theodore Schatzki's *Social Practices: A Wittgensteinian Approach to Human Activity and the Social* [Cambridge: Cambridge University Press, 1996]. The account offered there parallels closely, although in more depth, the account of practices offered here.)

practice; and though not all the participants may be able to articulate exactly what makes the right way right, they know it when they see it. (The people who can articulate what is right and wrong about various aspects of a practice are often thought of as the experts in that practice.) When teaching one's kid how to ride a bike, for instance, one may find oneself saying something like, "When the bike goes this way, do *this,*" where *this* is some sort of twist of the body.

The normative governance of practices must also be social. That is to say, just as there is no such thing as a private language, there is no such thing as a private practice. Now, the socially normative governance of a practice does not entail that the practice itself must be social. Diary writing, for instance, is a solitary activity. It is both socially and normatively governed, however. There are ways one writes diaries, types of topics that are considered, potential readers (if even only oneself) that are kept in mind, and so forth. These ways are socially recognized as constitutive of the practice of diary writing. If one does not conform to these norms, one cannot be said to be engaged in an instance of the practice of diary writing.[38]

Some may worry about the social aspect of the normative governance of practices. Must what is to count as a practice be socially recognized as being one (not necessarily by everyone, of course, but by a significant portion of that part of the population that can be expected to recognize such practices)? Does this not lead to some kind of totalitarianism of the social? I do not believe it does. The point in isolating the concept of practices is not to tell people how to act. There is no implicit commitment here to an idea that practices are good and behaviors that are not engagements in instances of practices are bad. As will be discussed below, some practices are good and others are bad. What I am getting at here is the proper level of analysis for understanding what it is to be in a community. Introducing the concept of practice allows us to see both what constitutes a community and what it is about communities that is constitutive of individuals.

The concept of a practice, then, lies at the intersection of individuality and community, as significantly constitutive of the former and perhaps fully constitutive of the latter (although I am not sure about that). As such, it will naturally have a social aspect. This social aspect—the social nature of a practice's normative governance—does not require us to take any normative stand pro or contra practices, and it does not give the members of a

---

38. I am grateful to an anonymous reader for clarifying this point, which in turn has led me to revise an earlier definition of a practice.

community any special power in delegating to them the say-so over what are and are not practices. It merely allows us to discover the social aspect of practices at the right point. If that is right, then there need be no worry that the requirement that practices be socially recognized as such to be such carries any insidious dangers in its wake.[39]

The third characteristic of a practice is that it involves a regularity of behavior. In order to be a practice, the various people engaged in it must be said to be "doing the same thing" under some reasonable description of their behavior. What constitutes a reasonable description in a given situation can be some matter of debate; and we can begin to see the pitfalls that might befall attempts at description when we recognize that, under a suitably abstract description, people we would want to say are engaged in very different practices might be said to be doing the same thing. For instance, a person handing a letter to a postal clerk and a person holding up that same postal clerk can be said to be doing the same thing under the description "interacting with a postal clerk." But we would surely want to say that mailing letters and robbing post offices are two different practices.

I will not address that conundrum here, because for a couple of reasons I do not think it affects the general thrust of the account. First, I do not want to deny that practices can be composed of other practices, so the general issue of level of abstractness does not introduce any particular problems. Second, I see no reason to deny that practices have fuzzy borders and that it is difficult determine when someone marginally involved in a practice passes over into not being involved in it. This fuzziness is not a defect of the account but a fact about practices. As regularities, they allow for variation in the kinds of behavior that can be considered part of the regularity; and those variations, in turn, need to be assessed in order to say whether someone is involved in a particular practice. A person who approaches a church by walking slowly up the church steps can be said to be engaged in the same practice, attending church, as the person who approaches a church by bounding up the steps. But how about the person who stands in the doorway and half listens to the sermon? This is a matter for deliberation, not be-

---

39. One could worry here that there is another problem attaching to social recognition. Social recognition of a practice may not be recognition of it explicitly *as a practice*. There is a difference between, say, a recognition, "They're playing chess," and a recognition, "They're engaging in an instance of the practice of chess playing." I do not believe that this difference causes any great difficulties for the account I am trying to give, however, since there seems no reason to bar implicit recognition of practices as practices from being a form of such recognition.

cause practices are not regularities, but because what variations on behavior count as being within the range of a regularity is not always clear.

That said, however, there is a clarification here that needs to be made. In practices, the regularities that different people are engaged in may not be identical but instead complementary. For instance, in baseball there are often at least ten people on the field at the same time (not including managers, the people in the dugout, etc.). They are all engaged in the practice of playing baseball, and indeed are all engaged in the same instance of that practice. However, they are not all "doing the same thing" in the sense of displaying the same regularity. (Note that this issue of doing the same thing is different from the one just discussed. There it was a question of different practices that may have similar descriptions; here it is a question of different regularities in the same instance of a practice.) Each of the roles taken by the players is socially and normatively governed, and each involves its own regularities. Taken together, those regularities are complementary; they constitute that instance of the practice of playing baseball. Thus, we need to understand the regularities of a practice as being either regularities of identity or regularities of complementarity.

In addition to the three characteristics cited in the definition, there is a fourth characteristic that practices possess, one that does not appear in the definition but is entailed by it. Practices are discursive, by which I mean that they involve the use of language. It is easy to see why practices must be discursive. Since a practice is socially normatively governed, it must involve some sort of communication between participants in order that they may either learn or coordinate the activities that the practice involves. (This does not imply that all the norms of a practice must be articulable by each participant in the practice, but only that some of those norms must.) Moreover, this communication must be potentially accessible to nonparticipants, since without such accessibility the practice would cease to exist when its current participants dropped out. The communication required by a practice, then, must be linguistic. The idea of linguistic communication can be broadly construed here, needing only a set of public signs with assignable meanings. But practices do require language.

This idea of practices as discursive—in later chapters I use the term "discursive practice" to emphasize the linguistic component of practices—is akin to Wittgenstein's idea that language games are central components of forms of life. Although my term "practice" can be read either as "language game" or as "form of life" (Wittgenstein was notoriously obscure about these notions),

I believe that the approach to community that I am advocating is of a piece with Wittgenstein's own perspective. The discursive nature of practices, however, requires something to be said about language in order for the concept of practices to be more deeply understood. At this point, let me offer a promissory note on that score. Although I address the issue of the discursivity of practices a bit further on in this chapter, the positive rearticulation presented in the next chapter outlines in more detail how to think about language and about semantic terms from a perspective that takes practices to be linguistic in nature and language to be fundamentally "practical."

Before turning to the question of how practices constitute communities, it is important to recognize that there can be crucial divergences between the goals a practice has in view and the results it actually achieves, even when it does meet its goals. Otherwise put, the effects of a practice (or of an instance of one)[40] can be other (or more) than the ends promoted by those engaging in that practice. This can happen in at least a couple of ways. First, practices in a society are not isolated. They occur in the presence of—and often in interaction with—other practices. In combination with those other practices, a practice may have unintended effects in areas that are not its normal purview. As we will see, Michel Foucault describes some of these unintended effects in showing how oppressive power arrangements can emerge in a particular practice through the course of its interaction with other practices.

These unintended effects are often opaque to the actor who has helped produce them, but not because he or she cannot in principle become aware of them. In a world of intersecting practices, it is difficult (perhaps impossible) to reflect upon the effects of one's practices upon others who are engaged in practices remote from one's own. This is because the complexity of the effects of interactions of practices that occur within a given society presents formidable obstacles to such a reflective project. This does not entail, however, that one cannot make *some* assessment of effects, or that assessment, inasmuch as it can reasonably be made, should not be attempted. Rather, the implication is that there are likely to be effects of one's engagement in practices that one is not in a position to recognize.

There is another, related way in which the effects of one's practices can be other than the goals one has in view in participating in those practices—a way to which thinkers such as Foucault, Gilles Deleuze, and Jean-François

---

40. For ease of exposition, I will henceforth use the term "practice" to cover both the general practice and its specific instances. I do not think this will occasion any problematic confusion in what follows.

Lyotard have called our attention. We often think of power as a negative, repressive force, serving to limit our actions and our thoughts but not to determine them in the first place. This way of thinking about power, which
Foucault calls "juridico-discursive,"[41] masks other and at times more important ways in which power operates. For instance, power can be a factor
not only in the limitation, but in the constitution, of a practice, in its terms
and in the justifications it gives itself. In turning to Foucault's analysis below, we will see this idea of power as a constitutive force as well as a negative, restricting one.

If power is constitutive as well as restrictive, this implies that there can be
effects—effects of power—that emerge from practices and that are opaque
to those who engage in those practices, at least in their role as participants
in the practice. If, for instance, the terms in which psychological practice is
carried out, terms such as "normal" and "deviant," help create the objects
of psychological study (normal and deviant people), then it is impossible
within the parameters of psychological discourse to become aware of the effects of power that engaging in this discourse has. For Foucault, Deleuze,
and Lyotard, the goal of a genealogical approach to certain practices is precisely to locate the unrecognized creative aspects of power within the practices that are the objects of a genealogy.

We are now prepared to turn to the question of the relationship between
practices and communities. This question can be straightforwardly answered: a community comprises its practices or intersections of practices.
Since practices are socially normatively governed, a given practice may define a community. Often, however, a community is defined by the intersection of several related practices. An instance of a single-practice community
would be people working in a particular political campaign. They are engaged in a common task, recognize their compatriots as being so engaged,
and are bound by this engagement, this recognition, and the norms of their
practice. Everyday talk reflects the use of the term "community" in this way:
we speak of political, religious, and even economic communities in referring
to communities comprising specific practices.

In many cases, however, it is an engagement in several overlapping practices that forms a community. Within the world of political organizing, for
instance, communities are formed not just among the people working on
specific campaigns, but among those within those campaigns who also work

41. Michel Foucault, *The History of Sexuality*, vol. 1, *An Introduction*, trans. Robert
Hurley (New York: Random House, 1978; or. pub. 1976), 82.

on other campaigns and who—often as a consequence of this—socialize with one another away from political work. As another example, people who work at the same institution may form a community, but in addition communities are formed among those who are engaged with one another outside the workplace, whether in socializing, volunteer work, raising children, churchgoing, or whatever. The members of these types of communities are in general probably more self-consciously aware of themselves as members of a community than those who share only a single practice, although there are exceptions here (as, for instance, in the case of a community of actors who define themselves by their abandonment to their art).

Now, in the former case, we might want to refer to these communities as communities of communities, communities composed of single-practice communities. There is no bar to doing this, provided that we refrain from ascribing any ontological or metaphysical significance to such a reference. Such a community of communities is not (or at least not necessarily) a "meta-community." It is just another type of community.

Much of what I have said so far in my positive rearticulation of community may sound pretty pedestrian to those who have followed the convolutions of my discussion of Nancy. Good. I believe that there are complications involved in thinking through community, and I treat a couple of them below. But I also believe much that is useful can be said about community by calling our attention to some noncontroversial facts about the ways in which we live our lives.

It might be objected here, however, that my treatment of community renders community vague. It may be difficult to tell sometimes whether or not there is a community at hand, since communities depend on practices and, as noted, the borders of practices are themselves vague. As in the case of practices, however, the borders of communities just are vague. Where one community leaves off and another begins, and whether there is a community in the first place, can be difficult questions to answer. And however they are answered, it cannot be by recourse to a set of finely honed specifications to which the object of investigation can be submitted. It should be noted, moreover, that the vagueness that characterizes practices and communities has at least some passing similarity to the idea, promoted by Nancy, that community cannot be signified. Although I think there is much more to be said about the nature of community than Nancy does, we agree that what can be said is exhausted before the point of absolute clarity. Otherwise put, there can be no foundationalism when it comes to articulating community, for the reason (among others) that the borders of community cannot be precisely fixed in a way that a foundationalism would require.

Having discussed what a community is, I have not yet answered the question of what it is to be in community. I want to turn to that question—but not just yet. First, I want to call attention to the fact that as the view I am constructing has proceeded, it has, in addition to explicitly addressing practices and communities, at the same time implicitly offered a conception of the social. This conception sees the social as a network of intersecting practices (and thus communities) with no single binding principle (e.g., the economic substructure) by which it is to be explained. Although there may be nodes or practices in the network that are particularly important to study in order to see what the network is all about—nodes where many or particularly important practices intersect—there is no privileged point of view from which the whole may be surveyed from "above" or "outside" the specificities of the various component practices.

This conception of the social is central to the writings of Foucault, Deleuze, and Lyotard. Deleuze, in collaboration with Felix Guattari, has called attention to it with the striking image of the rhizome. Deleuze and Guattari contrast rhizomatic conceptions with "arboreal" ones, conceptions that look for a single root from which structures arise and which, once understood, yields the principle for grasping the entire structure. In depicting the rhizomatic approach, Deleuze and Guattari state:

> Let us summarize the principal characteristics of a rhizome: unlike trees or their roots, the rhizome connects any point to any other point, and its traits are not necessarily linked to traits of the same nature; it brings into play very different regimes of signs, and even non-sign states. The rhizome is reducible neither to the One nor the multiple. It is not the One that becomes Two or even directly three, four, five, etc. It is not a multiple derived from the One, or to which One is added ($n + 1$). It is composed not of units but of dimensions, or rather directions in motion. It has neither beginning nor end, but always a middle (*milieu*) from which it grows and which it overspills.[42]

This image of the rhizome, of practices (which involve both discursive and nondiscursive aspects—"different regimes of signs, and even nonsign states") that are always evolving and possess no defining or constraining center, is the best image I am aware of to picture what is meant by the term "contingent holism." Contingent holism sees the social world as composed of practices

42. Gilles Deleuze and Felix Guattari, *A Thousand Plateaus: Capitalism and Schizophrenia*, trans. Brian Massumi (Minneapolis: University of Minnesota Press, 1987; or. pub. 1980), 21.

that intersect with and affect one another (although not every practice intersects with every other practice), that change over time, that form the parameters within which we understand ourselves and our world, but that do not offer a foundation from which the world can be exhaustively or indubitably understood.

Individuals, moreover, living as they do in social worlds, are largely constituted by the practices of those worlds. This constitution is not only a causal one, in which engaging in certain practices causes one to be a certain kind of individual. To think that practices are only causally related to who one is assumes that one can separate the entirety of who one is from the practices one is engaged in. That is an untenable assumption. I, for instance, am engaged in a number of practices: philosophy teaching and research, political organizing, the raising of children. Ask me who I am outside of these practices I engage in, and I begin to stumble. It is not that I cannot come up with anything about myself that is not part of a practice; rather, it is that most of the important aspects of who I am are tied up with the practices I am engaged in. Otherwise put, I am in part conceptually as well as causally constituted by the practices in which I am engaged.[43]

To be so constituted is to be constituted by the communities of which one is a member, since communities are themselves constituted by practices. In this way, then, communities are partly constitutive of individuality. Now, one might be tempted to object at this point that this form of community constitution is too voluntarist. After all, do we not choose our practices, and thus our communities? And does this not allow the possibility of a preformed individuality that only later chooses practices, in contrast to the deeper form of constitution that Nancy was after? We will see momentarily another form of individual constitution by communities, one that is closer to the kind of constitution Nancy has in mind. But even here it would be conceding too much to admit a deep voluntarism into this type of community constitution.

Individuals are not brought into this world with preformed personalities that only later get involved in some of the practices of their society. Individuals are plugged into practices from the moment of birth. At first, they are more passive than active participants in those practices. But they are being constituted nonetheless by practices they have not chosen and about which

43. This conception of an individual's relationship to community has affinities with Honi Fern Haber's concept of "subject-in-community," outlined in the fourth chapter of *Beyond Postmodern Politics: Lyotard, Rorty, Foucault* (New York: Routledge, 1994).

they have no say. Those practices are partly, but not solely, familial—a point Deleuze and Guattari have emphasized.[44] And later, when one chooses other practices, the process of choice does not occur by means of removing oneself completely from the practices that heretofore have had a hold on one. Choosing practices always comes from within practices. And in that way, practices are constitutive of oneself causally as well as conceptually.

Here one might be tempted to raise a larger question, which I intend to duck. The question is how much influence practices have on one's choices. To what extent is someone able to choose one's practices divorced from the hold one's past and current practices have on one? Alternatively, are one's choices wholly determined by the effects of those practices? These are large and important questions that relate to the large and important question of freedom and determinism. I have no light to shed on this matter, and fortunately do not require it. My point here is the more modest one that who one is and how one gets to be that way are in good part a matter of the practices in which one engages, and that the practices in which one engages are influential in the choices one makes about what further practices to engage in.

Having seen, then, how community is in good part constitutive of individuality, we can recognize as well that individuals often belong to different communities at the same time, because they often belong to widely divergent practices. This seemingly obvious and pedestrian point has two ramifications that have often been overlooked. First, it allows us to recognize that individual uniqueness need not be conceived as a matter of who one is outside of one's practices, as though uniqueness were a matter of what is left over after the common social (or individual, but socially normativized) projects in which one is engaged are removed. This is not to claim that uniqueness is reducible to the practices in which a person participates, but that uniqueness can derive in part from—rather than apart from—the unique array of one's practices.

Second, and more important, this conception of individuals in community points the way toward a resolution of one conundrum that has haunted political theorists regarding the proper way to conceive of minority identities. One example of this conundrum is the following: There seems to be something shared by many, if not all, of those in U.S. society who are of African descent—something more than the fact of having darker skin than some other members of that society. But how to conceive what is shared is

44. Especially in *Anti-Oedipus: Capitalism and Schizophrenia,* trans. Mark Seem, Robert Hurley, and Helen Lane (New York: Viking Press, 1977; or. pub. 1972).

a bit difficult. Oppression, surely. But if that is all, then African-Americans are definable in their uniqueness only negatively, only by means of something bad that has happened to them. One of the responses to this problem has been to say that there is something about being an African-American that is positive and to be valued above and beyond the common experience of oppression. This response runs the danger, however, of saying that there is something to the darkness of the skin or the fact of descent that provides the basis for a positive valuation. The former is problematic because it plays into the hands of racist ideologies; the latter is problematic because the connection many African-Americans have with Africa is very tenuous. The idea of descent by itself is empty, and the history of African-Americans is, aside from the commonality of oppression, very different from that of Africans over the past two hundred years. Thus the question arises, how can African-Americans (or other traditionally marginalized groups) conceptualize their communities positively without falling prey to various ideologies that are better off avoided?

The answer, I believe, lies in turning to the concept of practices. African-Americans have shared a set of practices in which non-African-Americans have had only a marginal presence. One of those practices, for instance, is jazz. African-American identity is bound up with jazz in a way that non-African-American identity is not. This does not mean that jazz develops from some deep essence of blackness, or that non-African-Americans cannot make a contribution to jazz. Rather, it means that this is one of the practices that has been defining for much of African-American identity: one of the practices that have constituted the individuality of many African-Americans. The value, then, in studying topics like African-American history lies in coming to understand what it is to be of African descent in this society, coming to understand the practices in which people of African descent have been engaged. Looking at matters this way helps get past the bouncing back and forth between essentialist affirmations and denials of all positivity that has characterized discussions of the identities of traditionally marginalized communities.[45]

So far, we have seen how community is constitutive of individuality inasmuch as it is one of the things that is defining for identity. There is another way individuality is constituted by community. This has to do with the dis-

---

45. This view of culture as characterizable in terms of practices seems to inform Kwame Anthony Appiah's book on African identity, *In My Father's House: Africa in the Philosophy of Culture* (Oxford: Oxford University Press, 1992).

cursivity of practices. Earlier I claimed that practices must be linguistic, or else the social nature of a practice could not be had. Tyler Burge has argued that this discursivity is constitutive of individuality in the sense that language is determinative not only for identity but also for a person's mental content. Again, this determination is not merely causal but also conceptual. What a person is thinking is conceptually dependent on what is going on outside a person. In terms closer to Burge's own idiom, individuation of mental content cannot be conceived individualistically. It must be conceived as well by reference to the language of one's communities and even to the external physical world. I turn now to his arguments in order to show how we can conceive of community as deeply constitutive of individuality at a depth that competes with Nancy, while avoiding the untoward consequences of embracing Nancy's own conception.

Before turning to the specific arguments, let me situate Burge briefly, since readers more steeped in the Continental tradition may be unfamiliar with his work. Burge's work is primarily in the philosophy of mind, and specifically in that area of intersection between philosophy of mind and philosophy of language that goes by the name of *mental content*. He has been concerned to show that mental content is not simply a matter of what goes on within a person's mind or brain, but also a matter of what is going on outside, specifically in that person's environment and language. The interest of this for us is that, to the extent that he can show this, he has developed a position similar to—although perhaps better in its development than—Nancy's position that there is an economy of "inside" and "outside" that resists any strict delineation of borders. Otherwise put, individuality is constituted at least in part by community.

Burge's argument is that mental content—what a person is thinking about, feeling, believing, and so forth—cannot be accounted for solely by an examination of the state of that person's "internal qualitative experiences, his physiological states and events, his behaviorally described stimuli and responses, his dispositions to behave and whatever consequences of states (non-intentionally described) mediated his input and output."[46] Burge offers an array of arguments, mostly in the form of thought experiments, to make his case; however, these arguments can be divided broadly into three types: social, physical, and dialectical.

---

46. Tyler Burge, "Individualism and the Mental," in *Studies in Metaphysics*, Midwest Studies in Philosophy, vol. 4, ed. Peter French, Theodore Uehling Jr., and H. Wettsten (Minneapolis: University of Minnesota Press, 1979), 79.

Burge's social argument is offered most forcefully in his paper "Individualism and the Mental." Burge asks us to consider a person who has a small set of true beliefs about arthritis, including the belief that he has arthritis. This person, however, also believes—falsely, of course—that he has arthritis in his thigh. Arthritis is an ailment that only affects the joints. Now, suppose the social situation of this person were different, such that in his society the term "arthritis" were used to refer to a variety of rheumatic ailments, and that therefore the person in question were using the term correctly. In that case, the person would not have thoughts, beliefs, or feelings about arthritis—that is, arthritis as we use the term. There is, in the counterfactual situation, neither an individuation of his mental content that corresponds to our notion of arthritis nor a linguistic individuation of our notion of arthritis. When he says, "I think I have arthritis," he will not mean arthritis, but instead a general rheumatic ailment.[47]

What is crucial to this thought experiment is not simply that someone raised in a different society would have concepts different from ours, but more deeply that one has them even though one would have the same physiological, behavioral, and mental experience. Nothing has changed in this thought experiment except the outside social environment; that change, however, has changed the mental content of the "arthritic" individual. He no longer has thoughts, beliefs, and feelings about arthritis, some of which were right and some wrong. He now has a mental relationship to something else—albeit a something else that is called "arthritis."

Burge offers an analogous argument regarding the composition of the physical environment. He relies on Hilary Putnam's Twin-Earth experiment in "The Meaning of 'Meaning'" to argue, in an extension of Putnam's own analysis, that not only would the term "water" not mean water on the planet of the doppelgänger (where its chemical composition is XYZ instead of H_2O), but the doppelgänger would in fact not have propositional attitudes toward water at all. "[I]t is hard to see how Adam(te) [the doppelgänger] could have acquired thoughts involving the concept of water. . . . There is no water on Twin-Earth, so he has never had any contact with water. . . . Further, no one on Twin-Earth so much as uses a word which means *water*."[48] Putnam, therefore, though correct on the analysis of the meaning of natural-kind terms, is wrong when he assumes in his thought

47. This thought experiment is given and analyzed on pages 77–79 of "Individualism and the Mental."

48. Tyler Burge, "Other Bodies," in *Thought and Object: Essays on Intentionality,* ed. Andrew Woodfield (Oxford: Clarendon Press, 1982), 109.

experiment that the earthling and his doppelgänger have the same thoughts.[49] Different physical environments determine different thoughts.

Burge's last argument against individualism in the individuation of mental content relies not upon the physical or social environment but upon how we learn language and what the status of that learning is.[50] He claims that the learning of many words, if not most, consists in a back-and-forth movement between "normative characterizations," which are guidelines dictating what something must have or be in order to be counted as a member of the set covered by a certain term, and "archetypal applications," which are exemplary members of that set.[51] The primary thrust of his argument is that since this dialectic exists, it is often not incoherent or self-contradictory to doubt statements that a community considers true by virtue of meaning. The dialectic precludes in many cases a tightness of fit between accepted synonyms, so that room for doubt or correction remains.

What this room for doubt implies, however, is that two individuals, identical except for their social environments, can have two different thoughts. The thought experiment Burge relies upon to show this is to imagine two people who think their respective communities are wrong in their beliefs about the meaning of a term. However, one of the skeptics is correct in what he or she holds the accepted meaning of that word to be, and the other is not. In the latter case the meaning that the skeptic thinks is the correct one is, by coincidence, in fact the one his community agrees is the correct one. Now, both skeptics are in the same physiological position, but both have different thoughts. The skeptic who is correct about what he or she thinks is the accepted meaning has doubts about the meaning of that very term. The other skeptic has no thoughts about that meaning, since it nowhere appears in his or her community's language.

There is a negative conclusion to be drawn from Burge's thought experiments: mental content is not purely an "internal" affair. There is a positive conclusion to be drawn as well: mental content relies upon a person's social and physical surroundings. Together, these conclusions point to a fact

49. In setting up his thought experiment, Putnam asks us to assume that the earthling and his doppelgänger "were exact duplicates in appearance, feelings, thoughts, interior monologue, etc." ("The Meaning of 'Meaning,'" in *Mind, Language, and Reality*, vol. 2 of *Philosophical Papers* [New York: Cambridge University Press, 1986; or. pub. 1975], 224).

50. The fullest articulation of this argument is given in Tyler Burge, "Intellectual Norms and the Foundations of Mind," *Journal of Philosophy* 83, no. 12 (1986): 697–720, esp. 703–10. See also idem, "Wherein Is Language Social?" in *Reflections on Chomsky*, ed. A. George (London: Basil Blackwell, 1989), esp. 181–84.

51. "Intellectual Norms," 703.

about community that runs close to the perspective Nancy wants to defend, but diverges in crucial ways. What is going on inside an individual, the mental content of that individual, is constituted not only by the individual's physiological states but also by the discursive practices—and thus the communities—in which that individual is engaged. To put the claim in Nancy's terminology, the individual (or singularity) is exposed to the community, and thus is not a self-enclosed whole. Earlier, in assessing Nancy's argument against self-enclosure, I said that although the idea of self-enclosure is not self-contradictory, it is false. Now we can see why. The idea of self-enclosure can be conceived without contradiction, but so to conceive it would miss the important distinction between the existence and the content of an individual's mental states. The existence of an individual's mental state may indeed be self-enclosed, at least conceptually (although not causally, as we saw earlier); but the content of an individual's mental state cannot even be conceptually self-enclosed.

This way of arguing for exposure has several advantages over Nancy's approach. First, it allows for a much finer grained approach to exposure than Nancy's approach does. In fact, one of the implications of Nancy's approach is precisely that anything more than a very partial account of community cannot be given. In contrast, Burge's approach, if embedded in a larger account of community, allows us to say much more about what a specific community is, what binds it together, and what its limits are. All this would occur by way of accounting for its particular discursive practices. Second, this approach to exposure does not face the problems that Nancy's approach, constitutively interpreted, faces. Unlike Nancy's approach, it does offer arguments for its position; those are the arguments here rehearsed. In part, it is able to offer such arguments because it does not endorse the Derridean view of language that Nancy endorses, and thus does not face Derridean problems of generalization. (The next chapter will offer a view of language that fits neatly with this view of community.) Finally, it gets the phenomenology of community right. Although Burge's argument that mental content is partially determined by a community's discursive practices may initially be counterintuitive, it converges with the larger idea that who someone is, is in good measure a matter of specific recognizable bonds that he or she shares with others in his or her community.

In addition to the two conclusions I have cited so far, there is another positive conclusion as well that can be drawn from the third thought experiment. This last conclusion concerns the nature of meaning, and will become of deeper interest to us both in the final part of this chapter and in the next chapter. If the dialectic Burge describes is an accurate account of the learning of meaning, then linguistic meaning is normative in the sense that it tells us how, among various possibilities, we should use our words. An account of meaning that precluded this dialectic (or something analogous to it) and considered meaning to be fixed by community usage would not be normative in this rich sense. On this latter account, there could be no debate over correct word usage, because the fact of community usage would be the final arbiter of any disagreement. For Burge, however, the field of linguistic meaning is more open than that: community usage is a recommendation rather than a legislation, and thus the normativity of linguistic meaning can be seen as a field of struggle rather than merely a binary opposition between correct and incorrect use.

It is the failure to understand the normative underpinnings of Burge's conception of language that has motivated much of the criticism of his work. Andrew Woodfield, among others, raises the question whether Burge has elided a distinction between the ascription of mental content and that content itself, and argues that the preservation of that content would subvert the power of Burge's thought experiments.[52] "[T]he same practices reveal that our *ascriptions* of content are sensitive to all sorts of background information, including information about the social environment of the subject, yet we do not, or should not, treat such variability as proof that the content in itself varies."[53] Woodfield argues that mental content should be considered as analogous to linguistic content in the sense that a concept is defined by its inferential role, and concludes from this that the first patient in Burge's arthritis example—the patient who shares our linguistic situation— was no more thinking about arthritis than the person in the counterfactual situation. This is because the inferences that the person drew from what he thought was arthritis were different from the inferences compatible with the concept of arthritis. Thus, not only did the patient misuse the term "arthritis" in the self-ascription of mental content; the content of his intentional life did not contain arthritis, but something else. Moreover, that something else was the same content that the person in the counterfactual situation intended. Neither of the two people in Burge's thought experiment were thinking about arthritis.

Burge's conception of language, however, raises doubts about the analysis

52. Andrew Woodfield, "Thought and the Social Community," *Inquiry* 25, no. 4 (1982): 435–50. See also Kent Bach, *Thought and Reference* (Oxford: Clarendon Press, 1987), esp. 262–80.

53. "Thought and the Social Community," 447.

Woodfield offers. Woodfield assumes that in deciding upon mental content one can reinterpret one's having a mistaken assumption about a term as actually thinking about something else.[54] If the meaning of linguistic terms is conceived normatively, however, this is not the case. Meaning is not merely a matter of describing, it is also a matter of commitment. To say of oneself or someone else that one is thinking about arthritis is to say that one is committed to a certain inferential pattern. If one draws an inference from the term that flies in the face of community usage, then one can either defend one's use of the term or abandon it. If one abandons previous usage, then one admits that one was thinking about that term mistakenly. But it makes no sense to say that one was actually thinking about something else. While it may be true that at the physiological level certain events were occurring that would not occur if one had the correct idea of what arthritis is about, this is irrelevant to Burge's argument. The force of his thought experiments relies on the fact that physiology can be distinguished from mental content. What cannot be distinguished, if Burge is right, are linguistic ascriptions of content from content itself.

One might want to object here that the normativity of meaning as I have interpreted it undercuts the idea that a community's discursive practices are partially constitutive for an individual's mental content. After all, if the dialectic Burge cites is right, then what a community thinks the meaning of a term is does not necessarily determine what goes on in a person's head. And if that is so, then a person's mental content is not necessarily determined by the practices of a person's linguistic community.

Although the first conclusion of this objection is true, the second one does not follow. It is true that meaning cannot be reduced to community beliefs. If meaning could be so reduced, it would not be normative in the sense the dialectic implies. However, this fact does not mean that the practices of a community play no role in determining mental content. When a person engages in questioning the meaning of a term as used by a community, he or she must do so on the basis of other terms the community uses that he or she accepts (even if those terms arise within the context of practices of another community). Questioning meaning, then, can only be local; it cannot be global. Thus, even though a community may be wrong in a specific instance about the meaning of a term—which implies that its beliefs are not

54. This assumption is also central to Bach's critique. "At any rate, if [the patient in the thought experiment who shares our linguistic situation] misunderstands the word 'arthritis' and does not associate it with the concept of arthritis, there seems to be no reason to suppose that the concept of arthritis figures in his belief" (*Thought and Reference*, 267).

constitutive of mental content—nevertheless its discursive practices remain generally determinative, since that error can only be conceived on the basis of a background of correct meaning use. Moreover, if a community is vindicated against a challenge of meaning by a member of that community, then it can be said in that specific instance that what is believed by the community does partially determine that person's mental content. We must be clear, however, that this determination does not arise because the community believes it, but rather—and this is the normative point—because the community is correct in its belief.

An alternative objection one might want to raise here concerns the claim I made earlier that there is a separation between the constitutive and normative questions regarding community. By introducing normativity into the constitutive account, have I not collapsed the two questions in my own approach, just as I accused Nancy of doing in his? In order to see why I have not, we need to recall first that the normativity at issue affects not so much the question of what a community is, but the question of how it is constitutive of individuality. The next step is to see that what it is to be in a community is a matter, in part, of how one's mental content is determined by a community. (It is also a matter, in part, of one's being what one's practices are, which involves no normative issue.) Recognizing that, we can further recognize that although what that constitution is in a given case is a normative matter—inasmuch as meaning is normative—the fact of such constitution is not. Thus the answer to the question of what it is to be in a community is not normative, although there is normativity in the answer to the question of what it is to be in *this* community, regardless of which community *this* community is. Therefore, while there is a point of contact between the normative and constitutive questions, there remains a strict distinction between asking what it is to be in a community and how community should be conceived.

The positive rearticulation of community I have been sketching here has, so far, addressed the questions of what it is to be in a community and how individuality is constituted by community. That is, I have only been addressing the constitutive issues. Lingering in the wings, however, is the normative question; and it is a question of no less urgency than the constitutive one. Recalling that I have argued that the constitutive and normative questions are separable, it is entirely coherent to argue that although I have gotten the constitutive approach right, to conceive things aright constitutively would bring all sorts of normative problems in its wake. Put in Nancy's terms, the constitutive approach I have offered might run the risk of totalitarianism. In closing the positive rearticulation, I would like to turn to this question. I do not want to be interpreted as holding that whatever practices a community embraces either dictate who we are and how we must act or are immune from critique. My argument here is that there is nothing that leans toward totalitarianism in this approach; in fact, it allows us to conceive a progressive politics that avoids totalitarianism. This allowance is exemplified by applying a specific Foucaultian analysis to the considerations to which Burge has drawn attention. All of this does not imply, however, as I pointed out before, that this approach necessarily resists all totalitarianism. Rather, it implies that the alleged bent toward totalitarianism possessed by every approach toward community that views community in terms of common substances is missing in this case.[55]

The entry into some of the normative possibilities of this approach is via the normativity of meaning, the third conclusion of Burge's thought experiments. This normativity invites not only questions of the rational coherence of decisions about meaning but also questions of historical and political emergence. Otherwise put, the issue of normativity can be viewed as a matter of getting it right not only according to the epistemic standards of a community but also according to its moral and political standards. Although Burge recognizes a social factor in determining what "goes on in our heads" and derives part of that recognition from an analysis of the social openness of semantic decisions, he neglects at least two political questions that can impose themselves in the wake of that recognition and that analysis.

First, what political and historical factors need to be taken into account in understanding why our linguistic meaning structure is the way it is? Although Burge opts to discuss pragmatic features of most rational usage in showing how the dialectic works, his thought experiment hints at another direction that his work opens up. He refers to someone who believes that the use of the term "sofa" to indicate a specific type of furnishing serves to "conceal, or represent a delusion about, an entirely different practice."[56] Here it is not a pragmatic consideration that is at issue in deciding what meaning a term should have, but rather a political one. What Burge recognizes in this passage, although that recognition remains undeveloped in his work, is that if linguistic meaning resists reducibility to community beliefs,

55. Were it to imply the former, then there would not be the strict separation between the constitutive and normative questions that I have argued there is. Thus, what follows must be read not as an entailment of the view of community I have outlined, but as one direction in which normative questions about community can be worked out without leading toward totalitarianism.
56. "Intellectual Norms," 707.

then the question of why certain meanings, rather than others, have been adopted by a community may admit of answers of a more politically controversial nature than the idea of pragmatic features of usage would lead one to believe.

The second question is related to the first. How do we come to understand what "goes on in our heads" as a purely internal affair? Here the issue is not the meanings of specific terms but a misconception about the social (and thus political and historical) dimension of meaning (and thus mental content, individuality, and community) itself. In our society, certain perspectives on meaning and mental content have been privileged at the expense of others. In particular, an approach to mental content that conceives it—mistakenly, as we have seen—as a purely internal affair (and, concomitantly, an approach to linguistic meaning that has ignored or overlooked its normative dimension) has privileged inquiry into individuals, rather than into social surroundings, as the arena of explanation of individual experience.[57] The social constitution of experience and the political dimension of discursive practices have been ignored in favor of individualizing epistemic approaches. Inseparably, what "goes on in our heads" has come to be seen as the product of a fixed an unchanging nature rather than as the product—at least in part—of conflict and struggle.

These two questions converge on the status of the discipline of psychology,[58] asking first what its relationship to the surrounding disciplines is and second why that relationship has not received the scrutiny it might deserve. Psychology, in other words, rather than be accepted solely as a paradigm by means of which discovery takes place, must as well be investigated as the product of historical contingencies and the source of social and political effects.

That Burge accepts the psychological paradigm without political or historical question is evident in his article "Individualism and Psychology."[59] There, in arguing from perception that individuation of mental content is nonindividualistic, he admits that his analysis assumes both that there are such things as psychological states that represent the world and that "there

57. Oddly, Derrida, whose project is a radical questioning of accepted approaches to linguistic meaning, also neglects this social dimension, as we will see in the next chapter.
58. At least, psychology in its normative dimensions, which includes not only psychopathology but perceptual and cognitive psychology, personality theory, child psychology, and so forth.
59. Tyler Burge, "Individualism and Psychology," *Philosophical Review* 95, no. 1 (1986): 3–45.

is a scientific account to be given that presupposes certain successes in our interaction with the world . . . and that explains specific successes and failures by reference to these states."[60]

Broadly, Burge's anti-individualistic thought experiment in this last text hinges on the fact that what is perceived is socially determined in the way that what is thought is socially determined in the articles cited above. Here, however, he makes explicit the idea that it is *successful* perception that provides a model for what is perceived. He writes: "Theories of vision, of belief formation, of memory, learning, decision-making, categorization, and perhaps even reasoning all attribute states that are subject to practical and semantical evaluation *by reference to standards partly set by a wider environment.*" The political implications of such standards are hinted at by Burge when he claims that while psychological theories are not of themselves evaluative, "they often individuate phenomena so as to make evaluation readily accessible *because* they are partly motivated by such judgement."[61]

In arguing that mental content is nonindividualistically individuated, that social and linguistic standards inform that individuation, and that the dialectical process by which those standards are arrived at precludes in many cases the possibility of their closure, Burge has opened the door to questions of the historical emergence and the political orientations of those standards, of what "goes on in our heads," and thus of the ways in which individuals are communally constituted. That he has not engaged those questions, and indeed accepts the psychological framework within which he asks them, is probably due to the fact that the story he tells is conceptual rather than causal. However, the very conceptual story he tells leads naturally to causal questions concerning the status of discourse about the mental, questions that have been addressed by Michel Foucault's genealogy of psychological discourse.

Foucault's project regarding psychology is one that shows how it arose, what other discourses and practices it intersected with, and what political effects it has had. In his most sustained discussion of the genealogy of psychology, *Discipline and Punish*, he writes of the modern soul that "it exists, it has a reality, it is produced permanently around, on, within the body by the functioning of a power that is exercised on those punished—and, in a more general way, on those one supervises, trains and corrects, over madmen, children at home and at school. . . . On this reality-reference, various concepts have been constructed and domains of analysis carved out: psyche,

60. Ibid., 44.
61. Ibid., 25.

subjectivity, personality, consciousness, etc."[62] A genealogy of psychology, then, will reveal at least some of the social, historical, and political conditions whose convergence determined the idea of the soul, or the mind, as we currently conceive it. Thus, like Burge, Foucault attempts to remove the mind from its moorings in the state of the individual; and like Burge, that removal focuses upon the concepts we use in order to determine what is going on inside a person's head. However, unlike Burge, Foucault's target is not mental content as a conceptual matter but the mind as a political concept.

The details of Foucault's genealogy of psychology cannot be recounted in detail here.[63] The part of the story offered in *Discipline and Punish*, however, can be given a brief summary. Torture, as the preferred method of punishment before the nineteenth century, often had effects unintended by the punishing authority and the king in whose name punishment was performed. Its gruesome details served not only as a deterrent against further crime but also as a source of resentment against regal authority and as a symbolic martyrdom of the criminal. Reformers emerged who called for gentler forms of punishment, both as a more humane practice and as more conducive to social order. At the time of these reformers' writings, however, a set of disciplinary practices that had been spread about in different regions of the social field—for example, monasteries and the military—came to the attention of punishing authorities.

What distinguished discipline from torture was, among other things, the change from destroying the body to manipulating it down to its last detail. This manipulation allowed it to be made both maximally conforming and maximally productive. These changes, moreover, coincided with the rise of industrial capitalism and its need for disciplined labor. With this newfound focus upon manipulation, which was adopted in the prisons and in the factories (and was refined in the military), the goal of punishment was no longer that of eliminating what was criminal but that of reforming what was out of order. Practices of normalization came to replace practices of torture; observation and manipulation replaced random spectacle and execution; psychological intervention replaced regal authority. As Foucault writes, "These two great 'discoveries' of the eighteenth century—the progress of societies and the genesis of individuals—were perhaps correlative

62. Michel Foucault, *Discipline and Punish*, trans. Alan Sheridan (New York: Random House, 1977; or. pub. 1975), 29.
63. These details occur not only in *Discipline and Punish* but also in the treatment of psychiatry and psychoanalysis in the first volume of his *History of Sexuality* and in interviews and discussions during the last years of his life.

with the new techniques of power, and more specifically, with a new way of administering time and making it useful, by segmentation, seriation, synthesis and totalization." [64]

Thus the concept of the mind as a discrete substance belonging to an individual whose nature it is the project of psychology to discover is inseparable from an intersecting set of politically charged practices within which it emerges. To the first of the two questions raised earlier regarding the political and social factors that determine the emergence of linguistic structures, Foucault offers the structure of an answer with his genealogical method. [65] To the second question, why we understand the mind as a purely internal affair, Foucault responds with a specific genealogy that isolates the practices and motivations that are intertwined in the emergence of psychology as a therapeutic discipline.

Foucault's approach to psychology does not, of course, tell the whole story about how to conceive community. In fact, if the view I have been articulating is correct, that question is best answered—aside from some of the generalities I have offered in this chapter—by means of a lot of local analyses. If community is a matter of practices, then the urgent normative question facing most communities is not, How should we conceive community? but rather, How should we conceive *our* community? It is those specific conceptions that will be determinative not only for how the community will look, but also, because of their discursivity, for the landscape of the mental content of the individuals engaged in that community.

Although Foucault works along a different register from that of Burge—the latter dealing in mental content and the former in the concept of the mind—they converge in their articulation of how the mental defies individualistic approaches. Foucault's causal story expands and deepens, and at points questions, the conceptual story offered by Burge; Burge's story offers a picture of language that renders Foucault's genealogy more plausible. Taken in their complementarity, and in combination with the general picture of community with which I opened the positive rearticulation, these stories offer a picture of community that has both the normative and constitutive virtues that Nancy seeks but does not find, without confusing the

64. *Discipline and Punish*, 160.

65. Although I have only referred to *Discipline and Punish* here, Foucault offers another, only slightly less direct historical analysis of our perceptual categories in his archaeology of medical perception entitled *Birth of the Clinic*, trans. A. M. Sheridan Smith (New York: Random House, 1973). In that text, he articulates some of the ways in which social relations help to constitute the emergence of the perceptual orientation—the medical gaze—which characterizes current-day diagnostic practice. I am indebted to Thomas Flynn for calling my attention to this point.

normative and constitutive dimensions of conceptions of community. Moreover, in contrast to Nancy, for whom specific political recommendations seem to be impossible, since they would imply an appeal to principles of common substance, which he rejects, the view of community that I am pressing here allows—as the Foucault example illustrates—specific analyses with specific recommendations based upon specific principles. (We will see in more depth the application of a specific principle in Chapter 3.) Therefore, not only does the view I am proposing here contain the normative virtues of nontotalitarianism that Nancy desires, it does so without exacting the cost of precluding specific political analyses and recommendations.

Finally, the proposed view, although saying much more about community than Nancy thought either possible or safe, avoids the foundationalism that Nancy's account eschews. It does so by distinguishing between the idea that a community defines itself by means of a common substance or, more often, common substances and the idea that those common substances must be signified in the full sense both Nancy and Derrida reject. Common substances arise in the context of practices, which are both historically contingent and evolving. Communal identities are not the product of a transcendental operation, and they receive no transcendental guarantee. Instead, they emerge in the unfolding history of practices that form communities, and vanish as those practices change. Some of those identities are beneficial, others insidious. Since, however, they are anchored in no deep foundations, they remain as distant from the totalitarian projects of signification as the concept of community Nancy develops.

Jean-Luc Nancy's work has done much to call the attention of Continental philosophers to the importance of a conception of community in our philosophical work. It has also done much to raise the issues of the community's role in constituting individuality and of the totalitarian dangers of communal self-perceptions. The argument of this chapter is that, however important the issues he raises, his approach to them is inadequate. What one needs in order to address these issues is not a view of community as unsignifiable exposure, but a view of community as practice or practices. In addition, one needs to embed this view of practices in a contingent holism, an approach that rejects both foundationalism and reductionism and stresses instead the historically changing, politically invested, and socially interactive characteristics of practices. It is this view of community that underlies the positive rearticulations in the following three chapters, and that must be kept in mind so that the positions articulated in those chapters are not taken to be a return to the traditional philosophical project of providing unsurpassable foundations for thought.

2

From Linguistic Difference to Linguistic Holism

Jacques Derrida

Fashions in philosophy, as elsewhere, tend to wax and wane for reasons that have little to do with the strength or weaknesses of specific philosophical positions. Not only are philosophical problems rarely "solved," but the dominance of a particular approach or cluster of issues is usually superseded by something other than refutation of the approach or resolution of the issues. This is probably fortunate, since it allows philosophers to think about what fascinates them instead of binding them to any particular current research program. In addition, the offering of new perspectives on our lives and our world seems to be at least as important a task as any full assessment of a particular perspective might be; if so, then the proliferation of perspectives need not await the assessment of any particular one.

As far as the deconstructive position staked out by Jacques Derrida goes, however, I think assessment has fallen short. If I may speculate a bit, it seems entirely possible that Derrida's philosophical approach will be superseded without the philosophical world's taking enough of a critical view of his work. The reasons for this may have to do with the combination of the "Heidegger affair," the "De Man affair," and a general uneasiness about the political commitments (or lack thereof) of deconstruction. Or it may just be that something else new comes along that goes better with cappuccino. For whatever reason, if the passage from deconstruction to the next philosophical fashion occurs without more of a critical grappling with Derrida's thought, we will all be worse off for it, and for several reasons.

First, the scope and power of Derrida's rereading of the classical philosophical canon are rarely matched. Regarding its scope, Derrida has claimed that what he has called into question, logocentrism, has controlled not only "the concept of writing" but also "the history of (the only) metaphysics" and "the concept of science or the scientificity of science." [1] Regarding its power, many reflective people have been drawn to this rereading, and it would be a shame merely to go on to the next thing without trying to discover what is worth preserving in such an influential philosophical approach. Second—and this is both the opposite and the complement of the first reason—the effect of Derrida's work will not be erased without (forgive me) a trace. His influence, however concealed, will continue to be felt not only in philosophy but in literature, architecture, the social sciences, and elsewhere. Whether such effects operate for good or ill depends on an assessment of the adequacy, in whole or in part, of his philosophical approach. We need such assessment, then, not only to do justice to him but in addition to do justice to the fields his work has affected.

Finally, closer to the specific concerns of this book, Derrida has been a leading member, along with Foucault, Deleuze, and Lyotard, of the contemporary French approach that focuses upon the often neglected role of difference in philosophical thought. If difference does play such an important role in our thinking—or ought to—we would do well to understand that role; and such an understanding cannot afford to bypass Derrida's proposals. Therefore, even if we were to agree that philosophy needs to think more seriously and more doggedly about—and in terms of—difference, we would still need to know how to do so. And for that reason, too, we must ask whether Derrida's treatment of difference is one we can embrace.

In assessing Derrida's thought, we must first understand that his philosophical concerns are, above all, metaphilosophical. This is, I think, uncontroversial, and has been emphasized by the currently standard approach to Derrida offered by Rodolphe Gasché in his *The Tain of the Mirror*.[2] I will not belabor the point now, since I intend to return to it frequently enough to fill it out by the end of the chapter. Instead, let me just summarily call attention to the fact that Derrida has focused his energies on the Western philo-

1. Jacques Derrida, *Of Grammatology*, trans. Gayatri Spivak (Baltimore: Johns Hopkins University Press, 1974; or. pub. 1967), 3.
2. Rodolphe Gasché, *The Tain of the Mirror* (Cambridge: Harvard University Press, 1986).

sophical tradition as it has unfolded, and has tried to bring to light repressions that that tradition has historically, if unconsciously, ratified, repressions that work not merely by banishing certain themes that are then placed outside of the space of philosophy, but also by attempting to banish certain themes that refuse to leave the space of philosophy, and indeed are partially constitutive of it.

Next, I want to call attention to the point that Derrida's metaphilosophical position hinges on his view of—and his view of the philosophical tradition's view of—language, and especially linguistic meaning.[3] This point, and especially the "especially," need some spelling out. For Derrida, the philosophical tradition, and the ways of thinking it has bequeathed to us, are the product of the workings of linguistic signification. "From the moment there is meaning there are nothing but signs. *We think only in signs.*"[4] If we are to understand our philosophical tradition—and ourselves, to the extent that that tradition remains a part of who we are—we must understand the ways in which language operates in the tradition.

It is important to be clear on this point. The issue is *not* one of understanding the language in which philosophy expresses itself. To put the issue this way would be to assume that there is such a thing as philosophical reflection before or beneath language, an assumption Derrida's analyses are at pains to reject. Nor is the issue one of coming to a better view of language in order to articulate better philosophical positions than the ones previously articulated. To put matters this way would be to assume that one can move from a better view of language to a better take on the ways things are and/ or should be. This assumption does not consider the possibility, which Derrida argues is a fact, that once we obtain a better understanding of how language operates, we will realize that it is impossible to get the kind of take on the ways things are and/or should be that philosophy has always striven for.

As a corollary to this, Derrida does not talk about the way things are or are not. In denying that being is presence—a denial that will occupy us momentarily—Derrida is asserting neither that being is absence (a mistake that only a cursory reading could yield) nor that it is *differance* (a more common misreading). Rather, he is asserting that the operation of language is such that there is always a play between presence and absence. Moreover, that

---

3. As Gasché puts the point, "Whereas Heidegger's discovery of the finite transcendentals is the result of his philosophizing logic, the logos of Being, Derrida's quasi-transcendentals are a function of his inquiry into the conditions of possibility and impossibility of the logic of philosophy as a discursive enterprise" (ibid., 317).

4. *Of Grammatology,* 50.

play operates such that we are precluded from ever attaining a realm of pure presence through our language. And, since "we think only in signs," we are precluded from attaining such a realm by jettisoning language either.

Finally, in talking about the operation of language, what we are referring to, the "especially," is linguistic meaning. It is not—as Derrida emphasizes time and again—marks on a page or vocalized sounds, nor is it the diachronic movement of linguistic change that concerns Derrida. The operation of language to which Derrida wants to turn our attention concerns the way linguistic meaning is produced, or, more accurately, the way what there is of linguistic meaning and nonmeaning in their interconnection is produced.

Derrida's focus upon the centrality of linguistic meaning to philosophy is, of course, not new. It has been an abiding theme of both Continental and Anglo-American thought since at least the turn of the century. What is new in Derrida, and what makes him at once so controversial and so compelling, is the claim that once we understand how linguistic meaning operates, we will also understand that giving philosophical accounts of ourselves and our world is—at least in an important sense, the sense philosophers construct theories about—impossible. As he puts the point, "The history of being as presence [which, as we shall see, is the entirety of the philosophical tradition as Derrida reads it], as self-presence in absolute knowledge, as consciousness of self in the infinity of *parousia*—this history is closed. . . . As for what 'begins' then—'beyond' absolute knowledge—*unheard-of* thoughts are required, sought for across the memory of old signs." [5]

The question I want to raise concerns this larger claim of Derrida's.

In order to make such a claim stick involves defending three comprehensive views: (1) a view of the operation of linguistic meaning, (2) a view of the philosophical project, and (3) a view of their relationship. If any of these three views turns out not to be compelling, then Derrida fails to make his case. If the first view is not compelling, then philosophy can proceed as Derrida thinks it has all along, as soon as it can come up with a suitable view of language, and especially linguistic meaning. If the second view is not compelling, then even if one accepts Derrida's account of the operation of linguistic meaning, there are other tasks left to philosophy. If the third view is not compelling, then even if Derrida is right in his accounts of both linguistic meaning and philosophy, the conclusions he wants to draw in moving from the former to the latter are questionable.

5. Jacques Derrida, *Speech and Phenomena and Other Essays on Husserl's Theory of Signs*, trans. David Allison (Evanston, Ill.: Northwestern University Press, 1973; or. pub. 1967), 102.

In some sense, I want to take issue with all three views of Derrida's. To anticipate a bit, I want to argue that, *even if Derrida's treatment of specific thinkers is right,* he has no basis to move from his specific analyses to general conclusions about either the operation of language or the philosophical project (and thus about their relationship). Otherwise put, although Derrida *may* have put his finger on an important strand in the philosophical tradition and on the way in which language operates in that tradition, he has not made his case that either language or philosophy operates in such a way that the giving of philosophical accounts—including philosophical accounts of language—is impossible in the way he claims it is. At no point do I want to enter into the debate about the merits of Derrida's reading of other figures.[6] I take it that even if Derrida is not completely right about them, he is onto something important in the philosophical tradition. Rather, my complaint is with the implications he sees as stemming from those readings, and my argument is that not only are accounts of language and of philosophy other than those offered by Derrida possible, but that to a large extent they exist and are part of current philosophical discussion.

More specifically, I want to argue that Derrida shares at least two fundamental commitments with the tradition he sees himself as rejecting—two "dogmas" that have characterized traditional philosophical views about linguistic meaning. Neither of these views is necessary either to philosophy generally or to the task of articulating a philosophical account of meaning. Once this has been seen, then the door is open to doing philosophy again in ways that Derrida has neither argued against nor even considered.

In order to understand what Derrida thinks the operation of linguistic meaning is, we will need to recall several specific Derridean texts, specifically several deconstructions. It will not do to remain at the level of general Derridean pronouncements, because without specific deconstructions in hand, the pronouncements will seem unmotivated. Although many different texts might serve the purpose of illuminating the general Derridean position, I have chosen three that are not only individually revealing but also collectively provide all the significant elements of a reconstruction of Derrida's view.

Those three texts are *Speech and Phenomena,* "Violence and Metaphysics: An Essay on the Thought of Emmanuel Levinas" (from the collection *Writing and Difference*), and "Signature Event Context" (from *Margins*

6. For an example of *that* debate, see J. Claude Evans's criticism of Derrida's reading of Husserl, in *Strategies of Deconstruction* (Minneapolis: University of Minnesota Press, 1991), and a reply by Joshua Kates in *Philosophy Today* 37, nos. 3–4 (1993): 318–35.

of Philosophy and later *Limited Inc.*). The first two complement each other well, since the former treats the Husserlian attempt to found a philosophical position in presence, and the latter, Levinas's attempt to escape from presence. If, as the former text argues, absence is inextricably bound to presence, it is just as much the case, as the latter text shows, that presence is never simply surpassable. Derrida points this out in an interview in *Positions:* "*On the one hand,* expressivism [the view of language as composed of signifiers that simply translate their signifieds into words] is never simply surpassable, because it is impossible to reduce the couple inside/outside as a simple structure of opposition. . . . *On the other hand,* and inversely, I would say that . . . expressivity is in fact always already surpassed, whether one wishes it or not, whether one knows it or not."[7] The juxtaposition of the text on Husserl and the one on Levinas displays this tension well, and thus leads to the heart of Derrida's view of the operation of linguistic meaning.

The third text, along with the additional comments in *Limited Inc.,* clarifies several important ambiguities in Derrida's approach to the operation of linguistic meaning. It offers an opportunity not only to confirm the conclusions drawn on the basis of the first two studies, but also to tie up some of the loose ends that lend themselves to tying.

Turning first to *Speech and Phenomena,* it must be recognized at the outset that the Husserlian project is, above all, to use phenomenology in order to put philosophical thought on a firm foundation. For Husserl, philosophy must be the foundational science, and all other sciences must take what justification they can from it. As the foundational science, however, philosophy has to be self-justifying. If philosophical claims were justified by reference to something else, then that something else would be foundational; thus, philosophy must found itself. The goal of phenomenology is to offer a path to that self-foundation that will allow philosophy to assume its rightful place. As Husserl says in a work later than the one *Speech and Phenomena* treats: "Thus the idea of an all-embracing philosophy becomes actualized— quite differently than Descartes and his age, guided by modern natural science, expected: Not as an all-embracing system of deductive theory, as though everything that exists were included in the unity of a computation, but—with a radical alteration of the fundamentally essential sense of all science—as a system of *phenomenological* disciplines, which treat correlative

7. Jacques Derrida, *Positions,* trans. Alan Bass (Chicago: University of Chicago Press, 1981; or. pub. 1972), 33.

themes and are ultimately grounded, not on an axiom, ego cogito, but on an *all-embracing self-investigation*." [8]

Among the hurdles that any philosophy that attempts to be self-founding must face is its relationship to the language in which it offers its claims. After all, language is an evolving, unstable, empirical reality. As Derrida put it in an earlier text on Husserl, "[T]o the extent that language is not 'natural,' it paradoxically offers the most dangerous resistance to the phenomenological reduction, and transcendental discourse will remain irreducibly obliterated by a certain ambiguous worldliness." [9] How ought a philosophical project whose goal is certainty—absolute knowledge, apodicticity—to deal with the empirical, "nonnatural nature" of the language in which its claims are cast? In Derrida's view, the heart of that dealing occurs early on in Husserl's texts, in the *Logical Investigations,* and specifically in the chapter entitled "Essential Distinctions." There Husserl develops a view of the relation between language and thought that, according to Derrida, he never significantly modifies.[10]

For Husserl, the attempt to found philosophical thought occurs by means of trying to locate a precommunicative stratum of thought and experience, a realm where experience can appear to itself immediately—in an unmediated

8. Edmund Husserl, *Cartesian Meditations: An Introduction to Phenomenology,* trans. Dorion Cairns (The Hague: Martinus Nijhoff, 1977; or. pub. 1950), 156. It may be argued here that the application of thoughts offered in 1929 to the project of understanding the *Logical Investigations* is anachronistic, especially since at the time of the *Investigations* Husserl had not yet developed *transcendental* phenomenology. Although it is true that the aims of the *Investigations* were more limited, what they share with almost the entirety of the Husserlian corpus is the project of founding the object of their studies apodictically, and doing so through a process of self-grounding reflection (even if the nature of that reflection changed somewhat with the introduction of transcendental phenomenology).

9. Jacques Derrida, *Edmund Husserl's Origin of Geometry: An Introduction,* trans. John P. Leavey Jr. (Lincoln: University of Nebraska Press, 1978; or. pub. 1962), 68–69.

10. Derrida writes at the outset of *Speech and Phenomena:* "[A] patient reading of the *Investigations* would show the germinal structure of the whole of Husserl's thought. On each page the necessity—or the implicit practice—of eidetic and phenomenological reductions is visible, and the presence of everything to which they will give access is already discernible" (3). Derrida further confirms this reading in his later essay on *Ideas I,* "Form and Meaning: A Note on the Phenomenology of Language," in *Margins of Philosophy,* trans. Alan Bass (Chicago: University of Chicago Press, 1982; or. pub. 1972): "Husserl begins by delimiting the problem [of the relation of thought to language], by simplifying or purifying its givens. He then proceeds to a double exclusion, or if you will, to a double reduction, bowing to a necessity whose rightful status was acknowledged in the *Investigations,* and which will never again be put into question. *On the one hand,* the *sensory face* of language . . . is put out of circulation. . . . *on the other hand,* he defers—forever, it seems—the problem of the unity of the two faces" (161).

fashion. If there is such a realm of thought, and if philosophy can begin to study and articulate it, then it will have achieved a level of apodicticity that can ground (by way of self-grounding) the philosophical project. How so? At the level of immediacy, before the distortions produced by an empirically given system of significations, one comes face to face with one's experience. What one experiences in that realm is indubitable, since it is purely, undistortedly, immediately present to one. This attempt to achieve pure, unmediated presence is the "principle of principles" of phenomenology, which Derrida sums up as "the original self-giving evidence, the *present* or *presence* of sense to a full and primordial intuition." [11] If this realm exists, and if it can be harnessed to the philosophical project, then philosophy will have found a way to ground itself in absolute—apodictic—evidence, and will indeed be the self-grounding discipline that Husserl seeks as the foundation for all other sciences.

In order to isolate this realm, Husserl distinguishes between "expression" and "indication," or, more accurately, between expressive and indicative signs. Both types of signs are meaningful, in the sense that they convey meaning. But there is a crucial difference between them. Indicative signs are meaningful only because of the content of the sign, that is, because the sign is caught up in a social network that a community understands and that is thus meaningful to that community. Alternatively, an expressive sign is one that is animated by the intention that produced it. Its meaningfulness resides not in its being able to be *taken so* by a certain community, but rather in its being *given as such* by a certain intentional life. Otherwise put, an indicative sign is a sign *to* something, to a community that understands it as such; an expressive sign is a sign *of* something, of an animating intention that it is expressing.

For Husserl, only expressive signs are truly meaningful, which entails, as Derrida points out, that "meaning (*Bedeutung*) is always *what* a discourse or somebody wants to say." Alternatively put, for Husserl, "[t]he essence of language is in its telos; and its telos is voluntary consciousness as meaning (*comme vouloir-dire*)." The question, then, for Husserl, becomes whether it is justifiable to hold that there is a realm of experience and especially of thought, unaffected by indication, that is the basis for communicative linguistic usage—language expressed in the form of indications—and thus constitutes the basic object for philosophical reflection. Such a realm would have to be, as Derrida points out, a realm of pure self-contained presence:

11. *Speech and Phenomena*, 5.

"[M]eaning is therefore *present to the self* in the life of a present that has not yet gone forth from itself into the world, space, or nature. All these 'goings-forth' effectively exile this life of self-presence in indications." [12]

It is important to be clear here that Husserl's distinction between expressive and indicative signs is not a distinction between two different sets of sounds or marks, some of which would be indicative and some expressive. The distinction, rather, is between using signs indicatively and using them expressively. When signs are used indicatively, they have merely their socially accepted content as their "meaning"; used expressively, they have their animating intention as their meaning. (Derrida flags this point by saying that the distinction is "more *formal* than *substantial*.") [13] For Husserl, only the latter use of the term "meaning" (*Bedeutung*), its expressive use, is, in the end, the correct one.

Can there be a realm of self-presence that would form the animating core of linguistic meaningfulness? According to Derrida, Husserl's own philosophical commitments forbid this. The two sets of Husserlian commitments Derrida points to presage Derrida's later discussion of *differance* as spacing and as timing; they have to do with the role of absence in intersubjectivity and in temporality.

Turning first to temporality, Derrida argues that it is a requirement on Husserl's thought that, if there is to be a full presence of the type that will underwrite a concept of expressive meaning, then such a presence must present itself temporally; and moreover, temporality itself must possess a point of full presence in which presence can occur. The reason for this is not difficult to see. The kind of experience that allows for apodictic judgment is, for Husserl, an immediate experience. Such an experience is one of full presence. Temporally rendered, the presence of an experience is one rendered in a present—a present that confronts one without the mediation of memory or expectation. It is there, before one, indubitable in its content. Such a present, however, is precluded in Husserl's own thinking.

For Husserl, the present as a now-point distinguishable from immediate retentions of the past and protentions of the future is only an ideal point (like a geometrical one) and not a real one. The movement of time is such that the immediate present shades off into the past and thus into retention (primary memory, as opposed to the secondary memory that calls up previously retained temporal passages); thus, the presence of a temporal object is

12. Ibid., 18, 36, 40.
13. Ibid., 20.

given in good part by way of a nonpresence—the memory of it given in retention. As Husserl says, "[I]t pertains to the essence of the intuition of time
that in every point of its duration (which, reflectively, we are able to make
into an object) it is consciousness of *what has just been* and not mere consciousness of the now-point of the objective thing appearing as having duration." [14] Furthermore, from the other temporal direction, the present is
always immediately expected in a protention that directs itself toward a future that passes indistinguishably into the present.

If this is right, then what is called temporal presence is riven by an absence internal to it. In Derrida's words, "[T]he presence of the perceived
present can appear as such only inasmuch as it is *continuously compounded*
with a nonpresence and nonperception, with primary memory and expectation (retention and protention)." [15] Otherwise put, there is no pure presence
given temporally, because all temporal presence requires absence *even to be
present*. If there were not the nonpresence of retention within presence, temporality would unfold as a series of unconnected now-points that are infinitely small in their "temporal width": there would be no temporality.

This alone would be enough to raise serious doubts about the Husserlian
attempt to extricate expressive signs from indicative ones, and thus to found
apodicticity on pure, immediate experience. But there is more. It concerns
the reflective capacity that a consciousness must possess in order for the
content of its reflections to have an apodictic status. As with temporality,
reflectively achieved apodicticity requires full presence. One must be fully
present to oneself if the contents of one's experience are to be rendered immediately. Specifically, if the content of one's thoughts is to be rendered apodictically, then that content must appear immediately. (We need to recall
here that the challenge Husserl is trying to meet is that of articulating a
thought undeniably present to itself, in order to render plausible the distinction between expressive and indicative signs.) The question is, Can this requirement be met?

Derrida points out—and this is a central theme in his work—that the
idea of a thought immediately present to itself is bound to the privileging of
speech or the voice over writing. This is because writing is clearly a mediated use of language; the content of a written text is understood by way
of the socially accepted meanings of the sentences (words, phonemes, etc.)

14. Edmund Husserl, *The Phenomenology of Internal Time-Consciousness,* trans. James S.
Churchill (Bloomington: Indiana University Press, 1964), 53–54.
15. *Speech and Phenomena,* 64.

in it. Therefore, writing cannot yield the immediate relationship to one's thought that any philosophy seeking to ground itself apodictically in subjective experience requires. Speech or the voice, alternatively, seems to possess the possibility of an immediate rendering of precommunicative thought, since it is, on many traditional models of language, the first translation of thought into language. Derrida calls this purported intimacy between speech or the voice and precommunicative thought "auto-affection" or "hearing oneself speak." And he argues that the purported intimacy of auto-affection is illusory.

The reason for this returns to the analysis of temporality. In reflective consciousness, the relationship of the reflecting self to the reflected-upon self is purely temporal. This is because the reflecting self does not look at its reflected-upon self from somewhere else, from the point of view of another self. Instead, the reflecting self looks *back* at the reflected-upon self, through time. But, as Derrida has already shown, the nature of temporality precludes full presence; thus, auto-affection, as the presence of self to self, rests on a basis constituted by the intertwining of presence and nonpresence, presence and absence. "The process by which the living now, produced by spontaneous generation, must, in order to be a now and be retained in another now, affect itself without recourse to anything empirical but with a new primordial actuality in which it would become a not-now, a past now—this process is indeed a pure auto-affection in which the same is the same only in being affected by the other, only by becoming the other of the same." [16]

We can see, moreover, that the nonpresence of temporality introduces a "distance" between the reflecting self and the reflected-upon self. In not being immediately in the same time, they are not exactly the same thing. And in that sense, contrary to what I claimed a moment ago, the reflecting self is a self different from the reflected-upon self; it is "outside" the reflected-upon self. Thus there is, by the same movement by which there is nonpresence as noncoincidence-with-self of temporality, there is a nonpresence as noncoincidence-with-self of auto-affection: a spacing between oneself as reflecting self and oneself as reflected-upon self. This temporal and spatial noncoincidence is what Derrida refers to in the term *differance*: "[W]hat is supplementary is in reality *differance*, the operation of differing which at one and the same time both fissures and retards presence, submitting it simultaneously to primordial division and delay." [17] And since one's own

16. Ibid., 85.
17. Ibid., 88.

identity is formed through reflection, it can be said paradoxically that identity is formed on the basis of a nonidentity with oneself, temporally and spatially. One is oneself by way of never quite being oneself.

If all this is right, then the Husserlian project of distinguishing expressive from indicative signs, and thus of isolating a precommunicative realm of thought that would form the basis for philosophical reflection, is bound to fail. It fails because the project of full presence upon which Husserl pins his philosophical hopes cannot provide a basis for meaningfulness. The upshot of this is twofold. First, there cannot be a philosophy that is self-grounding in the way that Husserl sought. To be self-grounding in that way requires apodicticity; apodicticity requires immediacy; immediacy is a matter of full presence; and there is no such thing as full, unmediated presence. Second, and related to this, linguistic meaning must be mediated. The picture of linguistic meaning as a "translation" from the sphere of apodictic self-presence to the sphere of socially constructed signification is illusory, since the former does not exist.[18]

For Derrida, then, Husserl's project of philosophical apodicticity falters because it stumbles across problems of language and linguistic meaning. But Derrida does not read this failure as uniquely Husserl's. "Signs can be eliminated in the classical manner in a philosophy of intuition and presence. Such a philosophy eliminates signs by making them derivative; it annuls reproduction and representation by making signs a modification of a simple presence. But because it is just such a philosophy—which is, in fact, *the* philosophy and history of the West—which has so constituted and established the very concept of signs, the sign is from its origin and to the core of its sense marked by this will to derivation and effacement."[19] In this passage we can anticipate two significant generalizations from individual analyses that Derrida makes, one concerning linguistic meaning, and the other, bound to it, concerning the project of philosophy.

The generalization concerning linguistic meaning is that theories of meaning are bound to commitments about presence. In the passage just noted, Derrida continues by citing the alternative to the "classical manner." The

18. Earlier in *Speech and Phenomena,* Derrida gives an independent reason to think that the translational model is a failure: he points out that all signs are repetitive in their nature, which precludes them from offering an adequate translation of singular intentions unless those intentions are already formed on the model of language. This a point to which I return in discussing "Signature Event Context."

19. *Speech and Phenomena,* 51.

alternative involves, not a competing theory of linguistic meaning, but the playing off of the classical manner against itself:

> Thus, to restore the original and nonderivative character of signs, in opposition to classical metaphysics, is, by an apparent paradox, at the same time to eliminate a concept of signs whose whole history and meaning belong to the adventure of the metaphysics of presence. This also holds for the concepts of representation, repetition, difference, etc., as well as for the system they form. For the present and for some time to come, the movement of that schema will only be capable of working over the language of metaphysics from within, from a certain sphere of problems inside that language.[20]

Not another theory of signification, of linguistic meaning, but the continuous undoing of the presuppositions and effects of the classical theory. There are, in other words, no candidates for a theory of linguistic meaning other than the one embodied in that philosophical tradition—the only philosophical tradition there is, according to Derrida—that goes by the appellation "metaphysics."

In order to get from the specific critique of Husserl that Derrida has offered to the conclusion that there can be no competing theories of linguistic meaning involves three significant inferences, each of which is controversial. First is the inference that there are no alternative, more sympathetic readings of Husserl that can salvage his theory of linguistic meaning. As I noted above, I do not wish to intervene on that point. Second is the inference that Husserl is representative of the entire philosophical tradition. Now, Derrida has, of course, offered readings of many more philosophical figures besides Husserl, and would probably defend himself here by pointing to those readings. But let us recall that his claim, here and elsewhere, is a sweeping one. It involves not only a commitment to there being a dominant trend in the Western philosophical tradition that has articulated linguistic meaning in terms of presence, but more deeply a commitment to the idea that even non-dominant trends have so articulated linguistic meaning. That sweeping commitment would require much more philosophical analysis than Derrida has yet offered. Yet I do not wish to challenge it.

The third inference, the one I do intend to challenge, is from what has

20. Ibid.

happened in the history of philosophical theories of linguistic meaning to what possibilities there are. Derrida assumes that since no theory of linguistic meaning apart from theories committed to presence has been offered, there can be none. That is why the alternative to the classical manner is deconstruction. Further on, I illustrate two particular theories of linguistic meaning, both of which are currently discussed in philosophical circles, one of which I try to defend a bit, and neither of which has the classical commitments with which Derrida wants to saddle theories of linguistic meaning.

Something else that neither of these theories shares—and this goes to the heart of the problem—is Derrida's view of what the philosophical project necessarily involves: absolute self-grounding, foundationalism. To anticipate later discussion, the commitments to presence that Derrida wants to saddle *any* theory of meaning with are more plausibly ascribed to theories of linguistic meaning that want to buttress foundationalist philosophies, philosophies that want to provide a system of exhaustive and indubitable claims regarding their subject matter (which, for philosophers like Husserl, is the subject matter to which all other subject matters must refer for their justification). However, the extent to which philosophy can be conceived and practiced nonfoundationally is also the extent to which projects of articulating theories of linguistic meaning in terms of presence seem less urgent. Otherwise put, Derrida's constricted view of the operation of linguistic meaning is inseparable from a constricted view of the philosophical project.

Before these claims can be made to sound more compelling, however, more needs to be accomplished in the way of interpretation of specific Derridean texts. I want to turn next to his essay on Emmanuel Levinas, "Violence and Metaphysics." Although I treat Levinas more fully in a subsequent chapter, a thumbnail sketch of his view would not be out of place here. Levinas is in an important sense the opposite and complement to Husserl. While Husserl seeks to reduce experience to a scope of a single transcendental ego, Levinas wants to lay hold of an experience that necessary escapes such an ego. Otherwise put, while Husserl wants to set himself the project of articulating experience in ways that can be captured categorically, Levinas sets himself the counterproject of showing that philosophical categories fail in (quite literally) the face of a certain recalcitrant experience. That experience, the one to which Levinas dedicates his major writings, is the experience of the other.

For Levinas, the experience of the other, and specifically of the other as *other,* as irreducible to my own experience, is the ethical experience *par excellence.* It is the confrontation with what resists the imposition of my own categories, and thus my own conceptual control. The fundamental ethical decision everyone must confront is whether to recognize and come to terms with this experience, with what Levinas calls the experience of the "infinite" (because the other is infinitely outside the stretch of my own cognitive or emotional categories), or instead to refuse this experience and try to force the other into one's own categories, a project that Levinas calls "totality" (and that is not unrelated to the project of political totalitarianism).

At the outset of his essay Derrida emphasizes three aspects of this perspective. First, Levinas is attempting a "dislocation of the Greek logos,"[21] a dislocation of the reduction of philosophy to sameness or oneness. Levinas seeks a radically nonreductive mode of thought. Second, this thought, however, continues to call itself "metaphysical" and therefore to play a role in our thought not unrelated to the role metaphysics plays. Finally, Levinas calls upon the ethical relationship, the relationship to the other or the other, to be the cornerstone of this new, nonreductive thought that is still metaphysical. In all of these characteristics, Levinas sees himself as diverging from a philosophical approach that includes, among others, Husserl and Heidegger.

For Levinas, the relationship to the other must be, if ethics is to be thought nonreductively, a relationship characterized by something other than the presence of the other. The reason for this is not far to seek, especially in light of the considerations just adduced regarding Husserl. If the other is to be articulated on the basis of something that is not reducible to my own perspective and categories, then he/she/it cannot be reducible to a presence arrayed before me. There must be some reserve that leaves the other *as other,* that calls me out of myself toward the other without my being able to hold the other in my grasp, be that grasp conceptual, political, or otherwise. "It can be said only of the other that its phenomenon is a certain nonphenomenon, its presence (*is*) a certain absence. Not pure and simple absence, for there logic could make its claim, but a *certain* absence. Such a formulation shows clearly that within this experience of the other the logic of noncontradiction, that is, everything which Levinas designates as 'formal

---

21. Jacques Derrida, "Violence and Metaphysics: An Essay on the Thought of Emmanuel Levinas," in *Writing and Difference,* trans. Alan Bass (Chicago: University of Chicago Press, 1978; or. pub. 1967), 82.

logic,' is contested at its root. This root would be not only the root of our language, but the root of all western philosophy, particularly phenomenology and ontology." [22]

This absence, this nonphenomenon, is not a lack but rather an irreducibility to presence. It reveals itself—as this absence—in the face of the other. The face of the other beckons me, calls me away from my own self-enclosure and from the presence that supports that self-enclosure, toward an I-can-never-know-what of the other. Such a call is the call of ethics; my acknowledgment of that call is the respect that instantiates an ethical relationship.

There are clear affinities between this thought of Levinas and the Derridean project. Both abjure the traditional philosophical project of offering a conceptual reduction of how and what things are; and both believe that that project is undermined because it requires a reduction to presence that violates some important "phenomenon." [23] Where they part paths, however, is where they locate these "phenomena." For Levinas, the "phenomenon" is located in the otherness of the other. For Derrida, the "phenomenon" is a matter of the operation of language. Thus it is not surprising to read the opening of Derrida's critical reflection on Levinas: "The questions whose principles we now will attempt to indicate are all, in several senses, questions of language: questions of language and the question of language." [24] These questions are, in the end, questions of the linguistic status of Levinas's own discourse.

The key problem for Levinas, since the otherness he seeks to articulate is outside of language, is that it cannot be articulated. It cannot be stated; therefore, it cannot be thought. (Recall Derrida's view of the connection between language and thought.) Why not? The absence Levinas seeks to call our attention to is not, as Derrida points out, pure absence. It is a certain kind of absence. But if the other is to elude our own categories, he/she/it must be presented only in terms of pure absence, only negatively. To render the otherness of the other positively, in terms of categorial language, would be to violate that very aspect of the other to which Levinas wants to call our attention. But if the otherness of the other, the part of the other that outstrips my conceptual categories and that Levinas calls "infinity," cannot be

22. Ibid., 91.
23. I use the term "phenomenon" in this instance widely and loosely, not in the strict phenomenological sense. This use of the term must, obviously, cover "certain" absences as well as presence.
24. "Violence and Metaphysics," 109.

stated negatively without inaccuracy and cannot be stated positively without betrayal, then it cannot be stated at all. "The positive Infinity (God)—if these words are meaningful—cannot be infinitely Other. If one thinks, as Levinas does, that positive Infinity tolerates, or even requires, infinite alterity, then one must renounce all language, and first of all the words *infinite* and *other*." [25]

Thus Levinas, in positing an otherness that is not mere negativity but a certain kind of otherness, loses the ability to say what it is the moment he wants to move outside our conceptual categories. "Levinas *in fact* speaks of the infinitely other, but by refusing to acknowledge an intentional modification of the ego [i.e., the other as *in some way* present to oneself]—which would be a violent and totalitarian act for him—he deprives himself of the very foundation and possibility of his own language." [26] This deprivation prevents him from seeing out his project—the discovery and articulation of an ethical relationship that escapes and subtends the ontological or categorial one—because it forbids him access to the language in which such an articulation could occur.

Does this mean that we should abandon the approach Levinas takes toward ethics, that we should regard the categorial subsumption of the other under the rubric of my own selfsameness to be unproblematic? Hardly. What Derrida argues is not that Levinas has missed the ethical relationship, but rather that he has misarticulated it. What needs to occur, in order for Levinas's insight to be preserved, is the casting of that insight in intralinguistic terms. Rather than be seen as an otherness to language, the other must be seen as an otherness *within* language. Otherwise put, Levinas's own thought must be articulated within the Husserlian and (perhaps) Heideggerian framework he rejects, rather than in competition with it.

This is the thrust of Derrida's remark that "language can only indefinitely tend toward justice by acknowledging and practicing the violence within it. Violence against violence. *Economy* of violence . . . an economy which in being history, can be *at home* neither in the finite totality which Levinas calls the same nor in the positive presence of the Infinite. Speech is doubtless the first defeat of violence, but paradoxically, violence did not exist before the possibility of speech." [27] Like Levinas, Derrida senses the danger of the

---

25. Ibid., 114. I should note that although it is God that is in question here, for Levinas the question of otherness, or alterity, does not lie solely in God but in all the otherness that transcends my categorial space.

26. Ibid., 125.

27. Ibid., 117.

reduction of otherness to categories of the same. For Derrida, this danger
lies specifically in the reduction of absence or nonpresence to presence. Although the analysis of Husserl offered above argued that the reduction to
presence in Husserl's case was mistaken rather than dangerous, Derrida has
provided a number of statements over the years to show that such a reduction is also ethically problematic.[28]

Where Levinas goes astray, then, is not in locating an otherness that is irreducible to full presence, but in citing it as an alterity *to*, rather than an alterity *within*, presence. This alterity provides the possibility of both violence
and nonviolence because, without otherness inhabiting the same, there is
neither anything toward which violence can occur nor the possibility of at-
tentiveness toward an other. Moreover, without an otherness that inhabits
the same, there cannot be sameness, because there is no other from which
to distinguish oneself as selfsame. "In effect, *either* there is only the same,
which can no longer even appear and be said, nor even exercise violence
(pure infinity or finitude); *or* indeed there is the same *and* the other, and
then the other cannot be the other—of the same—except by being the same
(as itself: ego), and the same cannot be the same (as itself: ego) except by being the other's other: alter ego."[29]

Now, all this, let us not forget, is a question of language. It is a question
of what is going on inside language, of how language operates. If language
were to be a matter of full presence, the possibility of otherness would be
excluded—as would the possibility of sameness. What Levinas and Husserl
seem to share, according to Derrida, is this commitment to language as full
presence. Their purposes are diametrically opposed. Husserl wants to be
able to reduce experience to conceptual certainty; thus he seeks to found
linguistic meaning on presence. Levinas wants to resist precisely this reduction; thus he turns away from language. But for both, the tie between language and presence persists. It is this tie that Derrida questions. *Against*
Husserl, he argues that absence—nonpresence—precludes the project of
full and final foundations. *Against* Levinas, he argues that presence is necessary for any articulation at all, and thus for the articulation of the ethical
relationship. Alternatively, he argues *with* Levinas that the reduction to full
presence is a danger, and that it is a danger language seems to permit as an
abuse of itself. And he argues *with* Husserl that presence, if not full pres-

28. See, for example, Derrida's recommendation for a deconstructive politics as a strategy
against "the violent relationship of the whole of the West to its other" ("The Ends of Man," in
Margins of Philosophy, 134).
29. "Violence and Metaphysics," 128.

ence, is inescapable. In the end, then, language is the source of both violence and nonviolence because it is the unstable play of presence and absence, of presence to self and absence from self, in which absence can always be made to appear to be an illusion or derivation or impure rendering of full presence.[30]

The danger, then, the ethical danger, the one that Levinas has his finger on, lies not in reducing alterity or otherness to language, but in exorcising language of its own alterity or otherness. That danger, which is the project of what Derrida calls "the history of metaphysics," is met not by exiting from language but by turning the violence of language against itself: an economy of violence. To cast the issue in terms Derrida uses later, one has *at the same time* to "attempt an exit and a deconstruction without changing terrain" and "to decide to change terrain, in a discontinuous and irruptive fashion, by brutally placing oneself outside." If the danger of relying solely on the first strategy is that of always confirming what is deconstructed, the danger of relying solely on the second strategy—Levinas's strategy—is one of "inhabiting more naively and more strictly than ever the inside one de- clares one has deserted, the simple practice of language ceaselessly reinstat- [ing] the new terrain on the oldest ground."[31]

The analysis of Levinas provides the counterpart to the analysis of Hus- serl. Whereas the latter displays the inescapability of absence as constitutive of presence, the former displays the inescapability of presence as constitu- tive of absence: not absence as lack, but as other-than-presence. And it is, above all, a question of language. Language operates in such a way that it requires the play of presence and absence, presence and nonpresence, in or- der to be meaningful. Without each, there can be no act of meaning. And yet what gives rise to meaning, this play, cannot itself be rendered meaning- ful, because to do so would be to reduce the play to presence, which is pre- cisely what the play escapes. This play, which is *differance,* is neither pres- ence nor absence: it is neither the identity of self-presence nor the difference of what cannot be brought to presence.

And here it is important to distinguish difference from *differance.* Differ- ence is one element of the play of *differance.* It is the unrecognized and his- torically repressed element, which is why it is so closely associated with

---

30. Compare *Of Grammatology:* "To recognize writing in speech, that is to say *differance* and the absence of speech, is to begin to think the lure. There is no ethics without the presence *of the other* but also, and consequently, without absence, dissimulation, detour, *differance,* writing. The archi-writing is the origin of morality as of immorality" (139–40).
31. "Ends of Man," 135.

Derrida's thought. But it is *differance*, not difference, that is the productive (non)basis of meaning.

We are close to arriving at an understanding of Derrida's view of the operation of language, and specifically of linguistic meaning. In order to cement that understanding, I want to turn finally to the article "Signature Event Context," which provides a crucial element of Derrida's view that I have not yet discussed: iterability.

In the discussion of the relationship between thought and signs thus far, the emphasis has been on the side of thought. The treatment of Husserl focused on the idea that thought is never entirely present to itself; the engagement with Levinas emphasized that thought cannot treat what is entirely absent to it either. This does not mean, of course, that the discussion has been about thought *as opposed to* language, but rather that in the thought/language chiasm less has been said about the nature of signs. "Signature Event Context" offers a discussion of what Derrida considers the crucial aspect of signs, the aspect that finally renders signification a practice that eludes the grasp of any theory of meaning that would reduce it to presence.

Iterability is, at first glance, simple repeatability. When Derrida ascribes iterability to signs, he means that signs can be repeated. But he means more than just that. What he is after in the concept of iterability is meaningful repeatability. He addresses it first in the context of writing. "The possibility of repeating and thus of identifying the marks is implicit in every code, making it into a network that is communicable, decipherable, iterable for a third and hence for every possible user in general. To be what it is, all writing must, therefore, be capable of functioning in the radical absence of every empirically determined receiver in general. . . . What holds for the receiver holds also, for the same reasons, for the sender or producer."[32] Writing, if it is more than mere scratches on a page, must convey a meaning that is a product of the code—the social system of signification—from which that writing draws its significative resources. That meaning is independent of the communicative intention of the person doing the writing in this specific sense: the writing has a meaning, a socially accepted signification, regardless of what the person who did the writing wants that writing to mean. The writer's intentions here are, in that specific sense, irrelevant to the meaningfulness of the writing.

The proof for this is simple. Imagine you discover a piece of paper on the

---

32. Jacques Derrida, "Signature Event Context," in *Limited Inc.*, trans. Samuel Weber and Jeffrey Mehlman (Evanston, Ill.: Northwestern University Press, 1988; or. pub. 1972), 8.

street that says, "I love you, Johnny." Now, you do not need to know who wrote that note, or who Johnny is, to be able to make some sense of what it says. It is meaningful, and is so even if Johnny is not there, even if you did not happen across it, and even if the writer himself or herself has died. Iterability is precisely this quality of being meaningful in a repeatable way regardless of any intention of the writer or any status of the addressee.

As Derrida points out, this ability for writing to be meaningful is tied intimately to the language's capacity for quotability. "Every sign, linguistic or nonlinguistic, spoken or written (in the current sense of this opposition), in a small or large unit, can be *cited,* put between quotation marks; in so doing it can break with every given context, engendering an infinity of new contexts in a manner which is absolutely illimitable." [33]

One might object here that Derrida has underplayed the role of the writer's intention. When I want to communicate one thing, I write one set of words; when I want to communicate something else, I write a different set of words. So the words are intimately connected to what I want to write. Derrida does not—nor does he need to—deny any of that. His claim is not that we are not capable of writing various words depending on what it is we want to say (more on wanting-to-say momentarily), but rather that the meaningfulness of those words is not reducible to the intention that motivated our writing them. They are meaningful independent of whatever the intention was in writing them.

Now, one might want further to object here, not to Derrida, but to the interpretation I have offered of Derrida. Is not Derrida's project exactly the opposite of the one I have ascribed to him—a project of denying the idea of an independent meaningfulness rather than positing it? The evidence for this lies in the continuation of the citation above about quotation: "This does not imply that the mark is valid outside of a context, but on the contrary that there are only contexts without any center or absolute anchorage. This citationality, this duplication or duplicity, this iterability of the mark is neither an accident nor an anomaly, it is that (normal/abnormal) without which a mark could not even have a function called 'normal.' What would a mark be that could not be cited? Or one whose origins would not get lost along the way?" [34] One might want to claim here that, since there are only contexts without a center, it is mistaken to talk about a certain meaningfulness that is carried from context to context.

33. Ibid., 12.
34. Ibid.

I do not think Derrida can be understood that way, even though I am prepared to concede that he might so understand himself. This latter interpretation, the one that competes with my own, necessarily undercuts Derrida's argument, and in two ways. First, if there are only contexts in the sense this passage seems to indicate, then meaning becomes reducible to those contexts; and if it is reducible to those contexts, it is not iterable. In order for iterability to occur, there must be something (although this something may yet be a nonpresent or nonpresentable something) that carries over from context to context and is independent of them. This does not entail that all meaning is reducible to that something, to what is iterated in various contexts. Instead, it entails that whatever the context provides, it cannot provide everything.

Second, if meaning is reducible to context in the way the competing interpretation would have it, it would also seem to be reducible to presence. This is because the meaningfulness would be reducible to what is there at that present moment, before the speakers and receivers. Now, one might claim that at that present moment, within the context, there is absence or nonpresence that inhibits a situation of full presence. But that claim would require an independent argument, one that Derrida does not provide and does not seem interested in providing in the context of this piece.[35]

It is crucial to note here, although this is a point whose implications will become clear only later, that although Derrida is committed to the idea that there must be something, some kind of meaning, that transcends contexts and provides iterability, this does not commit him to saying in any case what that transcending meaning is, or even taking a stand on whether one can say in any case what that transcending meaning is. It is possible—and this indeed is the Derridean position—to say that something transcends contexts but that that something eludes any account we can give of it. That this is the Derridean position will become clear momentarily when I consider his larger position on language and linguistic meaning. But it must equally be borne in mind that no part of Derrida's argument *in this essay* precludes the possibility of giving an account of linguistic meaningfulness that captures the content of what is iterated from context to context by specific utterances. It is possible for someone to accept what Derrida says about the iterability of signs, while rejecting Derrida's arguments that one cannot give an account of what is iterated.

---

35. Moreover, even if he were interested in providing it, he would still have to do so in a way that preserved the iterability that is his primary concern.

Although the considerations Derrida adduces on behalf of iterability, once considered, may strike one as obviously true, Derrida claims that the entire tradition of philosophical approaches to writing has, at least since Condillac, missed them. In that tradition, "communication is that which circulates a representation as an ideal content (meaning); and writing is a species of this general communication." [36] Here we can see a convergence with Derrida's examination of Husserl's expressive/indicative distinction at the level of writing rather than of speech. Derrida, however, does not restrict the concept of iterability to written texts alone. He claims, in a move that should surprise nobody, that the iterability so clearly evident in the case of writing is also characteristic of speech. "[T]his unity of the signifying form only constitutes itself by virtue of its iterability, by the possibility of its being repeated in the absence not only of its 'referent,' which is self-evident, but in the absence of a determinate signified or the intention of the actual signification, as well as of all intention of present communication. This structural possibility of being weaned from the referent or the signified (hence from communication and from its context) seems to me to make every mark, including those which are oral, a grapheme in general." [37] Inasmuch as speech uses signifying marks, that is, inasmuch as it participates in a socially sanctioned code, it is suffused with iterability. Thus what can be seen clearly in writing holds also for speech. Linguistic meaning is not a mere translation from intention to (oral or written) marks; it is a product of those marks as well.

This sort of analysis, complementary to Derrida's treatment of Husserl, occurs not only in the essay "Signature Event Context" but also in *Speech and Phenomena*. In the chapter "Meaning and Representation," Derrida writes, "A sign which would take place but 'once' would not be a sign; a purely idiomatic sign would not be a sign. . . . it can function as a sign, and in general as language, only if a formal identity enables it to be issued again and to be recognized." [38] Here Derrida is considering—focused upon the sign rather than (but not exclusive of) the intention—the irreducibility of signification to intentions. In the bulk of the book, Derrida makes the same point by focusing, as we saw, more on the intention than on the sign. But the analyses converge upon the idea that linguistic meaning is irreducible to the self-presence of an intention; it is suffused with something intention cannot capture or master.

36. "Signature Event Context," 6.
37. Ibid., 10.
38. *Speech and Phenomena*, 50.

Having examined several specific Derridean texts, we are now in a good position to see what Derrida's more general position is on language and linguistic meaning. To do that, I want to work primarily with the concept of *differance*, although, as Derrida points out, the concepts of supplementarity, *pharmakon*, trace, and re-mark play a similar role in his thought. Although Derrida claims that *differance* is "neither a *word* nor a *concept*,"[39] he offers what can be called a general "definition" or at least perspective on it in his essay *"Differance"*: *"Differance* is what makes the movement of signification possible only if each element that is said to be 'present,' appearing on the stage of presence, is related to something other than itself but retains the mark of a past element and already lets itself be hollowed out by the mark of a relation to a future element. This trace relates no less to what is called the future than to what is called the past, and it constitutes what is called the present by this very relation to what it is not, to what it absolutely is not; that is, not even to a past or future considered as a modified present."[40]

Differance, then, lies beneath signification in the sense that it makes it possible.[41] And it makes it possible by means of presence. And yet presence is never wholly present, because of the suffusion of an absence that is both spatial and temporal. The absence is spatial because the meaningfulness of any given element in language is had only by reference to other elements that are not present. This is the lesson of Saussure's showing that, phonemically as well as phonetically, language is a formal system of differences.[42] The absence is temporal because, as the considerations on Husserl have shown, the intention to mean something cannot ever be fully present to itself.

But if *differance* lies beneath presence, if it is what gives us whatever of presence there is, and if signification—linguistic meaningfulness—is a matter of presence, then three implications follow from this. First, *differance* itself cannot be subject to signification; it is beneath presence, and thus cannot be brought to presence. Second, the philosophical project of rendering language transparent in signification necessarily fails, since the very source

39. *"Differance,"* in *Speech and Phenomena,* 130.
40. *"Differance,"* 142–43.
41. "[T]he movement of *differance,* as that which produces different things, that which differentiates, is the common root of all the oppositional concepts that mark our language, such as, to take only a few examples, sensibleintelligible, intuitionsignification, natureculture, etc. As a common root, *differance* is also the element of the *same* (to be distinguished from the identical) in which these oppositions are announced" (*Positions,* 9).
42. Cf. *Positions,* 18: "By emphasizing the *differential* and *formal* characteristics of semiological functioning . . . Saussure powerfully contributed to turning against the metaphysical tradition the concept of the sign he borrowed from it."

of language, inasmuch as it is *differance,* eludes the transparency of signification. Third, the philosophical project itself, inasmuch as it is one of offering a final accounting for our world and our experience, remains always in-
complete, since such a project requires language in order to articulate itself
and the very language it uses eludes any final accounting.

All of this relies on the role that difference, in the form of absence, plays
in *differance,* or in any of the terms Derrida employs in order to mark what
lies beneath but resists linguistic signification or meaningfulness. "Presence,
then, far from being, as is commonly thought, *what* the sign signifies, what
a trace refers to, presence, then, is the trace of the trace, the trace of the erasure of the trace. Such is, for us, the text of metaphysics, and such is, for us,
the language which we speak."[43] "The language which we speak": it is a
theme Derrida sounds elsewhere, for instance, in an essay on Bataille and
Hegel. "There is only one discourse, it is significative, and here one cannot
get around Hegel."[44] Derrida's view is that literal talk, discourse, is of one
type. That type is characterized by presence. And presence is suffused with
an absence that cannot be brought to presence, and thus cannot be articulated meaningfully.[45]

None of this implies that (a) language is somehow a chaos, or (b) there is
a space outside of language to which thought must return, or (c) difference
as absence is the source of presence. The Derridean project itself is a refutation of the first. It tries to locate *precisely* where and how language cannot
be transparent to itself, where meaningfulness is an effect of what lies beneath it. In this sense, one can indeed give an account of language and of linguistic meaning, if by this one means that one can give an account of how
language operates to produce linguistic meaning by means of that which resists it. What one cannot give an account of is the meaningfulness of lan-

43. Jacques Derrida, "*Ousia* and *Grammē*: Note on a Note from *Being and Time,*" in *Margins of Philosophy,* 66.

44. Jacques Derrida, "From Restricted to General Economy: A Hegelianism Without Reserve," in *Writing and Difference,* 261. The original French here is "Il n'y a qu'un discours, il
est significatif et Hegel est ici incontournable" (*L'écriture et la différence* [Paris: Editions du
Seuil, 1967], 383).

45. Derrida makes these claims not only for *differance* but for other terms he uses that play
an analogous role for him. For example, supplementarity: "The supplement is neither a presence nor an absence. No ontology can think its operation" (*Of Grammatology,* 314). And also
pharmakon: "And if one got to thinking that something like the *pharmakon*—or writing—far
from being governed by these oppositions, opens up their very possibility without letting itself
be comprehended by them . . . one would then have to *bend* into strange contortions what
could no longer even simply be called logic or discourse" (*Dissemination,* trans. Barbara Johnson [Chicago: University of Chicago Press, 1981; or. pub. 1972], 103).

guage itself, because what produces meaningfulness at the same time produces a nonmeaningfulness that resists all accounting.

As for (b), the considerations I have brought forth on Levinas are a refutation of this possibility. Although the "text" of language is riven by an absence that it cannot master linguistically, this does not entail that thought can seek for someplace other than language in order to articulate itself. This is the import of Derrida's oft-misunderstood remark, *"There is nothing outside of the text."*[46] And regarding (c), this is the significance of the distinction between difference and *differance*. It is not solely difference—difference as absence—that lies beneath linguistic meaningfulness. It is *differance*, the play of presence and absence, of identity and difference.

There are two implications to this line of thought to which I want to draw attention before offering a synoptic overview of the Derridean view of language and its relationship to philosophy. The first implication is that, given *differance* (supplementarity, archi-writing, etc.), philosophy as it has been traditionally conceived—in Derrida's terms, "metaphysics"—is a failure because it relies on a concept of presence that is unachievable. The evidence for this view runs like a leitmotif across Derrida's texts. "[M]etaphysics has always consisted in attempting to uproot the presence of meaning, in whatever guise, from *differance*"; "the philosophical text, although it is in fact always written, includes, precisely as its philosophical specificity, the project of effacing itself in the face of the signified content which it transports and in general teaches"; "*sense* (in whatever sense it is understood: as essence, as the meaning of discourse, as the orientation of the movement between *archē* and *telos*) has never been conceivable, within the history of metaphysics, otherwise than on the basis of presence and as presence."[47]

Although philosophy, as traditionally conceived, cannot succeed (at least cannot succeed at what it would like to succeed at), a pure and simple turning away from philosophy is just as impossible. The reasons for this were given in the discussion of Levinas. If one is to be able to talk about issues

46. *Of Grammatology*, 158.

47. *Positions*, 32; *Of Grammatology*, 160; *"Ousia* and *Grammē,"* 51. Although, as I note momentarily, Derrida often uses the French term *vouloir-dire* when referring to signification, here he uses the term *signification*. This is an indication of his thinking of linguistic signification on the Husserlian model of expression of a pregiven sense. The full French original here is "aucun *sens* (en quelque sens qu'on l'entende, comme essence, comme signification du discours, comme orientation du movement entre une archie et un *telos*) n'a jamais pu être pensé dans l'histoire de la metaphysique autrement qu'à partir de la presence et comme presence" (*Marges de la philosophie* [Paris: Les Editions de Minuit, 1972], 58).

that have traditionally concerned philosophers, talk about language and ethics and knowledge and the nature of reality, then one cannot avoid recourse to a discourse that always eludes our mastery. "There is only one discourse, and it is significative." The philosophical work that must be done must be done from within the resources of the traditional conception, as a reworking of that conception from within its own resources. "There *is not* a transgression, if one understands by that a pure and simple landing into a beyond of metaphysics . . . even in aggressions or transgressions, we are consorting with a code to which metaphysics is irreducibly tied." [48]

The task of deconstruction, baldly put, is that of reworking the text of philosophy from within its conceptual resources, putting its claims in questions even as it ratifies them.

I want now to try to pull all of the threads of my discussion together and to offer, against all odds, an argument structure for Derrida's treatment of language and its relation to philosophy. This may strike some as bald-faced chutzpah; it may strike others as an exercise in futility. However, I believe that, at least in broad outline, there is a structure that accurately sums up the Derridean position. And if it does not, I suspect that it catches enough of it that someone more subtle than I will be able to turn it into something that does.

There seems to me, in any case, something independently worthwhile in the attempt. The elusiveness of Derrida's writings make it difficult to give an assessment of him. This tends to divide people into two camps: one more or less uncritically accepting his perspective, the other more or less uncritically rejecting it. In neither case is Derrida's thought given a fair shake. And this contributes, I believe, to the possibility, mentioned at the outset, that Derrida's influence will come and go without his having had the kind of assessment his thought deserves. I hope, then, to serve two purposes by offering this argument structure: to sum up my own considerations on Derrida's approach to philosophy and its relationship to language, and to provoke discussion on the question of just where Derrida thinks he has gone and how he thinks he has gotten there.

I start the argument structure with the broad metaphilosophical claim that I argued at the outset is the central concern of Derrida's work, and try to show the role that various parts of his work play in addressing and drawing implications from that metaphilosophical claim.

48. *Positions*, 12.

The Fundamental Derridean Argument Structure Regarding Philosophy
and Its Relationship to the Operation of Linguistic Meaning

1. Philosophy, as traditionally conceived, is a foundationalist project; it attempts to provide knowledge that is both exhaustive and absolute, indubitable, or unsurpassable.
2. Since the philosophical project must be articulated in language, in order to succeed it must be able to give an account of linguistic meaning or signification that renders meaning transparent.
3. No account of linguistic meaning or signification can render linguistic meaning or signification transparent.
    3.1. Linguistic meaning is a matter of the relationship between a signifying intention and the signs to which it gives rise.
    3.2. If linguistic meaning can be rendered transparent, it must be because (a) the sign is a faithful translation of a signifying intention and (b) that signifying intention is able to become transparent to a reflecting consciousness.
    3.3. The sign is not a faithful translation of a signifying intention, because signs are part of a code of iterability that is outside any necessary relationship of a signifying intention to a sign.
    3.4. The signifying intention cannot become transparent to a reflecting consciousness because it lacks the necessary self-presence to do so.
        3.4.1. Signifying intentions are constituted partially by absence; they are constituted by a play between presence and absence.
        3.4.2. Therefore, no signifying intention can become present either to itself or to a reflecting consciousness.
        3.4.3. There is no other way for an intention to become transparent.
        3.4.4. Therefore, signifying intentions cannot become transparent to a reflecting consciousness.
4. Therefore, the traditional philosophical project cannot be carried out successfully.
5. Any alternative to the traditional philosophical project must come to terms with the language in which it is articulated.
6. This coming to terms requires a recognition that linguistic meaning always eludes any account that attempts to render it fully transparent.
7. However, this coming to terms cannot take the form of stepping outside linguistic meaning, without undercutting itself, specifically without lapsing into silence.

8. Therefore, whatever else the philosophical project involves, it must continuously unwork from within itself the assumption that the claims it makes signify in any stable way. This unworking is the task of deconstruction.

Up until this point, I have not tried, except in passing, to offer any critique. Having rendered what I see as the Derridean position, I can now point precisely to the steps I think are mistaken. The primary problem, as I will try to show, is with step 3.1. I will later relate that attempt to what I think is a mistaken assumption in the passage from step 5 to steps 6 through 8. But before I do so, I need to make my case more solid that Derrida is committed to step 3.1 as I have articulated it.

Finding the evidence for this is not difficult. Not only is it, as I have tried to show, implied in his analyses, it is explicitly stated several times by Derrida. In *Positions*, for example, he says that "I try to *write* (in) the space in which is posed the question of speech and meaning. I try to write the question: (what is) meaning to say?"[49] The French expression Derrida uses, *vouloir-dire*, is a significant clue to his view. Although there are several French terms that might be used to signify linguistic meaning—for example, *sens* or *signification*—Derrida chooses a term whose literal English translation is "to want to say."[50] It is as though he opts for an intentional view of meaning, which lends itself to a deconstructive analysis. Derrida is not unaware of his choice, but I believe is unaware of the implications of this choice.

In "Limited Inc.," for instance, which is the continuation of "Signature Event Context" by way of a reply to a critique by John Searle, Derrida writes: "One of the things *Sec* ["Signature Event Context"] is driving at is that the minimal making-sense of something (its conformity to the code, grammaticality, etc.) is incommensurate with the adequate understanding of intended meaning. I am aware that the English expression 'meaningful' can also be understood in terms of this minimum of making-sense. Perhaps even the entire equivocation of this discussion is situated here. In any case, incommensurability is irreducible: it 'inheres' in intention itself and it is riven with

49. Ibid., 14. The French original reads "J'essaie d'*écrire* (dans) l'espace où se pose la question du dire et du vouloir-dire. J'essaie de'écrire la question: (qu'est-ce) que vouloir-dire?" (*Positions* [Paris: Minuit, 1972], 23).

50. He even chooses the term *vouloir-dire* to translate Husserl's German term *bedeuten* in *Speech and Phenomena*.

iterability."[51] The question is, however, whether linguistic meaning can be understood in terms of a "making-sense" that need not refer to any intention, that is, whether meaningfulness is something wholly other than a never-quite-consummated relationship between intentions and signs. I argue that it is. And even Derrida hints at this possibility in the afterword to *Limited Inc.*: "I believe that no research is possible in a community (for example, academic) without the prior search for this minimal consensus and without discussion around this minimal consensus. Whatever the disagreements between Searle and myself might have been, for instance, no one doubted that I had understood at least the English grammar and vocabulary of his sentences."[52] If it can be said what that understanding consists in, what that "minimal consensus" is about, then Derrida is incorrect in claiming that a philosophical theory of linguistic meaning is beyond our reach. He might be right that the articulation of that minimal consensus cannot be had by a theory that starts from intention-sign relationships. And moving away from intention-sign relationships may necessitate a move away from understanding philosophy as a foundationalist enterprise. Both of these moves, however, are within the scope of philosophy itself. Philosophy, as well as philosophical theories of meaning, has more options open to it than the deconstructive one that Derrida cites at the end of the argument structure given above.

In order to see how open the field is for theories of linguistic meaning that do not fall prey to the Derridean critique, it is important to see that, by limiting linguistic meaningfulness to the intention-sign relation, and specifically to presence, Derrida is making two assumptions, both of which are optional to theories of language and linguistic meaning. The two assumptions are these: (1) If there is to be an adequate theory of meaning, it must rely on an adequate theory of truth. (2) If there is to be an adequate theory of truth, it must involve some kind of correspondence relation. Without a commitment to *both* of these assumptions, Derrida's claim that deconstruction is the only viable philosophical approach fails, and with it much of the force of his metaphilosophical views. Now, I do not want to claim that Derrida recognizes himself as making a commitment to either of these assumptions. In fact, he shows no evidence of having formulated matters the way I just did. Rather, I want to show that there is evidence for them in his work and, more important, that the larger claims he makes for deconstruction depend upon a commitment to them.

---

51. "Limited Inc.," in *Limited Inc.*, 64.
52. Afterword to *Limited Inc.*, 146.

Before showing how both of these assumptions are implicit in Derrida's thought, I would like to call attention to the fact that these are assumptions Derrida shares with the most traditional of philosophical approaches to language. Neither of these assumptions, for instance, would be rejected by Husserl. What distinguishes Derrida from Husserl is not a commitment to these long-standing assumptions—I believe we can go so far as to call them "dogmas"—but rather the fact that Husserl affirms the antecedent of both, while Derrida denies the consequent. For Husserl, there can be an adequate theory of meaning, therefore an adequate theory of truth, therefore a correspondence relation. For Derrida, there cannot be a correspondence relation, therefore no adequate theory of truth, therefore no adequate theory of meaning.

Where, then, do we see these assumptions, these dogmas, in Derrida's thought about language? The first one is derived from Derrida's view of the relationship between philosophy and language. If the philosophical project, as traditionally conceived, is to be carried out successfully, then, as step 2 in the argument structure points out, it must incorporate a theory of meaning that allows for meaning to be transparent. The motivation for the transparency is, in Husserlian terms, apodicticity. One wants to be assured that the meaning of one's words (sentences, etc.) are not eluding one, because, if they are, then they run the risk of falsifying one's thought. If, alternatively, one can ground meaning in truth, then the possibility remains that as long as one's thoughts are well grounded, there will be no slippage on the way from thought to language.

The same point can be put another way, and perhaps ought to be. In order for the traditional philosophical project to succeed, one must have epistemic control over one's semantic intentions. One must be able, in the vernacular, to "say what one means." Without this, there is no assurance that what one says will not be false even though what one is thinking is true. And philosophy, as a linguistic endeavor, not only has to think true thoughts, it has to be able to say them.

Grounding meaning in truth is the only way to preserve the connection between thought and language. To see why this is so, consider an alternative. Imagine meaning were grounded not in truth but in verifiability. Suppose, that is, that the meaning of a sentence were, broadly construed, the conditions under which it was justifiable to assert that sentence. Since conditions of justifiability are not conditions of truth, then what would make a sentence meaningful is different from what would make it true. This would admit the possibility of sentences that, to all appearances, justifiably reflect what one means to say, but do not truly reflect what one means to say. The apodicticity of the relationship between intention and language would be lost, and philosophy would be unable to realize its traditional project. The relation between intention and meaning has to be one of strict fit, then, and only a theory of meaning that grounds itself in truth is capable of providing that fit.

Derrida recognizes the internal relation that holds between meaning and truth. Although in *Speech and Phenomena differance* is said to be a condition of meaning,[53] in other texts he freely substitutes the word "truth" [*vérité*] for meaning. Thus, in "Plato's Pharmacy" we read that "*[d]ifferance*, the disappearance of any originary presence, is *at once* the condition of possibility *and* the condition of impossibility of truth."[54] Moreover, even in *Speech and Phenomena*, Derrida cites the intertwining of the truth and meaning: "We have experienced the systematic interdependence of the concepts of sense, ideality, objectivity, truth, intuition, perception, and expression. Their common matrix is being as *presence*."[55]

Now, one might object that, while Derrida sees an internal bond between meaning and truth, he never articulates it in terms of a theory of meaning having to depend on a theory of truth. Agreed. Derrida nowhere says outright that a theory of meaning must reside in truth. This seems, however, to be due less to his holding a different position and more to his subsuming the ideas of meaning, intention, and truth under the concept of presence. My argument is that this subsumption needs to be separated out into separate commitments—the dogmas—in order to see exactly what constrictions Derrida assumes in his reflections on language and linguistic meaning. When so separated, it can be seen that, given Derrida's argument structure, he must hold that meaning can be cashed out only in terms of truth, given that he wants to be able to undercut the traditional philosophical project and, *at the same time*, motivate deconstruction as the only alternative. This is because, if meaning can be cashed out some other way, then we are not forced to take up a deconstructive attitude toward our own language. (The cost of this other alternative is that we cannot engage in the traditional philosophical project, but, as I argue in a bit, that is a cost that can be paid—and may come cheaper than deconstruction.)

53. "The absence of intuition—and therefore of the subject of intuition—us not only *tolerated* by speech; it is *required* by the general structure of signification, when considered *in itself*" (93).
54. "Plato's Pharmacy," in *Dissemination*, 168.
55. *Speech and Phenomena*, 99.

The first dogma alone does not capture all of the constrictions that Derrida places on a theory of meaning, however. For Derrida, the grounding of a theory of meaning in a theory of truth is a special type of grounding because truth involves a particular kind of relationship between words and things. That relationship is one of correspondence.[56] If the first dogma issues from Derrida's metaphilosophical concerns regarding foundationalism, the second dogma issues from his metaphilosophical idea that the history of philosophy is a history of the privileging of presence.

That Derrida reads truth as primarily a matter of correspondence comes out in many places in his work. In a more recent essay, for instance, he writes that "[t]he great question, the generative question, thus becomes, for this epoch, that of the *value* of representation, of its truth or its adequacy to what it represents."[57] Earlier, in the essay "Plato's Pharmacy," he offers a convergent view: "But what the parricide in the *Sophist* establishes is not only that any *full, absolute* presence of what *is* (of the being-present that most truly 'is': the good or the sun that can't be looked in the face) is impossible; not only that any full intuition of truth, any truth-filled intuition, is impossible; but that the very condition of discourse—*true or false*—is the diacritical principle of the *sumplokē*. If truth is the presence of the *eidos*, it must always, on pain of mortal blinding by the sun's fires, come to terms with relation, nonpresence, and thus nontruth."[58]

One might want to object here that Derrida is not so much offering his own view of truth, but Plato's, and trying to show that Plato's view of truth—truth as presence—must be subtended by a play of untruth as nonpresence. Granted. However, it is this view of truth which Derrida supposes characterizes the entire philosophical tradition and without which philosophy as a foundationalist enterprise—as an enterprise of absolute and/or indubitable knowledge—would be inconceivable. He makes this commitment clear elsewhere, when, for instance, he writes in *Of Grammatology* that "[t]he *empty* symbolism of the written notation—in mathematical technique, for

56. Constantin Boundas raised the possibility that deconstruction might work against coherence theories of truth as well as correspondence theories. I do not believe so, because of Derrida's commitment to the idea of presence as central to language. Below, when I discuss Donald Davidson's theory of (a substitute for) meaning, I consider the possibility of reading Davidson as holding a coherence theory of truth. Read thus (or several other ways), Davidson's theory turns out to be immune from the deconstructionist critique.

57. "Sending: On Representation," in *Transforming the Hermeneutic Context: From Nietzsche to Nancy*, ed. Gayle Ormiston and Alan Schrift. Albany: State University of New York Press, 1990, 118.

58. "Plato's Pharmacy," 166.

example—is also for Husserlian intuitionism [as it is for Saussure, who is the object of the discussion] that which exiles us far from the *clear* evidence of the sense, that is to say from the full presence of the signified in its truth, and thus opens the possibility of crisis."[59] Or again, in *"Ousia* and *Grammē"*: "[I]t is the tie between truth and presence that must be thought, in a thought that henceforth may no longer need to be either *true* or *present,* and for which the meaning and value of truth are put into question in a way impossible for any intraphilosophical moment."[60]

For Derrida, what undercuts any theory of linguistic meaning is not only that theory must be articulated in terms of truth, but also that truth itself must be articulated in terms of presence. Thus the history of metaphysics as a history of presence: a history of the project of "auto-affection," as he puts it in *Speech and Phenomena.* If philosophy is to speak and yet to remain foundationalist, it must do so in such a way that the truth of its meaning is guaranteed through presence. Now, the exact operation of presence does indeed vary throughout the history of philosophy, which is why Derrida employs different terms for the disruption of presence depending on which philosopher he is examining. For instance, as Gasché points out, supplementarity is not exactly the same thing as archi-trace, because the former involves an other that is *added to* the same, while the latter involves an other that is *referred to* by the same.[61]

What all presence has in common, however, is *presence to,* that is, correspondence. For Plato and much of ancient philosophy, one might be present to an *eidos* if one is in truth; while for Descartes and the modern tradition, presence is articulated primarily in terms of presence to a subject. For both, however, presence is a matter of something broadly corresponding to or adequating with something else. Now, this correspondence relationship need not be one of similarity or copy. What goes on, for instance, in a subject need not be a process that replicates what goes on in the world or in the subject-world nexus. Correspondence can be much broader than that. But correspondence must involve, if it is a matter of presence, the "coming-into-contact" of a consciousness and its subject matter in a way that guarantees that that consciousness is not mistaken in its judgments about that subject

59. *Of Grammatology,* 40.

60. *"Ousia* and *Grammē,"* 38.

61. *Tain of the Mirror,* 206. This is also why, for instance, in "Plato's Pharmacy," Derrida writes in a footnote that "[w]ith a view precautions, one could say that *pharmakon* plays a role *analogous,* in this reading of Plato, to that of *supplement* in the reading of Rousseau" (96n).

matter. "In nonmeaning, language has not yet been born. In the truth, language is to be filled, achieved, actualized, to the point of erasing itself, without any possible play, for the (thought) thing which is properly manifested in the truth." [62]

Linguistic meaning, then, requires truth; and truth requires correspondence. Without correspondence, without presence, there is no truth; and without truth, there can be no stable meaningfulness and thus no account of meaning. Derrida's arguments around meaning have been marshaled precisely to convince us that indeed there can be no such thing as presence, at least not in a way that will support a philosophical theory of meaning.

I do not want to argue with Derrida regarding presence. For the record, I believe he is right about that. Any theory of meaning that requires presence is probably going to be mistaken, and more or less for the reasons Derrida adduces. But must a theory of meaning rely on presence? Or, to put the matter more broadly and in terms of the schema offered above, must a theory of meaning be a theory of the relationship between signifying intentions and signs? One might respond that indeed it must be so if philosophy as a foundationalist pursuit is to have any hope of success. Philosophy, after all, is bound to the language in which it is articulated. But what if philosophy can be done without being either a foundationalist enterprise or the deconstruction of one? What if it can be done in a more fallibilist mode? Then it would not require a theory of meaning that guarantees its truth or its infallibility.

In what follows, I would like to consider two approaches to language and linguistic meaning—both rather briefly—that do not have the relationship of signifying intentions to signs as their linchpin. In doing so, I not only offer competitors to Derrida's view of language that demonstrate how the alternative metaphysics/deconstruction is a false dilemma, but also give a picture of what philosophy can be like as a pursuit once one gives up the traditional project of philosophy that Derrida has rightly criticized. My argument against Derrida, then, is, to repeat what I said at the outset, not that he is wrong about the general run of the philosophical tradition, but that he is wrong about its possibilities. Moreover, that wrongness is bound to too constricted a view of the operation of language, or at least to too constricted a view of what counts as a decent theory of the operation of language and linguistic meaning. Thus, the presentation of these two approaches to language and linguistic meaning serve three related purposes at the same time:

---

62. Jacques Derrida, "White Mythology," in *Margins of Philosophy*, 241.

(a) to offer examples of theories of language for nonfoundationalist philosophy, (b) to offer theories of language that escape deconstruction, and (c) to show how deconstruction is committed to the two dogmas cited above.

I want to proceed first by describing—"sketching" would be a better term—a theory of language that holds to one dogma, the first one, without holding to both. The point of this sketch is to show that one can hold to the first dogma without running afoul of any Derridean arguments against the possibility of a theory of linguistic meaning. After that sketch, I want to present at slightly more length a theory of language and of linguistic meaning that holds to neither of the dogmas. In keeping with the project of this book, that theory will be articulated in terms of a contingent holism. My goal here, as elsewhere, is to provide a philosophical perspective that captures much of what current French philosophy is after without some of the incoherencies or untoward commitments that have characterized it.

The first theory of language is Donald Davidson's. Although Davidson can be said to hold to the dogma that meaning needs to be characterized in terms of truth, there is nothing in his position that commits him to the second dogma, that truth must involve correspondence. Before turning to this view, however, I should note that Davidson does not see himself as offering a theory of meaning so much as rendering one unnecessary. He believes that the concept of truth can do everything that the concept of meaning can, and without dragging along some of the metaphysical temptations (that meaning exists somehow apart from sentences) that have characterized theories of meaning. In a word, Davidson sees his proposal less as a truth-conditional theory of meaning than as a truth-conditional substitute for one. This distinction, however, does not matter to us here, since the upshot will be the same: meaning can be conceived in terms of truth without the necessity of deconstruction following.

For Davidson, the project of a theory of language is to allow someone who knows the theory to know what the speaker of a specific language is doing (meaning) when he or she makes a specific linguistic utterance.[63] In order to generate such a theory, one must start from scratch, observing the speaker of the language, and then figure out what that speaker is doing with his or her linguistic utterances. For Davidson, one cannot start any other way in generating a theory, since to do so would already presume that one

---

63. The details of Davidson's view can be gleaned from his articles collected in *Inquiries into Truth and Interpretation* (Oxford: Clarendon Press, 1984), especially the articles "Radical Interpretation" (or. pub. 1973), "Truth and Meaning" (or. pub. 1967), "Reality Without Reference" (or. pub. 1977), and "On the Very Idea of a Conceptual Scheme" (or. pub. 1974).

knows in some sense what the speaker means when speaking; and to base a theory of language on that knowledge would be to argue in a circle.[64] Thus, one has to start out with only the speaker's behavior in view, and generate a theory of language from there. This project Davidson calls, after Willard Quine, "radical interpretation": one is interpreting the behavior, in this case the linguistic utterances, of another, without benefit any prior knowledge of the meaning of that behavior.[65]

In the position of the radical interpreter, the only way one can make sense of the linguistic utterances of others is by relating those utterances both to other utterances of the speaker and to aspects of the world one already knows. If, for instance, one notices the speaker using the word "schnook" every time an elected officeholder is visible, and especially if the speaker looks at the elected officeholder when saying it, then one has some evidence that when the speaker uses the word "schnook," he or she means something that has to do with elected officeholdership.[66]

---

64. Actually, Derrida has a very similar approach to language in one of his later articles, "On Representation," esp. 109–14. There he asks us to imagine that French is a dead language and that later philologists are trying to decipher it, and particularly the word "representation" (*representation*). He concludes there, as we will see Davidson does, that representation is inseparable from translation, but also, unlike Davidson, that the necessary incompleteness of translatability requires the introduction of the concept of *différance*. The project of translation, writes Derrida, requires a desire for representation, which requires the following: "Under the diversity of words from diverse languages, under the diversity of uses of the same word, under the diversity of contexts or of syntactic systems, the same sense or same referent, the same representative content would keep its inviolable identity" (113). Since, for reasons we have seen connected with the critique of Husserl, the idea of a certain identical content beneath language cannot be maintained, we can only think of translation, and thus of representation, in terms of *différance*. If the following remarks on Davidson are right, then at least one other account of language and translation can be offered that does not require *différance,* and Derrida's commitment to the two dogmas prevents him from considering the possibility of a Davidsonian account.

65. For Davidson, the necessity of radical interpretation applies not only to the linguistic utterances of foreign speakers but to the utterances of those who speak the same language: "The problem of interpretation is domestic as well as foreign: it surfaces for speakers of the same language in the form of the question, how can it be determined that the language is the same? . . . All understanding of the speech of another involves radical interpretation" ("Radical Interpretation," 125).

66. Given the problem of the inscrutability of reference that Quine discusses in "Ontological Relativity" (in *Ontological Relativity and Other Essays* [New York: Columbia University Press, 1969]) and that is ratified by Davidson in his piece "The Inscrutability of Reference" (*Inquiries into Truth and Interpretation* [essay or. pub. 1979]), one can never be sure that it is exactly elected officeholdership that is referred to by the speaker. This is one of the reasons that radical interpretation is a theory of truth *rather than* a theory of meaning, instead of being a theory of truth *as* a theory of meaning.

Of course, people rarely speak in single words; they more usually speak in sentences. Furthermore, the interpretation that we give of people's specific words often comes from the context of the sentences they are uttering. Thus, in engaging in radical interpretation, what one looks for are ways to match up linguistic utterances of the speaker with the sentences that one holds true of the world in particular situations in order to get an understanding of what the speaker is doing or meaning in making those particular utterances. This presumes both that the speaker and the interpreter are not using systematically different schemes of thinking about the world[67] and that the speaker is not radically mistaken in his or her view of what is going on in the world.[68]

It also requires a lot of mixing and matching, since, for every situation in which a linguistic utterance occurs, there can be many true things said about that situation. So the interpreter has to cross-check utterances and situations in order to come up with a reasonable theory of language for that speaker.

Now, what is the goal of all this interpretation? It is to come up with a theory for that speaker's linguistic utterances. This theory could loosely be called a "translation manual," but only very loosely, since, for reasons Quine adduces and Davidson subscribes to, the translation manual may hook up true sentences in the speaker's language with true sentences in the theorizer's language (and false ones with false ones), but this correspondence between true sentences and true sentences (and false sentences and false sentences) does not guarantee correspondence of any other kind.[69] The manual, then, is a theory of meaning only on the condition that we do not assume that there are such things as meanings independent of the sentences being uttered. The manual itself would consist in large part[70] of sentences of the form (traceable back to the logician Alfred Tarski) "S is true if and only if p," where S is a linguistic utterance of the speaker and p is a true sentence (if and only if S is a true sentence)[71] in the theorizer's language. With such a

67. Davidson emphasizes this in "On the Very Idea of a Conceptual Scheme."

68. This is the (in)famous Principle of Charity, which, as Davidson argues, is not a way of interpreting people sympathetically, but a condition of interpreting them at all. If we did not see people as broadly right in their beliefs (i.e., broadly like us in them), then interpretation would be entirely unconstrained, and would thus not be able to get off the ground.

69. See esp. Willard Quine's *Word and Object* (Cambridge: MIT Press, 1960), chap. 2.

70. Although not exclusively, since there are special ways of dealing with, for example, logical operators. For a more exhaustive approach to the details of this aspect of Davidson's view, see Mark Platts's *Ways of Meaning* (London: Routledge & Kegan Paul, 1979).

71. The necessity of adding this parenthetical remark was pointed out to me by an anonymous reader.

manual in hand, someone would have a specific theorem—an empirical theorem, because later and better manuals based on more information are not impossible—about what a speaker means in producing a linguistic utterance.

Clearly, the Davidsonian approach to language reduces meaning to truth. In fact, it can be said to eliminate meaning in favor of truth, allowing truth to play the role traditionally allotted to meaning. In that sense, it subscribes to the first dogma. But does it need to subscribe to the second? (Here I want to leave open the question whether Davidson himself subscribes to the second, because it seems that an approach to linguistic meaning by way of radical interpretation allows for several accounts of truth, of which Davidson's own may be only one.)[72] Would, for example, a coherentist or deflationist account of truth—the latter being an account that sees truth as adding no independent significative content[73]—be consistent with the other tenets of radical interpretation?

There seems to be no reason to think otherwise. If, for example, a coherence account of truth—an account that holds that true claims are those claims that fit with other claims held true—were to be combined with Davidson's approach, then matters would look like this: The theorizer would come up with a "translation manual" for the speaker's language, complete with all its sentences "S is true if and only if p" and whatever else besides. In addition, the theorist (or, if the theorist were mistaken about truth, we theorists of the theorist) would hold that this claim can be further cashed out as something like "S fits with the rest of the claims the speaker believes (or, on other accounts, ought to believe) if and only if p." Alternatively, if a deflationist account of truth is embraced, the cashing out would be something like "S if and only if p." Neither of these approaches to truth seem inimical to the Davidsonian project, since they both allow interpretation and the construction of "translation manuals" to occur without introducing any inconsistency into the project.

Whatever its other merits or demerits, such a position would be immune from Derrida's deconstructive critique of theories of linguistic meaning. The reason for this is that such a position would not provide the toehold that deconstruction needs in order to scale a particular philosophical position.

---

72. For the record, Davidson seems to have a correspondence theory of truth, but, as he himself points out, his own particular view of correspondence is also coherentist. See "A Coherence Theory of Truth and Knowledge," in *Truth and Interpretation: Perspectives on the Philosophy of Donald Davidson*, ed. E. Lepore (Oxford: Basil Blackwell, 1983), and also "The Structure and Content of Truth," *Journal of Philosophy* 87, no. 6 (1990): 279–328, esp. 319–26.

73. I detail a particular deflationist account of truth below, pages 120–22.

Recall that, for Derrida, all metaphysics is the history of presence. Deconstruction is—and it cannot be otherwise—a deconstruction of presence. Davidson's approach to language, however, interpreted without a correspondence theory of truth, does not rely on presence anywhere in the account. Otherwise put, it does not embrace the second dogma. The theorizer's interpretation of the speaker is an empirical theory that, like other empirical theories, claims neither absolute exhaustiveness nor infallibility. Truth, if conceived along the coherentist model, would not be a relation between claims and something present to those claims, but a relation among claims themselves, a relation at least vaguely similar to that among words or phonemes in Saussure's structuralist linguistics. If, alternatively, truth is conceived along deflationist lines, then no relationality whatsoever is involved, and thus no relation of presence.

Now, one might object that the Davidsonian view presented here would not be able to support the traditional metaphysical project, since it would allow that theories of linguistic meaning can go wrong. This is true. And the implication of this is that inasmuch as a philosophical position relies on a Davidsonian semantics, it could not claim absoluteness or infallibility for itself. But this is only to say that such a philosophical position would have to be nonfoundationalist. Since I want to address the more general issue of nonfoundationalism in philosophy below, I will do no more than remark this point here.

I have offered this brief treatment of Davidson with a limited purpose in view, that of showing that Derrida must be committed to *both* of the dogmas I am trying to saddle him with, if he is to make deconstruction seem like the only viable philosophical approach. I want to turn now to a slightly more ambitious task: the sketch of an approach that avoids not one but both of the dogmas to which I argued Derrida is committed. I do not want to argue for the position here; to do so would require at least an entire separate volume.[74] Rather, I merely wish to describe a particular approach to theorizing about language and linguistic meaning that abandons the dogmas subscribed to by Derrida and the tradition he deconstructs.[75]

---

74. Two volumes have been written that articulate this approach in more detail: Robert Brandom's *Making It Explicit* (Cambridge: Harvard University Press, 1994) and Mark Lance and John Hawthorne's *Grammar of Norms* (Cambridge: Cambridge University Press, forthcoming).

75. The following section is a revision of part of a journal article coauthored with Mark Lance. The original draft of that part of the article I have revised for this book was written by Lance. Thus, although this reworking is mine and I take full responsibility for any mistakes it may contain, I cannot take full credit for its presentation. The following section must be considered coauthored.

This sketch begins with the approach to language articulated in the work of the Anglo-American philosopher Wilfrid Sellars, and is guided by some followers of Sellars's work, especially Robert Brandom. Both Sellars and Brandom can be seen as participants in the non-Rortian strain of neopragmatism that I cited in the Introduction. For them, discussions of language must recognize the Wittgensteinian point that linguistic meaningfulness occurs within the context of social practices, not above them. Thus, as we shall see, the *semantic* task of discussing linguistic meaning cannot be separated from the *pragmatic* task of showing how language operates in social practices.

Sellars conceived of language as fundamentally a normatively constrained human social practice, a "game of giving and asking for reasons." According to this view, we approach language as a sociological phenomenon and understand it in terms of the functionally characterizable normative structure governing the interactions within it. Although in the previous chapter I claimed that language should be seen as bound to a variety of practices—thus the term "discursive practices"—I believe that that modification is a friendly amendment to the Sellarsian view. Thus, in contrast to the tradition (at least on Derrida's reading of it), language does not lie beneath human our practical engagements as some sort of foundation for them, but rather is a natural phenomenon that ought to be treated in the way we treat other natural phenomena. There is an affinity here between Sellars's approach and the more familiar approach of Wittgenstein, who thought of language in terms of "language games" that were part of the "forms of life" in which people engaged. And, in fact, Sellars's article "Some Reflections on Language Games" explicitly takes the Wittgensteinian approach.[76]

In that article, Sellars identifies three broad types of "moves" within a language game that are central to its significance as a linguistic practice. The first type he calls language entrances. These are transitions from nonlinguistic acts, for example, looking in the direction of a red apple, to linguistic acts, for example, asserting "Yo, a red apple."

The second sort of move in a Sellarsian language game is the language-language move. This corresponds to inferences (of various sorts) such as moving from "Yo, a red apple" to "There is a colored fruit in the room." Finally, there are language-exit moves that involve transitions from linguistic to nonlinguistic acts, as in the move from asserting "I will now leave the room" to doing so.

---

76. Wilfrid Sellars, "Some Reflections on Language Games," in *Science, Perception, and Reality* (London: Routledge & Kegan Paul, 1963).

To understand a language, according to Sellars, is to grasp such constraints governing appropriate usage. This grasping can either be a matter of explicit theorizing about the structure of an actual practice or a matter of implicit competence in the employment of acts within the practice. On the face of it, then, this theory accounts for language not in terms of meaning but in the same sorts of terms that an anthropologist might employ for the characterization of any social practice. It is not a theory of meaning but a theory of how language works. Because of this, its starting point is significantly different from Derrida's.

Recall that Derrida's approach to language occurs by way of metaphilosophical issues of first philosophy: accounts of language have traditionally had as a constraint that they must support foundationalist philosophical positions. And Derrida, although denying that such support was forthcoming, did not rid himself of the implicit assumption that any adequate account would be able to do so.[77] The more broadly naturalist or empirically minded approach that Sellars is articulating does not fall within the Derridean purview, because it does not support the kind of philosophical approach that the philosophers Derrida thinks constitutive of the tradition are seeking. If language is to be conceived in practical terms—that is, as a practice or group of practices—it is difficult to see how it will be able to perform the foundationalist functions required by the "metaphysical" tradition Derrida deconstructs.

One result of this more naturalist view is that Sellars avoids ratifying the two dogmas. Though not a behaviorist, Sellars uses the idea of normative constraints on socially characterized moves in order to avoid an emphasis on semantic concepts like meaning and truth. If language is a special sort of social practice, according to Sellars, its specialty is to be found in the unique structural form had by the normative constraints definitive of it, not in the fact of its being foundational for the philosophical project. In particular, we ought to look for that which is uniquely linguistic in the existence of an *inferential* structure internal to language rather than in a truth-structure. On this account the semantic vocabulary of truth, reference, and meaning assumes a secondary importance here; and, as we shall see, this de-emphasis on semantic vocabulary issues out onto a view of meaning that does not tie it to truth and on a view of truth that does not tie it to a correspondence to reality.

---

77. One might object there that Derrida's deconstructive approach *is* an account of language, although not of linguistic meaning. Granted. But it is more accurately conceived as an account of why no adequate account can be given than as the type of account that the tradition—or, in a very different way, Sellars—is trying to offer.

To give a sketch of what this inferential structure is like, I want to turn to the philosopher who has taken this idea the furthest: Robert Brandom. In his paper "Asserting" he gives a detailed account of the sort of normative structure that must be posited in order to understand the act of asserting as a move within a language game. Essentially, Brandom sees an act of asserting in terms of the two normative dimensions of *commitment* and *entitlement*.

To assert *that P* is to undertake a commitment to defend P against reasonable challenges. If one succeeds in responding to any challenges brought against one's claim in the language game, then others in the linguistic community are bound to attribute entitlement to one's assertion. This implies granting the assertor entitlement to use the assertion in any of the three types of Sellarsian moves.

Along with this commitment undertaken in asserting a sentence comes an attribution of entitlement as well. When one asserts P, one issues a "reassertion license," one offers up to others a right, conditional upon one's own authority over the sentence, to reassert the claim and to make acceptable inferences from it.

In later articles and his recent book *Making It Explicit,* Brandom shows how to make inferential structures definable within such a normative system do much of the work of accounting for the semantic content of various linguistic entities. For example, he distinguishes singular terms from predicates on the basis of substitutional roles definable in terms of the inferential role of sentences; he provides accounts of the content of various propositional attitudes understood as devices for the attribution of commitments to others, and so forth.

When we move from Sellars to such Sellarsian philosophers as Brandom, we can see the emergence of a view that avoids the second dogma; these philosophers reject traditional accounts of meaning, reference, and truth as dependent upon relations between language and extralinguistic reality. They do not conclude, however, that such semantic concepts are empty or defective. They conclude, rather, that the traditional accounts were on the wrong track.

The tradition embodying the two dogmas that Derrida also accepts placed semantic concepts—and, of particular concern to us, the concepts of meaning and of truth—outside the linguistic, at least in the sense of thinking that there was an important conceptual distinction between semantic and nonsemantic vocabulary and that the former was to explain the significance of the latter. Concepts like meaning and truth were to be the cornerstones of any account of language, because it was through them that language's—and thus, in an important sense, *our*—relation to the world was to be understood. Philosophers of the Sellarsian bent, on the other hand, see semantic and nonsemantic vocabulary as on a par. Rather than derive our concept of truth from other terms, we derive it from the pragmatic use of "is true." For them, semantic vocabulary is very much a part of language and is to be explained in the same terms as any other bit of language, namely, in terms of its significance within the game of giving and asking for reasons.

As Brandom explains in his paper "Pragmatism, Phenomenalism, and Truth Talk,"[78] the Sellarsian approach is to begin with an account of truth not as a property of sentences founded upon relations between language and reality, but in terms of an investigation of the import of acts of making truth claims. This investigation is to be carried out in exactly the same terms as our overall investigation of language as a more or less natural phenomenon.

The first detailed theory of one of the semantic concepts to emerge from this view was the "prosentential theory of truth" of Dorothy Grover, Joseph Camp, and Nuel Belnap.[79] Rather than look at truth as a property of sentences, propositions, or whatever—one that is foundational to the semantic content of language and is attributed by the locution "is true"—they begin by supposing that we have some independent account of the significance of language. The account I have been promoting here is, of course, the Sellarsian one.

So we are given an account of the significance of sentences in terms of their role in a language game. Attaching to each sentence is a vast structure of normative constraints determining the bounds of competent usage—either in inference or in moves to and from nonlinguistic acts—of that sentence. As a useful and only slightly misleading shorthand, we can speak of this as the *inferential role* of the sentence.

What then is the inferential role of the sentence "It is true *that P*"? It is, leaving aside some pragmatic details, precisely that of the sentence P. Thus, to say that "it is true that electrons have negative charge" is simply to say that electrons have negative charge. Among the crucial points is a grammatical one: this sentence is not predicating anything of the sentence P. It is not commending a belief in P or ascribing some sociological property to P. To say that it is true that electrons have negative charge or, similarly, to say " 'electrons have negative charge' is true" is not to talk about language but instead to talk about electrons.

78. Robert Brandom, "Pragmatism, Phenomenalism, and Truth Talk," *Midwest Studies in Philosophy* 12 (1988): 75–93.

79. Dorothy L. Grover, Joseph Camp Jr., and Nuel D. Belnap, "A Prosentential Theory of Truth," *Philosophical Studies* 27 (1975): 73–125.

Such examples of the use of "is true" are only the simplest cases, of course. Traditional disquotational theories and redundancy theories of truth, of which the prosentential theory is an offspring, foundered on much more complicated examples as "Everything the Pope says is true." For the traditional redundancy theory of truth, for example, for which truth is merely redundant, the sentence "Everything the Pope says is true" would lose nothing if the "is true" were dropped. But dropping the "is true" leaves only "Everything the Pope says," which is not even a sentence. So the "is true" must perform *some* role. The sentence "Everything the Pope says is true" can be understood, however, as a quantificational claim, involving propositional quantifiers. "Is true" is seen as a disquotational operator that takes a name of sentence and produces the sentence.

Otherwise put, to say "Everything the Pope says is true" is to say "For any proposition *that P:* if the Pope says *that P,* then it is true *that P.*" Given the disquotational role of "it is true that," this sentence has as instances such sentences as "If the Pope says that it is raining, then it is true that it is raining," which is equivalent—in terms of its inferential role—to "If the Pope says that it is raining, then it is raining." Similarly, an acceptable instance would be "If the Pope says that the last assertion of President Coolidge is true, then it is true." Here, both the phrase "the last assertion of President Coolidge is true" and "it is true" are anaphoric *prosentences—* entities in the category of sentences that function just as do pronouns in the category of nouns—whose semantic content is determined by their anaphoric antecedent, namely, the last assertion of President Coolidge.

Thus, the primary role of "is true" in natural language is seen to be akin to that of pronouns; such a device allows for the construction of quantificational claims, which can be thought of, roughly, as big conjunctions. Just as it is important, as a matter of expressive resources, to go beyond the series Fa, Fa&Fb, Fa&Fb&Fc, . . . to the claim "For all x, F(x)," so a language that allows infinite conjunctions of the form "For all claims of P, then P" has increased its expressive resources over one that can only say, for example, "If the Pope says that it is raining, then it is raining, and if the Pope says that it is snowing, then it is snowing." Life is easier with prosentences.

The prosentential theory of truth, then, clearly articulates a view of how truth works that competes with the second dogma. While the second dogma sees truth as a matter of a relationship between language and the world, the prosentential theory sees it as an intralinguistic device that increases the expressive resources of a language. As noted above, such an account could be combined with Davidson's general approach—although Davidson does not do so—to yield an approach to language that, while embracing the first dogma, avoids the second. But I want to look at the current approach a bit more to see more clearly how the first dogma is avoided as well.

Before turning directly to the question of meaning, let me note that Brandom has shown that the same sort of internalist or intralinguistic account of reference can be given. In his "Reference Explained Away" he analyzes such singular terms as "the one referred to by Jones" not as presupposing a relation between words and objects, but as a kind of complex anaphoric pronoun, a longer version of "he" that wears its anaphoric antecedent on its sleeve.[80] Thus, to say that the one referred to by Smith as "that pinhead congressman" is Jesse Helms, is not to assert the existence of a relation between Smith's assertion and the honorable senator, but to assert a simple identity claim; it is like saying "he is Helms."

Again, the point of having such vocabulary is to increase the expressive resources of the language. In particular, we get the opportunity to piggyback our word usages on those of others—that is, to assert sentences in such a way that their inferential role is a function of the norms determining the other's use of the term—without ourselves knowing enough to use the words properly ourselves.

To deny that "reference" is a relation between words and objects is, of course, only to make a claim about the function of "refers" in language. It is not, in particular, to suppose that there are no relations between words and objects. There are all sorts of empirical relations between bits of language and bits of reality, but none of them is constitutive of linguistic content. As Brandom once put the point, to ask for the relation between language and the world is like asking for *the* relation between me and China. The problem is not that there is none, but that there are too many.[81]

While "refers" and "true" can be seen as vocabulary making it possible to form new compounds out of preexisting semantic contents, "meaning" can be seen as a bit of vocabulary designed to allow for the modification, through dialogue, of an existing structure of linguistic practice. On this view, to say that A means B is not to ascribe a property to A or to B, or to describe any sort of relation between A and B. Rather, it is to put forward a normative proposal (or to ratify an existing one) as to how to use the terms in the future. In particular, to say "A means B" is to say that one ought to use A as one ought to use B. Thus, such a locution presupposes an antecedent understanding of the use of B (competence at using B according to

---

80. Robert Brandom, "Reference Explained Away," *Journal of Philosophy* 81, no. 9 (1984): 469–92.
81. This point was put to Mark Lance in conversation.

the standards of the language) and advises the adoption of a rule to the effect that A be used in the same way.

Such a view of meaning contrasts sharply with Derrida's view. For Derrida, if there is such a thing as meaning, it is substantive rather than normative. To render the meaning of an expression is, for the most part, to render the content of the intention of the person who uttered the expression: meaning as *vouloir-dire*. This view of meaning, however, contrasts with his view, articulated in "Signature Event Context," that there is something social about the meanings of expressions that is irreducible to intentions. The contrast, however, is not a contradiction. As we saw, the "something social" that expressions possess is not something that can be rendered, beyond saying that it is iterable; and this iterability precludes any reduction of the meaningfulness of the expression to an intention animating it.

The substantive character of Derrida's view of meaning lies both in the animating intention and in the iterability. The meaning of an expression, for Derrida, is something it contains; and all expressions contain animating intentions and iterability—or, alternatively, presence and absence.[82] What the view of meaning I am describing here rejects is the possibility that there is anything substantive about meaning. To give the meaning of an expression is to say how one ought to use that expression. Meaning, like truth and reference, is an intralinguistic device that helps us navigate from some bits of language to others.

This view of meaning is also in keeping with the general inferentialist character of the account of language being offered. Saying that A means B can be read as saying that B ought to admit of exactly the same inferences as A does. Thus, the role of the term "meaning" is to tell us about the roles that the terms of a language ought to play within the inferential structure of that language. There is, on this view, no theory of meaning as a theory of what the meaningfulness of linguistic expression consists in; rather, there is a theory of what role of the term "meaning" plays in the practice or group of practices that we call language. This theory, as well as the inferentialist structure that supports it, is clearly holistic. Meaning and inference take place within a holistic structure, rather than in an atomistic relation to the world or to thought. It also involves contingency, since, as discursive prac-

82. It is worth noting that a substantive view of meaning involves commitment not only to the first but to the second dogma as well. If one were committed to the idea that meaning is to be cashed out in terms of truth, but that truth was to be understood, for example, prosentenially, then there would be no substantive commitments in one's account of meaning. Since, however, Derrida thinks of truth in terms of presence, he is committed to a substantive theory of meaning; or, more exactly, he is committed to the idea that could there be a theory of meaning, it would have to be substantive.

tices change, so do the inferences and the meaningfulness of their terms.[83]

Thus we can see that on this more or less naturalist view of language not only is the second dogma avoided, the first one is as well. Meaning is to be thought, not in terms of truth, but in terms of linguistic appropriateness. Of course, the point of thinking of meaning in terms of truth, for the traditional theories of language that Derrida deconstructs, is to be able to get from meaning to presence. Thus, by blocking the route from truth to presence, as the prosentential theory does, the motivation for the traditional reduction of meaning to truth is lost. However, it is important to see that even that first move is one that does not have to be ratified by an account of language. And thus both of the dogmas to which both Derrida and the tradition are committed turn out to be optional in philosophical accounts of language.

Having said this much about language, however, I want to close this chapter by returning to the question of the status of philosophy. This is especially urgent, since the view of language I have recounted here and Derrida's deconstructive approach to language share something important in their view of philosophy. For both, philosophy cannot be a foundationalist practice. The reasons for this in Derrida's case have been given. It is not difficult to see, however, how the account of language offered here also resists philosophical foundationalism.

For any philosophy to be foundationalist, it must seek some bedrock of certainty upon which to rest its claims. But the account here precludes such a bedrock. The reason for this is that while the giving and asking of reasons may be understandable behavior *within* the context of specific language games, there is nothing that allows for any ultimate support *for a language game itself*. Traditionally, the way to try to obtain that support was to interpret the semantic concepts—meaning, truth, and reference—in terms of word-world or word-intention relationships, and then to seek the way to fix those relationships so that they cemented into some form of absoluteness or indubitability. This was Husserl's project in trying to reduce meaning to ex-

---

83. It is worth remarking the similarity between this inferentialist view of language and the Saussurean view of language as an oppositional structure, also ratified by Derrida. For an inferentialist, understanding a bit of language is understanding the role it plays—or ought to play—in the general semantic structure of that language. For Saussure, words are meaningful only by taking up a differential position within the larger linguistic constellation, that is, in contrast to other words in the language. The two key differences between the inferentialist position and that of the Derridean/Saussurean here are that (1) the former view emphasizes the inferential connections rather than the oppositional differences between terms (although it does not preclude a recognition of those differences) and (2) the latter, not the former, combines this holistic approach to language with the two dogmas that preclude the possibility of ever achieving an understanding of language.

pressiveness and expressiveness to animating intention.[84] Since the account offered here sees semantic terms as on a par with nonsemantic ones, and not as foundational for them, this route to foundationalism is closed; and it is difficult to see how, given the closure of that route, a route could be opened from this account of language to foundationalism. Moreover, as Derrida has argued, any philosophy that purports to be foundationalist must have as part of its approach an account of language that shows how the language of philosophy can be rendered absolute or indubitable.

In contrast to Derrida's position, however, this approach does not necessitate the deconstruction of philosophical inquiry. In eliminating foundationalism, what is left is not a deconstructed foundationalism, but a nonfoundationalist philosophy. What distinguishes this nonfoundationalist philosophy from other, more straightforwardly empirical, sciences? The distinction, I want to argue, is more quantitative than qualitative. Philosophy is a more nearly conceptual practice than what are traditionally called the empirical sciences. It works more closely with how we think about things, whether those things are our lives, our world, our moral duties, our language, or whatever. If that sounds vague, it is. Wilfrid Sellars once defined the goal of philosophy as "to understand how things in the broadest possible sense of the term hang together in the broadest sense of the term."[85] I am not sure I can improve on that.[86]

The practice of philosophy is, like other discursive practices, one that has its own reasons and justifications within the context of its own network of commitments and principles of reasoning. That practice, however, is not supported by some absolute, indubitable, or unchanging foundation. The concepts it uses, the reasoning it engages in, the functions it performs among other cultural functions—all these evolve with the practice, in part due to the influence of other, more nearly empirical, epistemic, or scientific practices.

Among the implications of this view of philosophy is that there is no strict division between philosophy and other, more nearly empirical, epistemic

---

84. Of course, Husserl's indubitability was obtained at a cost. Since the anchor from language went into intention instead of the world, the contingency of the world's relation to language remained a problem. Husserl's solution to that problem, the transcendental reduction, assessed the cost of the problem to be payable in terms of idealism.

85. Wilfrid Sellars, "Philosophy and the Scientific Image of Man," in *Science, Perception, and Reality*, 1.

86. It is my not wholly considered opinion that there is little that does more damage to the practice of philosophy than people trying to come up with very strict answers to the question, What is philosophy? Among the effects propagated by those who have tried to give strict answers to that question has been to keep Continentalists and Anglo-American philosophers from respecting each other's work for nearly a hundred years.

practices. (Of course, perhaps we should have known this since Quine's "Two Dogmas of Empiricism.") The practice of science may have much to tell philosophers about the philosophy of science; we may use sociological evidence to inform us about political philosophy and to guide us in the formation of moral principles; empirical research on cognition may help us to solve problems of personhood or of moral responsibility. Once philosophy is no longer seen as founding for empirical knowledge, then the appeal to those sciences in the construction of philosophical positions is no longer any type of begging the question: we are not appealing to the founded in order to construct the foundations.

Reciprocally, philosophy as a practice of concepts may have much to say to various empirical sciences. It can no longer lay claim to providing their conceptual foundations, but it may still provide resources for often badly needed conceptual reflection. Consider, for instance, the now-resurrected debates in psychology and sociology about intelligence, intelligence tests, and race. It seems that among the contributants to (yet another) resolution of this issue ought to be some critical reflection on the terms "intelligence" and "race." Such reflection would not occur instead of or beneath, but rather alongside and intertwined with, empirical studies and research.

Thinking of philosophy as a practice, then, and specifically a discursive practice—a language game—allows us to allot a role to philosophy that is less than the grander role that much of the pre-twentieth-century tradition saw itself as performing, but is more than the end of philosophy that some philosophers, whether gleefully or ruefully, prophesy. It is also a way of thinking about philosophy very different from that proposed by Derrida. For Derrida, there is an important aspect of the philosophical tradition that is inescapable, at least directly: its foundational character. This inescapability is not something for which Derrida argues. Rather, it is an assumption that informs his argument structure. Specifically, it appears in the passage from step 5 to steps 6 through 8 in the structure I have laid out.

Step 5 says that "any alternative to the traditional philosophical project must come to terms with the language in which it is articulated." There is nothing in the proposal about language I have articulated that would deny that. In fact, it seems that one of the implications of my proposal is that philosophy must be nonfoundationalist, since there seems to be no place in the account of language for foundationalism to get a foothold. Step 6, however, claims that "this coming to terms requires a recognition that linguistic meaning always eludes any account that attempts to render it fully transparent." And after the Levinas-refuting step 7 moves in step 8 to conclude that "whatever else the philosophical project involves, it must continuously unwork from within itself the assumption that the claims it makes signify in any stable way."

After the foregoing considerations, it is not difficult to see the dogmatic assumptions underlying this movement. From the fact that philosophy must take into account the language in which it occurs, one can only infer a deconstructive conclusion if one assumes as true the two dogmas I have worked here to undermine. Put another way, only within the confines of a restricted view of language and linguistic meaning can it appear that the only alternatives are traditional philosophy and traditional philosophy deconstructed. The dilemma that Derrida presents us with is a false one, and its falsity lies in assumptions about language and specifically about linguistic meaning that are dispensable. There is an alternative to traditional philosophy that is not deconstruction: it is nonfoundationalist philosophy. And among the accounts it can give of itself, one candidate is the account given here.

This account does not claim that meaning *can* ever be rendered fully transparent, as Derrida's step 6 denies. Given the open and changeable structure of language, and given the open and changeable structure of the world in which practices of language operate, one would not expect such exhaustiveness. But the reason for the lack of closure has to do with the various types of limits such a project would face—empirical, political, and so forth—and not with, as deconstruction holds, the project's being internally riven from the outset.

One might object that the account of language sketched here may turn out to be false, and then query whether that would throw us back into the dilemma deconstruction stakes out for us. No, it would not. Even if the proposed account is wrong, it would be wrong for reasons having nothing to do with the deconstructive argument. That is because the deconstructive argument requires an adherence to the two dogmas for which a case has not been made. (That is why I call them "dogmas.") In order for deconstruction to be vindicated, it would have to show not only that the proposed program does not work, but that there is no good reason to believe that any program that does not adhere to the two dogmas can work. And only then, having shown that the consequents of the dogmas are false, it could go on to claim that deconstruction is the only viable philosophical alternative.

There is a final lingering issue that I have not yet discussed, and that may have passed through the mind of many readers who have borne with me so far. I have claimed that the deconstructive view of language assumes two dogmas that are dispensable, and have illustrated their dispensability by recalling research programs that actually dispense with at least one of those dogmas. But I have not given any reason, in comparing the deconstructive view of language and philosophy and the nonfoundationalist view, to pick the latter over the former. From the fact that deconstruction is not the only alternative open to philosophy, we cannot immediately conclude that whatever alternative competes with it is better. Why opt for the view I have presented here over deconstruction?

I have a confession to make. To me the reason is obvious. The view I have recounted here gives an account of linguistic meaning, truth, reference, and language that the Derridean view does not. Derrida's claim, rather, is that, given philosophical foundationalism, such accounts cannot be given. I find no fault with such a claim. But when a philosophical research program, or even an entire tradition, fails to give an adequate accounting of that for which it seeks to account, then, all other things equal, it is best to try a new philosophical research program or inaugurate a new tradition.[87] If the argument of this chapter is right, Derrida has not shown that philosophical accounts of language or alternatives to deconstructive views of philosophy are wrong, only that foundationalism and the views of language that support it are wrong. Why not seek to understand our linguistic practices then another way, a way that might work out?

If you will grant me the premise that, all other things equal, having access to an understanding of our world and our lives in that world is better than not having access to an understanding of them (and what philosophically oriented reader will not?), then a philosophical approach that offers some understanding presents a more attractive alternative than a philosophical approach that gives (dogmatically based) reasons why such an understanding will not be forthcoming.[88]

---

87. There are, of course, times when all else is not equal. If Michel Foucault's arguments in *Discipline and Punish* are right, then perhaps it would be best to abandon the search for a better psychological self-understanding than current ones provide. The reasons for such an abandonment, however, have to do with the deleterious political effects of psychological practice. In order to abandon the search for better linguistic and generally philosophical understandings, an argument would have to be made regarding their political perniciousness. I see none forthcoming, but I am open to the possibility.

88. This chapter cannot resist a last footnote. One might wonder how a Sellarsian view would see the relationship, so central to Derrida, between intentions and language. Sellars offers a view in "Empiricism and the Philosophy of Mind," in *Science, Perception, and Reality*, esp. 186–96. Roughly, the idea is that while language must provide the model for thought— we cannot render the content of someone's thought without recourse to language—that does not mean that all thought must occur *in* language. The mental process might occur any number of ways, but the content of that process must be articulated in language.

3

From Ethical Difference
to Ethical Holism

Emmanuel Levinas

This chapter discusses what is perhaps the motivation underlying the emphasis on difference in recent French thought: the project of valorizing—or at least protecting—difference or differences. It would not be understating the case to say that every major French thinker since the heyday of structuralism has had as a central preoccupation this valorization or protection of difference. This should not be surprising, given the European experience with what we might call in shorthand "the identitarian politics of fascism." This is the politics, highlighted during the time of the fascist dictatorships in Germany, Italy, and Spain but present everywhere around us, that privileges the practices, viewpoints, and discourses of one's own culture at the expense—often very concrete expense—of others. Today we can see identitarian politics not only in the rise of neo-Nazism, but in regional nationalisms, various fundamentalisms, renewed racism, and, in academic circles, the rejection of multiculturalism. Starkly put, identitarianism, a project of either marginalizing the other or reducing it to the categories and practices of the same, pervades our world.

The valorization or protection of difference against identitarianism, however, is not as philosophically straightforward or comfortable as might be hoped. It has faced a seeming trilemma that has driven thinking into some strange places.

The trilemma, straightforwardly and a bit simplistically stated, is this: First, if we refuse to accept the differences of others as of a worth equal to our own, then our thinking is identitarian after the fashion of fascism: we privilege our own discourse and practices at the expense of others'. Second, if we accept the differences of others on the basis of our own standards of tolerance (or some other value), then we covertly raise our own standards above those of others, and thus have not escaped from the first position. Finally, if we accept the differences of others on the basis of relativism, arguing that our own standards are not more acceptable than those of others, we lose the basis of judgment altogether. This is because, when faced with the question of why our own standards are not more acceptable than those of others, our only answer—if we are to answer at all—is to offer reasons that accord with our own standards, thus putting us back in the second position and ultimately in the first one. It seems, then, that we cannot evade a certain fascist identitarianism, no matter how we approach the problem. The trilemma, moreover, is both political and philosophical, since it goes to the heart of the status of "our" (whoever that "we" is) way of taking things, accounting for them, and justifying our accounts.

It needs to be seen that this trilemma affects not only how the moral position one embraces responds to difference, but the very status of one's moral position. There seems, in fact, to be something self-undermining about the moral or ethical project. If, on the one hand, one refuses to accept the differences of others (the first position), then one's moral position may justifiably be said to be flawed, insofar as an identitarian fascism can be considered a moral flaw. If, on the other hand, the moral position one holds forces one both to embrace a respect for difference and deny one's own position in doing so (realized in different ways in the second and third positions), then one faces a moral quandary: the more justifiable the principle of tolerance, the less justifiable the framework that justifies the principle.

Thus, in thinking about how to introduce the valorization of difference into philosophical and practical reflection, what is at stake is not merely one moral principle among others, but the very standing of one's own moral position and of morality itself. The thinkers I discuss in this chapter realize this, which is why their thought about difference opens out onto the larger questions of morality or ethics.[1]

1. Although I prefer the term "morality" to "ethics," philosophers like Levinas and Deleuze tend to opt for the latter term (although Levinas does use both). In this and the next chapter, I use the terms more or less interchangeably, letting context decide which term to employ. For the most part, I use the term "ethics" when discussing the work of the people I criticize, and "morality" when offering my positive alternative.

One of the perspectives that can be taken on the approach to difference, one that seemingly evades the trilemma, runs through absence. That perspective, associated with Derrida, Levinas, Nancy, and Lacoue-Labarthe, tries to circumvent the trilemma by offering a position not associated with one of the three just cited. Instead, it discovers difference to be a constitutive part of our most deeply held practices, a part that either cannot be eliminated or at least cannot be eliminated without transforming our practices into something unrecognizable.

The purpose of this chapter is twofold. First, I want to raise some doubts about the approach to difference through absence. Second, I want to show why embracing the second horn of the trilemma is both necessary and more benign than it seems. The valorization or protection of difference must be had by reference to our own standards or not at all. This second part itself involves two tasks: the articulation of a principle of respect for differences and the defense of such a principle within a view of morality that is necessarily identititarian in the sense just defined.

To accomplish the first task, I focus primarily on the thought of Emmanuel Levinas. I choose him for two reasons. First, he is the most dogged thinker of ethics in the recent French tradition. While the remarks on ethics by Derrida have been more allusive or programmatic, and while thinkers such as Foucault and Deleuze often resist discussions of ethics altogether—or at least the kind of ethics that has any resonance with the concern for others that has been the hallmark of traditional ethical positions—one's relationship with and responsibility to the other have been the centerpiece of Levinas's thought. It would be no exaggeration to say that he has thought nothing else besides this.

The second, and related, reason for choosing Levinas has been the influence of his ethical thought on recent French philosophy. In the last chapter, I detailed Derrida's critical view of Levinas's approach to ethics. In the course of that discussion, however, I noted that there are also deep confluences between the two thinkers. Simon Critchley has investigated this confluence and details the relationship between the Derridean recovery (but not recuperation) of the other that cannot be said in discourse and Levinas's responsibility to the other that can never be recuperated.[2] In addition to his influence on Derrida, Levinas has figured prominently in recent writings of Jean-François Lyotard, who articulates in *The Differend* a self-consciously Levinasian view of the logic of obligation and of the ethical genre of discourse.[3]

2. Simon Critchley, *The Ethics of Deconstruction* (Oxford: Basil Blackwell, 1992).
3. Jean-François Lyotard, *The Differend: Phrases in Dispute*, trans. Georges van den Abbeele (Minneapolis: University of Minnesota Press, 1988; or. pub. 1983), esp. 110–15. Levinas's

Before turning directly to Levinas, I want to spend a moment, as sort of an addendum to the last chapter, taking a critical look at the Derridean deconstructive approach to the trilemma cited at the outset. There has recently been much discussion about the ethical and political implications (or lack thereof) in Derrida's thought, and therefore it is probably worth a word regarding at least one of the purported ethical implications of deconstructive thought.

The deconstructive position banks, as we saw, on the discovery of absence at the heart of presence.[4] Rather than rehearse the entire argument of the last chapter, let me just draw its connection with identitarianism. Presence is self-presence; what is present is present to a self. As such, all presence is identitarian, in the sense that it exists within the parameters of a self-given identity that is taken to be the ultimate standard by which all difference or otherness is judged. If, however, presence is shot through with what is not present, then every self-given identity is fractured, and identitarianism is an illusory position. Difference, in the form of absence, is ineluctable.

To be sure, this does not mean that one can turn the tables and substitute difference for identity, because identity is just as ineluctable as difference if there is any discourse at all. Recall Derrida's claim: "There *is not* a transgression, if one understands by that a pure and simple landing into a beyond of metaphysics."[5] Recognizing that metaphysics is the identitarian project *par excellence*, the conclusion is that discourse always takes place within an economy of presence and absence, identity and difference.

The problem, according to Derrida, is that metaphysics—foundationalist philosophy—has attempted to deny the differences that help constitute its very possibility. In doing so, it denies nonconformity to the identitarian character of its project, to its reduction or rejection of difference. Moreover, in embracing identitarianism, it also denies in content those things which do not conform to the traditional philosophical identities: not merely difference per se, but the specific differences of gender, metaphor, writing, and so forth, in short, all differences that are characterized by an absence that suffuses the identitarian project. That seems to me to be part of the signifi-

---

influence also appears in Lyotard's book *Heidegger and the Jews*, trans. Andreas Michel and Mark Roberts (Minneapolis: University of Minnesota Press, 1990; or. pub. 1988).

4. In what follows, I will not rely on the arguments offered in the previous chapter regarding Derrida's approach to language. I believe that, even if that approach is correct, it provides neither the framework nor the ground for any defense of otherness or difference.

5. Jacques Derrida, *Positions*, trans. Alan Bass (Chicago: University of Chicago Press, 1981; or. pub. 1972), 12.

cance of Derrida's following claim in *Limited Inc.*: "Once it has been demonstrated, as I hope to have done, that the exclusion of the parasite (of divergences, contaminations, impurities, etc.) cannot be justified by purely theoretical-methodological reasons, how can one ignore that this practice of exclusion, or this will to purify, to reappropriate in a manner that would be essential, internal, and ideal in respect to the subject or to its objects, translates necessarily into a politics?"[6] Such an exclusion or denial is, of course, also a self-denial because, inasmuch as identity is constituted by difference, it is also constituted by the differences it denies. To give a simple but perhaps not inaccurate example, anti-multiculturalism is a position that privileges one form of discourse—generally Western, male, bound to certain types of rationality—at the expense of other discourses that both contribute to its constitution and, by their differences from it, to whatever self-recognition it has.

Thus, for Derrida, in recognizing the constitutive role of difference for all discourse, in recognizing its inescapability, one accords difference a place (although the word "place" is, of course, a bit misleading) that eludes the trilemma cited above. Since it is a difference that cannot be mastered, it eludes the first position; since it fractures our principles instead of underwriting them, it eludes the second position; and since it is an internal, rather than an external, limit placed upon our discourse, it eludes the third position.

Now, one might be tempted to offer a direct objection to Derrida's analysis, arguing that he has committed a version of the naturalist fallacy. Has he not started with a constitutive analysis, an analysis of what is, and wound up with normative conclusions, conclusions about what ought to be? Does the *fact* that difference constitutes identity imply—directly and without further argument, and especially further ethical argument—that we *ought* to accept difference, and specifically that we ought to accept the ways in which others are different from ourselves, even if those differences are partly constitutive of ourselves?

Matters are not as straightforward as this, however. Derrida can reply, in a move oddly similar to that of Habermas in his defense of discourse ethics, that to recognize the constitutive role of difference while denying concrete differences amounts to a performative contradiction. (Of course, readers of the previous chapter may ask themselves, as I have asked myself, whether the notion of contradiction can play any straightforward role in Derrida's

---

6. Jacques Derrida, *Limited Inc.*, trans. Samuel Weber and Jeffrey Mehlman (Evanston, Ill.: Northwestern University Press, 1988; or. pub. 1972), 135.

thought.) Thus, Derrida could say that the engagement in discourse is a normative engagement—it involves embracing or at least accepting the terms of the discourse in which one is engaged. But to embrace or to accept those terms is also to accept difference, since difference is constitutive of the terms of the discourse. Therefore, one accepts the terms of the discourse while at the same time denying the differences that constitute them, on pain of a performative contradiction.

I believe that this reply is correct, and in keeping with the general run of Derrida's thought. However, it does not allow Derrida to circumvent the trilemma. For we must ask, In being committed to difference as constitutive of discourse, to what exactly is one being committed? First, there is a commitment to antifoundationalism in epistemology. Second, there is a commitment to the idea that there are constitutive elements of one's discourse and one's identity that can never be made entirely clear. Third, there is a commitment to the idea that those constitutive elements involve repressions of some sort. But does it involve a commitment to the idea that the repressed elements of discourse, the repressed differences, ought to become less repressed? I do not see how it could. As Derrida himself points out, repression of difference is as necessary an aspect of discourse as the constitutive differences themselves. This is because, as absence, difference can never be brought to presence. In his terms, one never entirely escapes metaphysics. Therefore, although the identitarianism of metaphysics—as a project of reduction to presence—is necessarily a failed project, it is not necessarily a bad one, and indeed may be, on Derrida's analysis, a necessary one.

Now, here one might object on Derrida's behalf that he has pointed out certain repressions that philosophy and other forms of discourse live off of without according them their due, and that those repressions are a bad thing. Agreed. What is at issue, however, is not whether the repression of differences is bad, but whether the deconstructive approach offers a way to endorse difference without having to appeal to a principle of respect for difference *independent of* deconstruction. My argument is that it does not. The deconstructive approach to difference as an absence constitutive of discourse cannot give the proper normative force to a principle of respect for differences in a way that would circumvent the trilemma described at the outset. The deconstructive position cannot, without further ethical support, justify the position that we should respect difference; and once it has to rely on such support, we are landed back in the trilemma from which we had hoped it would liberate us.

Let me turn now to the central object of the chapter: Emmanuel Levinas.
Emmanuel Levinas is the Thelonious Monk of contemporary French
thought. Although some have long considered him to be a pioneering force,
as some in jazz understood Monk to be, it was not until comparatively recently that his pervasive influence came to be appreciated. Levinas's thought,
like Monk's music, was discordant to ears unused to the themes he was
sounding. Rereading him now, however, one immediately grasps why he has
been so influential to better-known figures such as Lyotard and recently
emerging ones such as Nancy. It is perhaps a shame that he did not play the
sax earlier in his career; jazz may have lost a good duet.

Levinas's primary influence unquestionably lies in staking out a sense of
responsibility each individual has to an otherness that cannot be reduced to
any of the categories one applies to oneself and to manipulable (or, for Levinas, enjoyable) objects in the world. It is not because we can comprehend
others or bring them into our sphere of understanding—whether by Husserlian analogy, Sartrean look, or Merleau-Pontian chiasm—that we are responsible to them; instead, it is precisely because we cannot. The other is infinite, his or her being (although the term "being" is rejected by Levinas here
as already too ontological) beyond the reach of our sensibility (at least for
the Levinas of *Totality and Infinity;* for the later Levinas otherness is partially constitutive of our sensibility) and our categories; and our responsibility is to that infinity or otherness rather than to that which we can master.

Levinas's account of otherness is in fact, however—or so I argue—two
accounts, mixed together in a way that vitiates the power of his thought. In
holding an ethical experience, as ethical, to precede and found ontology, Levinas winds up subsuming the ethics he sought to free from ontology under
the very ontological categories he sought to free them from. In the end, Levinas's ethics remains hostage to ontology. We have to think differently in
order to free ethics from the bondage he struggled against. Like Monk, his
discordance was productive; we need to go back and refashion moments of
the score, however.

Levinas's writings are extensive, yet much of his thought, particularly on
these matters, is offered in his two major works, *Totality and Infinity* and
Otherwise than Being or Beyond Essence,[7] so I focus almost exclusively on

---

7. References are to Alphonso Lingis's translations: *Totality and Infinity* (Pittsburgh: Duquesne University Press, 1969; or. pub. 1961) and *Otherwise than Being or Beyond Essence*,
2d ed. (The Hague: Nijhoff, 1981; or. pub. 1978).

them. Moreover, since the central point I want to make concerns what is common to those texts, I ignore, for the most part, the differences between them, such as the emphasis on diachrony in the latter work, the different interpretations of sensibility, and the more phenomenologically stratified approach of the earlier work. I proceed by recalling how Levinas considers ethics to precede ontology. Then I locate the weakness of the treatment. In doing so, I try to show both how Levinas's approach fails to navigate the trilemma cited at the outset of this chapter and how his account in fact repeats the very problem from which he sought liberation in the articulation of the experience of the other. Finally, as in the previous chapters, I offer an account of respect for otherness that relies not upon the privileging of difference but upon conceiving morality as a practice among other practices in a contingent whole.

Levinas wants to address, although not to describe (because description cannot be had) or even circumscribe (because it is infinite), an experience that, by itself, induces a sense of responsibility in those capable of it. That experience, the experience of the infinite other, is the foundation of what Levinas calls "metaphysics." This metaphysics is not to be confused with the metaphysics that has been the source of much of the deconstructive project—which Levinas calls "ontology"—and in an important sense subtends metaphysics in the latter sense.

In what sense does metaphysics precede ontology and what are the ethical implications of this metaphysical precedence? It is not, for Levinas, that the infinite other precedes (other) beings, in the sense that infinity either exists or is experienced before them. The enjoyment of beings and the experience of the other are coequal. "Just as the interiority of enjoyment is not deducible from the transcendental relation, the transcendental relation is not deducible from the separated being as a dialectical antithesis forming a counterpart to the subjectivity." [8] Moreover, there is no need for infinity to precede (other) beings, because what Levinas wants to call into question is not enjoyment but totality, the project of ontology.

What ontology seeks is a "a reduction of the other to the same by the interposition of a middle and neutral term that ensures the comprehension of being." [9] Ontology is a theoretical/practical project of bringing all otherness under the rule of the same, and thus of violence against all infinity or other-

8. *Totality and Infinity*, 148. As Alphonso Lingis argues in his introduction to *Otherwise than Being*, Levinas may have changed this view by the latter text, seeing alterity as founding for the enjoyment of beings. See esp. xxvi–xxviii.

9. *Totality and Infinity*, 43.

ness. If there is to be precedence, then, it need not be a precedence of the infinite over or before (other) beings, but of the infinite over or before totality. It is ontology, not beings, that must be shown to be deficient. And what renders ontology deficient is its neglect of an experience to which philosophical reflection owes a response. "Without substituting eschatology for philosophy, without philosophically 'demonstrating' eschatological 'truths,' we can proceed from the experience of totality back to a situation where totality breaks up, a situation that conditions totality itself. Such a situation is the gleam of exteriority or of transcendence in the face of the Other." [10]

It needs to be emphasized here, then, that the experience of the infinite, of the other in the other's otherness, is a pre-epistemic [11] and even prediscursive experience. In *Totality and Infinity*, Levinas remarks, in an echo of Descartes, that "the idea of infinity is exceptional in that its *ideatum* surpasses its idea, whereas for the things the total coincidence of their 'objective' and 'formal' realities is not precluded; we could conceivably have accounted for all the ideas, other than that of Infinity, by ourselves. . . . The distance that separates *ideatum* and idea here constitutes the content of the *ideatum* itself. Infinity is characteristic of a transcendent being as transcendent; the infinite is absolutely other." [12] As transcendent to discursive—and thus epistemic—categories, the ethical experience is a matter of a primordial relationship rather than a set of principles.

Levinas holds to this point, although he articulates it slightly differently, in *Otherwise than Being*. In this latter work, he emphasizes the ethical experience as being one of "substitution," in which I take complete responsibility for the other—not only for who he or she is but for what he or she does. "This passivity undergone in proximity by the force of an alterity in me is the passivity of a recurrence to oneself which is not the alienation of an identity betrayed. What can it be but a substitution of me for the others." [13]

10. Ibid., 24.
11. "The face to face is not a modality of coexistence nor even of the knowledge (itself panoramic) one term can have of another, but is the primordial production of being on which all the possible collocations of the terms are founded" (Ibid., 305).
12. Ibid., 49.
13. *Otherwise than Being*, 114. That the substitution involves my complete responsibility for the other is something Levinas makes clear in an interview: "You know that sentence in Dostoyevsky: '*We are all guilty of all and for all men before all, and I more than the others.*' This is not owing to such or such a guilt which is really mine, or to offenses that I would have committed; but because I am responsible for a total responsibility, which answers for all the others and for all in the others, even for their responsibility. The I always has one responsibility *more* than the others" (*Ethics and Infinity*, trans. Richard A. Cohen [Pittsburgh: Duquesne University Press, 1985; or. pub. 1982], 98–99).

This alternative articulation of the ethical experience as one of substitution is still beyond or beneath the realm of language and principles. "To say that the ego is a substitution is then not to state the universality of a principle, the quiddity of an ego, but, quite the contrary, it is to restore to the soul its egoity which supports no generalization."[14]

The experience of the other, then, is both prior to and subversive of totality, and indeed of representation. It is prior to totality because the totality cannot really be total unless it takes everything into account; and it does not take the infinity of the other into account. It is subversive because totality *cannot* take the other into account; infinity escapes representation, which is necessary for totalization: "The face of the other in proximity, which is more than representation, is an unrepresentable trace, the way of the infinite. It is not because among beings there exists an ego, a being pursuing ends, that being takes on signification and becomes a universe. It is because in an approach, there is inscribed or written the trace of infinity, the trace of a departure, but trace of what is inordinate, does not enter into the present, and inverts the *archē* into anarchy, that there is forsakenness of the other, obsession by him, responsibility and a self."[15]

If infinity's precedence, then, lies in its anteriority to the totalizing project of ontology, wherein does its ethical nature lie? For Levinas, it lies in the experience itself. The experience of the face of the other is the ethical experience *par excellence;* its normative force is derived from nowhere but itself. "It is in a *responsibility that is justified by no prior commitment,* in the responsibility for another—in an ethical situation—that the me-ontological and metalogical structure of this anarchy takes form. . . . The consciousness is affected, then, before forming an image of what is coming to it, affected in spite of itself. In these traits we recognize a persecution; being called into question prior to questioning, responsibility over and beyond the logos of a response."[16]

---

14. *Otherwise than Being,* 127.
15. Ibid., 116–17.
16. Ibid., 102. It is worth noting here how the idea of responsibility without commitment seems to flirt with ethical foundationalism. What Levinas seems to be commending here is a view of ethics that holds for everyone at all times regardless of their specific ethical practices. This does not mean that nonfoundationalism would have to underlie someone's voluntarily committing to ethical practices; in fact, that perspective might introduce an unwarranted foundation of freedom. The alternative to foundationalism to be considered here is rather that ethics arises from within practices, instead of beneath them.

The experience of the face of the other/Other,[17] as *the* founding experience for metaphysical reflection and *a* founding experience for all nonviolent reflection, justifies itself at the moment of its appearance, and by the very fact of its appearance. (Although we should be careful to understand the idea of appearance as one that does not involve an appearing to a consciousness.) "The 'You shall not commit murder' which delineates the face in which the Other is produced submits my freedom to judgement."[18] Thus the experience of the other, as an experience, plays a dual role. First, as the experience of someone (although a someone in part created by the experience), it is something that must be, if not accounted for, then at least accommodated by, any adequate reflection on experience. Second, as an ethical experience, it induces a sense of responsibility for whose normative power no other justification is necessary.

Now, Levinas does not always, or even often, distinguish these dual roles. He writes, for instance, that "[t]he idea of totality and the idea of infinity differ precisely in that the first is purely theoretical, while the second is moral." That view, however, misses the idea that for totality to betray infinity, or for ontology to presuppose metaphysics, there must be something about the experience that is ontologically relevant. One cannot claim that ontology presupposes metaphysics without also claiming that there is something metaphysical, in Levinas's sense, that it is the responsibility of ontology to respond to. Levinas seems to recognize this when he writes, "The ethical, beyond vision and certitude, delineates the structure of exteriority as such. Morality is not a branch of philosophy, but first philosophy."[19]

Perhaps the clearest evidence of the lack of differentiation appears in an interview in which he summarizes the key theme of *Otherwise than Being*: "Responsibility in fact is not a simple attribute of subjectivity, as if the latter already existed in itself, before the ethical relationship. Subjectivity is not for itself; it is, once again, initially for another. In the book, the proximity of the Other is not simply close to me in space, or close like a parent, but he approaches me essentially insofar as I feel myself—insofar as I am—

17. Alphonso Lingis, the translator, notes that Levinas uses both the personal term *autrui* and the impersonal *autre*. Lingis translates the former term as "Other" and the latter term as "other." Since I am concerned with the personal other—the other of other people—exclusively, I will drop the distinction and keep the term "other" in the lowercase. For Lingis's explanation of this, see *Totality and Infinity*, 24n.
18. Ibid., 303.
19. Ibid., 83, 304.

responsible to him." [20] In the final sentence of this quotation, Levinas collapses together the feeling of responsibility and the actual having of it. The feeling of responsibility is, in a certain way, a state of the subject. It is not, Levinas emphasizes, the interior emotional state of a self-contained subject, but rather the condition of a subject who is partially constituted by his or her "obsession" (to use the term employed in *Otherwise than Being*) with the other. The having of responsibility, on the other hand, is a normative ascription; it is not the characterization of a state, but the assigning of a duty.

Herein lies the rub for Levinas. The ethical experience, as experience, cannot possess the normative force of ethical justification. This is not to say that there is no experience of the sort Levinas calls our attention to. Nor is it to claim that that experience, or something like it, does not help us explain the ethical commitments we do have. Rather, it is to argue that the experience itself does not justify any ethical commitments, and that in holding that it does, Levinas repeats the very mistake he is warning us against: a reduction to, if not the ontological, then at least the theoretical. That is the case I would like to make.

We must first note that an experience, as such, cannot be justifying for any ethical claim. One might, for instance, experience another as vile or unworthy; surely that does not justify treating that person as vile or unworthy. Now, the experience of the other is, if anything, the opposite of that kind of experience. Moreover, as Levinas points out, the latter experience is founding for the former one. That is the meaning of his claim that "Violence can aim only at a face": [21] that to do violence to someone is to betray an experience of recognition that preexists the violence. While that may be true, it adds no *ethical* justification for a responsibility to that otherness. If, for instance, one's experience of another as infinite were founded on one's experience of that other as vile and unworthy, surely no one would take disrespectful treatment of that other to be justified simply in virtue of the fact that the latter experience was founded on the former one. Thus it is not the fact of something's being an experience, of whatever kind, that offers ethical justification for a relation to otherness. Ethical justification attaches to something other than experiences *as experiences*.

Some readers may be familiar with the criticism I am engaging in here under the rubric, referred to briefly above, in my discussion of Derrida's approach to difference, of the "naturalist fallacy." The naturalist fallacy, which

20. *Ethics and Infinity*, 96.
21. *Totality and Infinity*, 225.

traces its lineage—although not its appellation—as far back as Hume, actually covers a multitude of alleged sins, all of which share the attempt to "derive an ought from an is": that is, they move directly from a claim about some state of the world to a claim about the moral acceptability or unacceptability of that state. Those who consider the naturalist fallacy a fallacy do so because they hold that the direct move cannot be made. Otherwise put, one cannot argue validly from premises that are nonethical to an ethical conclusion.

Recently, however, some theorists in the Anglo-American tradition have taken issue with the idea that there is some sort of fallacy here. Peter Railton, Richard Boyd, and others argue that there are some states of the world that just are better or worse than others, and that when we are assured of obtaining those states of affairs, we can immediately come to a moral conclusion about them.[22] Levinas can be seen, perhaps, as operating in the same way. The ethical experience is just that: it is an experience that is ethical in its very nature. Thus, we can reject the naturalist fallacy and with it the argument that I am trying to make against him.

Matters are not so simple as that, however. Clearly, there are some states of affairs that are ethically better than others; so it cannot be enough to note that something is a state of affairs, without saying more about what kind of state of affairs it is, and then be able to come to some moral conclusion about it. One must say something about why certain kinds of states of affairs are ethically or morally superior or inferior to others, about what it is about those states of affairs that motivates the ethical ascriptions they have. Otherwise put, ethical judgments cannot be reduced to purely descriptive or explanatory judgments; giving an exhaustive account of the world does not yet tell us how we ought to react to it. Levinas recognizes this in his denial that we can reduce ethics to ontology. However, by saying that the ethical is foundational for the ontological, and by removing the ethical from representation—from semantic space—he may actually undercut that recognition. This is because, by making the ethical prerepresentational or prediscursive, he leaves the entire discursive field to ontology, and thus bars himself from philosophical reflection upon the ethical.[23]

22. See, e.g., Railton's "Moral Realism," *Philosophical Review* 95, no. 2 (1986): 163–207, and Boyd's "How to Be a Moral Realist," in *Essays on Moral Realism,* ed. Geoffrey Sayre-McCord (Ithaca: Cornell University Press, 1988).

23. I am here making the same point, although approached from a different direction, that Derrida makes in "Violence and Metaphysics" and that I referred to in the previous chapter ("Violence and Metaphysics: An Essay on the Thought of Emmanuel Levinas," in *Writing and Difference,* trans. Alan Bass [Chicago: University of Chicago Press, 1978; or. pub. 1967]).

Perhaps, though, I have moved too quickly here. On Levinas's behalf, it may be said that he is not just describing a piece of the world and saying, "Since that is a piece of the world, it has ethical significance." Rather, it may be pressed, the ethical experience is a special kind of experience, a special kind of state of the world. It is an experience of the infinite. Perhaps what Levinas is arguing is not that the mere fact of an experience is ethically justificatory, but that *this particular experience* is. If that were true, then the ethical experience he discusses *would* be both constitutive and normative at the same time. It would be constitutive because it would be what causes us to feel the pull of ethical obligation, or rather it would be the pull itself. And it would be ethical because it would underwrite the rest of ethical discourse. And, as at once constitutive and normative, it would be able to meet the objection that it reduces the ethical to the ontological: it would be ethical *and* ontological, rather than ethical *as* ontological.

The force of that reply depends, of course, on the specific character of the experience. The question, then, is whether alterity ought to be ethically compelling. Rather than ask the more ontological or constitutive question whether we in fact are compelled by alterity, we need to ask whether, regardless of the facts, we ought to be. If the answer is in the affirmative, then we can separate the ontological from the ethical status of the experience, and avoid reducing the latter to the former, in accordance with the requirements of Levinas's thought. Otherwise put, if the answer to the ethical question is in the affirmative, then it would be so for reasons other than those that would ground an affirmative answer to the causal or ontological question. The naturalist fallacy, then, in the weak fashion in which I have articulated it here, would be gotten around. The question, then, is this: Is one not responsible to that which in some way exceeds one's categories, or indeed any categories that one could possibly comprehend?

The answer to this question is no. The Anglo-American philosopher Thomas Nagel has argued forcefully for the idea that there must be something it is like to be a bat, but that, given our perceptual and conceptual makeup, we could never understand what it is like to be a bat.[24] Being a bat is infinitely other in the precise sense Levinas articulates. But that the experience of the bat transcends my own experience does not imply that there is some responsibility I have toward bats. To see why, we can appeal to two considerations.

24. Thomas Nagel, "What Is It Like to Be a Bat?" in *Mortal Questions* (Cambridge: Cambridge University Press, 1979).

First, if it were the fact of alterity, of being infinitely other to my own categories, that formed the basis of my ethical treatment of bats, then I would be under the same obligation toward bats as I would be toward other people. Since what undergirds my relationship to both is their alterity to my own experience, it is hard to imagine how the obligations stemming from that experience would be different. One might object here that it is indeed possible for the obligations to be different even while the experience is the same. This would be because the ethical experience is what grounds ethics itself, and not a particular set of obligations. For that, one needs to turn to more specific ethical theorizing. Such an objection would prove too much, however. For if the ethical experience does not ground any specific obligation, how would it ground ethics at all? To appeal to an experience that is divorced from the judgments ethics makes and install it as the ground of ethics is to posit an experience that plays no normative role in ethical considerations. Such an appeal would land one back in the position of finding the ethical experience to be constitutively but not normatively related to ethics, with all the attendant difficulties of that position.

The second consideration we can adduce in order to show that alterity does not ground our ethical treatment of bats is more phenomenological. In our ethical considerations of the treatment of other species, we do not appeal to their alterity to us as an ethically relevant consideration. If we do make an appeal, it goes precisely in the opposite direction: it is due to their similarities to us that we owe bats some measure of ethical consideration. Bats, after all, seem to feel pain, avoid threatening stimuli, and so forth. In short, it is in our similarities to bats, not in our differences, that we find the motivation to bring them into our ethical calculations. (Let us bear in mind here that the motivation I am currently discussing is constitutive and not justificatory.)

It is hard to imagine how it could be different. When I want to know how to treat someone or something—what my obligations are to it—what I seek are touchstones to understanding, so that I know how to move. I want to know how the person or animal feels, what causes him or her or it suffering, what is important in his or her or its life, what frustrations, joys, and passions are characteristic of him or her or it. These touchstones are ways of finding the other like me, or perhaps ways of finding me like the other. In any case, they are similarities that guide me in my comportment toward the other. For me to be told that there are no touchstones, that the other is infinitely other to me, is of no ethical help. It blocks the project of figuring out a proper ethical response.

This does not entail that I have to find the other to be exactly like me in order to be able to give it a full measure of respect. Others may be very different from me, but nevertheless different in ways that are describable and that thereby come into contact with some region of my experience. Indeed, this is the project of radical translation that we saw Donald Davidson engaged in in the last chapter. There is, I think, no bar to distinguishing that which is different from that which is infinitely other. In the former cases, the differences can be rendered to a greater or lesser extent in terms of my own categories; in the latter cases, such a rendering is impossible. What I seek in learning how to treat the other is not a complete reduction of the other to my own categories; rather, it is an understanding of the other from within them. To collapse that distinction in favor of an infinite other that eludes all categorial understanding is to fail to understand the difference between something's or someone's being other and something's or someone's being untranslatably other. This is an entirely unmotivated collapsing.

However, an objection might arise from a quarter utterly removed from this whole line of thought—what we might call the argument from battiness. This objection would not grant the first step of the argument. It would deny, contra Nagel, that there is anything like being a bat, that bats have something like an experience, and thus that they have, in any relevant sense, an experience infinitely other to our own.[25] If it is not the case that there is something it is like to be a bat, and only the case that there is something it is like to be a human being, then can we not vindicate Levinas's analysis after all, claiming that in pointing to infinite alterity he has indeed provided us with an experience that would ground our ethical relationship to others? After all, the objection would run, the alterity he has in mind is something that, if Nagel is wrong, only humans possess, and in respecting that, then would we not be respecting the otherness of other people, thus providing a ground for ethics (and at the same time successfully navigating the trilemma drawn at the outset of this chapter)?

I do not want to dispute the idea that there may be some fact about the experience of other people that can provide an ethical ground for the respect that we owe them. As long as we think of that fact as operating within—rather than beneath—ethical discourse, there seems to be no bar to using it. (More on the distinction between within and beneath below.) What I do want to dispute is, given the place at which we have arrived thus far in

---

25. John McDowell, who has some very different goals in view, offers this objection in his *Mind and World* (Cambridge: Harvard University Press, 1994), 121–22.

the discussion, the idea that that fact could be anything like the one Levinas sees himself as articulating.

For Levinas, let us recall, the ethical experience is the experience of the infinitely other. It is the experience of that which cannot be brought within my own categories, within my own cognitive sphere. "The Good cannot become present or enter into a representation." [26] On the interpretation we are currently considering, however, that experience cannot be elicited by bats and other nonhuman creatures. It can only be elicited by other human beings. [27] This is because, on the current interpretation, there is nothing it is like to be a bat or other nonhuman creature capable of eliciting an experience that is normatively grounding for ethics. If this is true, however, then the only beings that are capable of eliciting such an experience are those that are sufficiently like human beings that they share the relevant qualities. Otherwise put, only those beings sufficiently like me—beings of whom I can say that there is something it is to be like them in the relevant sense—can elicit in me the ethical experience. But with that restriction, we are removed from the realm of the infinitely other to the realm of the finitely other. The ethical experience is elicited in me by beings that are not so foreign to me as to be normatively incapable of eliciting in me the ethical experience.

This does not mean that those beings must be identical to me. I argued above that we can distinguish between otherness and infinite otherness. The point to which I want to call attention here is that if we reject Nagel's idea that there is something it is like to be a bat such that battiness is infinitely other to our own experience, then the ethical experience cannot be interpreted as an experience of the infinitely other, but only of others whose experience more or less lends itself to my understanding.

This interpretation of Levinas reads him as being hardly distinguishable from Hume, for whom the ethical relation was grounded in sympathy rather than otherness. [28] Now, I am sure that there would be few analyses to which Levinas would be more allergic than Hume's, since the latter sees the source of the ethical relation lying in the similarities among humans—especially

---

26. *Otherwise than Being*, 11.

27. For Levinas, a divinity or divinities can also elicit the experience. That point, however, is irrelevant to the question of how we treat others, which is what is at issue here.

28. David Hume, *A Treatise of Human Nature*, 2d ed., ed. L. A. Selby-Bigge (Oxford: Clarendon Press, 1978), esp. 317–20 and 618–19. At least on the standard reading of Hume, however, sympathy, while causally grounding for ethics, is not normatively grounding for it. On this reading, it is ethical practices, or "customs," that offer the normative grounding. My colleague Marie Martin informs me that this standard reading is currently under some scrutiny in Hume circles.

with regard to phenomena like suffering—rather than in their differences. For Levinas, on the contrary, "It is not because the neighbor would be recognized as belonging to the same genus as me that he concerns me. He is precisely *other*."[29] Once we restrict the capacity to elicit the ethical experience to beings that are human, however, as the current interpretation does, then the conclusion that the ethical experience lies at least as much in what we can recognize of ourselves in the other as in what we cannot seems difficult to avoid. At this point, then, we are far removed from the kinds of considerations Levinas was hoping to convince us of in founding the ethical relationship in the experience of the infinitely other.

To sum up this line of argument: Levinas is faced with a dilemma. If the experience he articulates is an experience of the infinitely other, it cannot play the normative role of grounding ethics. Alternatively, if he restricts the range of the experience in a way that allows it to become a candidate for ethical grounding, then it is no longer an experience of the infinitely other. It is, then, neither the ethical experience as such nor the experience as infinite that justifies the sense of responsibility that the ethical experience induces.

What, then, does justify having a responsibility, and, more specific to the trilemma cited at the outset, what justifies having a responsibility to respect people and practices different from our own? Momentarily, I turn from Levinas in order to provide an answer to those questions. At this point, however, I want to call attention in advance to one aspect of that account, since it allows me to treat a possible rejoinder that Levinas might make to the positive account I want to offer.

The aspect to which I want to call attention is this: ethical justification comes inescapably from within ethical discourse, within what might be called, with Wittgenstein, a language game. To say that a responsibility is justified is to say that it is in accordance with other responsibilities that are themselves justified. If I say, for instance, that I have responsibility to respect the transcendence of otherness when it is the otherness of, for instance, other people, I can justify that only by reference to other principles that I hold that can be seen as justifying for it.

Ethics, then, is not prediscursive, but rather is one among many discursive practices. Levinas does not always treat it so, and seems instead to view the ethical component of language as residing below, rather than within, the content of our speaking.[30] Thus: "The ethical sense of such an exposure to

29. *Otherwise than Being*, 87.
30. There is here an odd affinity between Levinas and Habermas's discourse ethics. Although the source of the obligations is different, both seem to want to locate ethical justification beneath,

the other, which the intention of making signs, and even the signifyingness of signs, presuppose, is now visible. The plot of proximity and communication is not a modality of cognition. . . . It is not due to the contents that are inscribed in the said and transmitted to the interpretation and decoding done by the other. It is in the risky uncovering of oneself, in sincerity, the breaking up of inwardness and the abandon of all shelter, exposure to traumas, vulnerability." [31] This passage, in keeping with Levinas's thought that the ethical lies beneath what can be cognized, precludes, rather than displays, the normative justification that attaches to the ethical. For if the ethical lies solely beneath the content of speech, then there can be no hope of ethical conversation or of having actions and situations decided by the weight of ethical reasons.

Herein lies the danger of Levinas's treatment of the ethical and of ethical responsibility. If ethics is either prediscursive or transcendent to cognition, then the content of our linguistic practices can never reach it; they can never make it a subject of discussion and debate. And if that is so, then ethics remains perpetually hostage to the ontological and to totality. If the content of our linguistic practices is not the site of ethical justification, then the ontological has triumphed, not through the suppression of the legitimate claims of the ethical, but through the willful withdrawal of the ethical from the field of discourse.

To see why this is so, it is worth recalling the central importance that twentieth-century thought has accorded to language, and specifically linguistic content, in structuring experience, social and political arrangements, and psychological constitution. Levinas, by founding the ethical in an experience that is prediscursive and transcendent to cognition, has precluded the legitimacy of ethical discourse and of ethical argumentation and reason. This is not to say that he has removed the ethical from speech altogether. In some sense, he has attempted the opposite: to see the ethical as founding for all speech, even speech that betrays it. "Meaning is the face of the Other, and all recourse to words takes place already within the primordial face to face of language." [32] However, by placing the ethical before, rather than within, the content of language, Levinas allows no recourse to those who would recuperate the ethical from its betrayal by the ontological, because he has shorn them of the possibility of justifying to others—of giving them

---

rather than within, the content of our linguistic practices. The danger for ethics in such a location is discussed below.

31. *Otherwise than Being*, 48.

32. *Totality and Infinity*, 206.

reasons they ought to feel compelled to accept—the preservation of the integrity of the ethical experience.

At this point, I want to turn to the rejoinder hinted at a moment ago to the position I am saddling Levinas with, a rejoinder that can be drawn from Levinas's own distinction between the saying and the said. In *Otherwise than Being,* Levinas makes much of the distinction between what he calls "saying" and what he calls "said."[33] The said is the content of speech, it is what is said in the saying. Returning to the terms of the last chapter, it is what is iterable in speaking. The saying, on the other hand, is the act of addressing another, and as such renders the speaker vulnerable to another. In saying, one exposes oneself to another, and in doing so opens the possibility of an ethical relationship to another. This exposure, which cannot be articulated in terms of the said, carries one beyond the realm of essence or of being to a realm of "otherwise than being, or beyond essence." "If man were only a saying correlative with the logos, subjectivity could as well be understood as a function or as an argument of being. But the signification of saying goes beyond the said. It is not ontology that raises up the speaking subject: it is the signifyingness of saying going beyond essence that can justify the exposedness of being, ontology."[34]

It might be argued here on Levinas's behalf that he has not ignored the discursive realm, but in his treatment of the said has accorded it a place. It is a secondary place, one predicated upon the saying—as, in the terms of *Totality and Infinity,* ontology is predicated upon metaphysics. But it has its own relative autonomy and can account for what it is I am trying to account for in appealing to the Wittgensteinian notion of language games.

And indeed, near the end of *Otherwise than Being* Levinas articulates, in his discussion of the third party, a position close to the one I have hinted at and develop momentarily. "The third party is other than the neighbor, but also another neighbor, and also a neighbor of the other, and not simply his fellow." The third party, although also in some sense an other that obsesses me, is distant enough from me that I must articulate my relationship with him or her in terms that are more political than ethical. "The other and the third party, my neighbors, contemporaries of one another, put distance between me and the other, and the third party." In order to cope with the third

---

33. Simon Critchley has read this distinction as a response to Derrida's critique of Levinas's earlier work, which I cited in the previous chapter. Cf. *The Ethics of Deconstruction.*

34. *Otherwise than Being,* 37–38. This is a theme carried over from *Totality and Infinity;* cf., e.g., 202: "Every language as an exchange of verbal signs refers already to this primordial word of honor. The verbal sign is placed where someone signifies something to someone else."

party, Levinas invokes the concept of justice, a political concept that, while predicated on the ethical relationship, goes beyond it in articulating principles whose meaning and balance rely upon the content of the said. "Justice is necessary, that is, comparison, coexistence, contemporaneousness, assembling, order, thematization, the visibility of faces, and thus intentionality and the intellect, the intelligibility of a system, and thence also a copresence [note the term "presence"] on an equal footing as before a court of justice." [35]

Could it not be argued that Levinas, far from denying the necessity of a resort to language games, has accommodated them in his notion of the said and, moreover, has shown how the said that is articulated in those language games rests upon something deeper that gives rise to them but cannot itself be brought to presence (logos, content) within them?

If the argument I have made so far is right, then aside from considerations of what Levinas calls "justice" and what I call the discursive practice of morality, there is no ground of ethics that lies beneath it in a saying or an ethical experience that is capable of giving it a normative foundation. To put the point bluntly, saying, like the ethical experience he describes, is a cog in the machine that performs no function. That has been the point of the arguments concerning the naturalist fallacy, battiness, and similarities to others. The normative role of ethics lies in the justifications one can give for what is and ought to be done within the resources of the said. Normative appeal outside of the said to a founding saying is either useless or illicit. [36] Contrary to Levinas's claim that the said is ethically founded in a saying, that the ethical experience is justificatory for ethical discourse, the ethical experience cannot perform the normative role that Levinas assigns it. Moral justification is had from within the context of a language game or not at all. There is no prediscursive realm that can found ethics.

For Levinas, the challenge that ethics provides cannot come from within the content of language; and if language betrays ethics, it is without resources to vindicate itself. This is hardly a strengthening of the ethical hand. If ethics is to challenge the dominance of the ontological, as indeed it must, that challenge must come, not through the withdrawal of the ethical from the realm of discursive justification, but rather through its claiming a place

---

35. *Otherwise than Being,* 157. Levinas emphasizes that justice is a matter of the said when he writes a bit further on, "Justice requires contemporaneousness of representation. It is thus that the neighbor becomes visible, and, looked at, presents himself, and there is also justice for me. The saying is fixed in a said, is written, becomes a book, law, science" (159).

36. Such an appeal would be an instance of subscribing to what Wilfrid Sellars and philosophers influenced by him call "the Myth of the Given."

alongside ontology. Ethical discourse and ethical justification must come to be seen as a practice as legitimate as ontological discourse and justification.[37] The anteriority of ethics to discourse and discursive justification that Levinas commends does not vindicate the ethical; instead, it is a further moment in the marginalization of the ethical. Such a marginalization cannot be what Levinas had in mind in calling attention to the experience of the infinite.

Before turning to my positive account, I would like to emphasize that the ethical experience to which Levinas has called our attention does play a role in ethics, contrary to the impression that might have been gained so far. Its role is not justificatory; it is constitutive. The experience he describes, the obsession that the face of the other induces, the constriction of our own lives that the otherness of the other displays to us, is an important moment in the formation of ethical discourse and ethical practice. It is legitimate to wonder whether, without it, there would be any ethical responsiveness at all. If all were selfsameness among us, the war of all against all would be more profound than it already is. In that sense, Levinas has recalled for us, and done so unflaggingly, an experience whose role may be to help elicit in us whatever decency we do possess. Here, then, in contrast to Nancy, for whom neither the constitutive nor the normative view of community seems adequate, Levinas does offer a constitutive view of the ethical relation that has promise.

There is, however, a difference, and indeed a gulf, between what causes us to be or constitutes us as what we are and what justifies us in being that way. If there were not, then anything that constituted us one way rather than another would be legitimate. And that, surely, is a position we should be loath to embrace. We should, then, read Levinas not as an ethicist but as, if the term will be permitted, a "metaphysico-ontologist," a thinker who has shown the irreducibility of what he has called the "metaphysical" moment to what he has called the "ontological" one, and who has recalled for our ethics the constitutive significance of that metaphysical moment. Such a reading would still grant him the discordance that is and ought to be the legacy of his thought, without ratifying the moments in which that discordance threatens to undo itself.

If all that has been said about Levinas and Derrida so far is right, it seems

---

37. It is worth noting that Lyotard attempts to reassert the legitimacy of the ethical alongside the ontological—or, as he terms it, the "cognitive"—in *The Differend*. However, by offering a Levinasian rendering of the ethical genre, he takes back with one hand what he has given with the other.

that there is no way out of the trilemma that respect for differences involves. What both try to articulate is a view of ethics that would allow for respect for otherness without subsuming otherness under one's own categories. Derrida tries to do so by discovering an ethical relationship within language, as he analyses it. Levinas tries to do so by discovering an ethical relationship beneath or beyond all language. Although differing in where they locate the relationship, Derrida and Levinas agree that it is nonconceptual, that it cannot be brought into the realm of linguistic categories. Both attempts, I have argued, fail to circumvent the trilemma. I believe that, indeed, there is no way out of that trilemma, but that the second horn of the trilemma can be grasped without one's being thrown directly onto the first horn, or at least not in any seriously damaging way. I turn now to the task of showing why that is so. Doing so engages, as it has for Levinas, not only questions about respect for difference but also larger questions regarding the status and nature of moral discourse. Although I have discussed some of those questions at more length elsewhere,[38] I will reiterate at least the results of some of those reflections here in order to provide the larger framework within which the valorization of difference can be articulated. The way I want to proceed is to grasp the second horn of the dilemma and then show why it does not have the untoward consequences that one might want to saddle it with. In brief, although the second horn does commit us to identitarianism in some form, it does not commit us to fascism.

Grasping the second horn of the trilemma, let us recall, involves committing oneself to the moral principle that *people ought to respect the differences of others, all other things being equal.* (I will explain the necessity of the *ceteris paribus* phrase in a moment.) Before proceeding to defend the principle, and the moral outlook in which it is embedded, let me offer a few words of clarification.

I intend the term "respect" to be ambiguous between "tolerate," "promote," and "enjoy." At the very least, respecting means tolerating the differences of others. I may not like what others are doing, but that fact gives me no justification for denying them the resources to do it. There may be times, moreover, when I would be called upon actually to promote those differences, specifically when there is a credible threat to them and I am in a position to lessen that threat without unreasonable cost or harm to myself. If, for instance, I am a college professor at a school in which the atmosphere

    38. Cf., e.g., my *Moral Theory of Poststructuralism* (University Park: Pennsylvania State University Press, 1995), esp. chap. 2.

is rabidly antihomosexual, and if an instance arises in which I can contribute to lessening homophobic sentiment on that campus, I may be called upon to do so. In that case, I would be not merely tolerating difference but also promoting it. Regarding enjoyment, I cannot see where one would ever be obliged to enjoy the differences of others—to be so obliged might involve having to reject the ways in which one is different from others, and thus underhandedly subvert the principle. Alternatively, I see no bar to enjoying those differences, since their enjoyment by members of other cultures or practices helps preserve them or at least protect them.

The term "differences" is meant to refer to behavior, ways of being, or, at the social level, practices (in the sense discussed in Chapter 1) that one does not recognize as possibilities for oneself. That one does not recognize them as possibilities for oneself should not be taken to imply that they are not possibilities for oneself or that they do not in fact constitute who one is without one's realizing it, but only that one does not recognize who one is or wants to be in those behaviors, ways of being, or practices. Finally, the *ceteris paribus* phrase seems a necessary part of this or almost any other moral principle, since cases arise in which the principle ought to be overridden. For instance, our (perhaps self-deceptive) failure to recognize ourselves in the practices of Nazi Germany or, more recently, the censorious projects of the anti-multiculturalists in academe would not motivate application of the principle.

Seeing what the principle is, I want now to turn to a justification of it, which will lead us to see how a commitment to it involves us in the trilemma.[39] It is not unreasonable to ask why one ought to hold such a principle, that is, to ask for a justification for it. For those who have studied recent French thought, especially in its non-Derridean strain, justifications are not far to seek. One thinks particularly of the historical studies of Michel Foucault, which detail the ways in which the project of normalization has served both to marginalize those who are different and to reinforce oppressive social arrangements. The first volume of his study of the history of sexuality, for instance, details how certain figures are created by the intervention of various institutions into sexuality, and how those figures have become the subject of constant vigilance and attention. "Four figures emerged from

39. That justifying the principle is what leads to that commitment should not be surprising. After all, as the second horn of the trilemma states, the problem arises when a respect for differences is had on the basis of reference to one's own standards, which in turn are seen as privileged relative to competing standards. It is in taking one's justifications seriously that one privileges them above competing justifications.

this preoccupation with sex, which mounted throughout the nineteenth century—four privileged objects of knowledge, which were also targets and anchorage points for the ventures of knowledge: the hysterical woman, the masturbating child, the Malthusian couple, and the perverse adult."[40] Since almost everyone can fall into one of the categories covered by these four figures, everyone is subject to institutional intervention, to make sure that sexual activity is not occurring in deviant (read: different) ways or giving rise to perverse (read: different) practices.[41]

Foucault's studies are not the only ones to detail the consequences of refusing to respect the ways in which others are different from ourselves. Without rehearsing the specific arguments, let me just recall Deleuze and Guattari's work on psychoanalysis, Robert Castel's studies on French and American psychotherapeutic practice, Michelle LeDoeuff's depictions of masculinism in philosophy, Jacques Donzelot's study of French medicine in the nineteenth century, and Jean-François Lyotard's work on the dominance of certain linguistic genres.[42] All of these works have contributed to a recognition that intolerable social conditions are promoted, supported, and even constituted by practices of power whose project is to constrain behavior and practice and to refuse to countenance differences.

But to offer the works of these thinkers as evidence for a principle of respecting difference is to found the principle on certain values, a commitment to which is required if one is to accept the principle. What values are these? Roughly, they are (1) the moral impermissibility of constraining people's behavior against their wishes, that is, a principle of autonomy, broadly construed, (2) the intolerability of at least certain capitalist social arrangements

40. Michel Foucault, *The History of Sexuality,* vol. 1, *An Introduction,* trans. Robert Hurley (New York: Random House, 1978; or. pub. 1976), 105.

41. Foucault's history of sexuality is not, of course, the only work in which he discusses the problem of rejecting difference. In *Discipline and Punish,* for instance, he points up the general social constraints attendant upon the creation of a criminal delinquent class that it is the job of the state and state-related institutions to surveil, supervise, and occasionally incarcerate.

42. Gilles Deleuze and Felix Guattari, *Anti-Oedipus: Capitalism and Schizophrenia,* trans. Mark Seem, Robert Hurley, and Helen Lane (New York: Viking Press, 1977; or. pub. 1972); Robert Castel, *The Regulation of Madness: The Origins of Incarceration in France,* trans. W. D. Halls (Berkeley and Los Angeles: University of California Press, 1988; or. pub. 1976), and idem, with Françoise Castel and Anne Lovell, *The Psychiatric Society,* trans. Arthur Goldhammer (New York: Columbia University Press, 1982; or. pub. 1979); of Michelle LeDoeuff's work, see esp. *Hipparchia's Choice: An Essay Concerning Women and Philosophy,* trans. Trista Selous (Cambridge: Basil Blackwell, 1991); Jacques Donzelot, *The Policing of Families,* trans. Robert Hurley (New York: Pantheon Books, 1979; or. pub. 1977); of Lyotard's work, see esp. *The Differend.*

(which itself involves the commitment to certain other values and principles), and (3) the unacceptability of using power to create behavior or practices in ways that are not transparent to those who are the objects of that power.

To see why a commitment to these principles—or principles like them—is necessary, imagine trying to convince someone of the principle of respecting differences who does not feel it morally impermissible to constrain people's behavior against their wishes, who does not find certain coercive capitalist social arrangements morally unacceptable, or[43] who does not feel it to be wrong to use power in ways that are opaque to the objects of that power. What *reason* would this person have to respect the differences of others? None, so far as I can see. For that person, involuntary behavioral constraint and devious applications of power are not morally problematic. They do not constitute reasons against a proposed course of action.

The point I am driving at is precisely a point about reason, or, perhaps more accurately, about reasons. In order to convince someone of the intolerable consequences of denying the principle of respecting difference, in order for that principle to be compelling, the someone being convinced has to be open to the justifications being offered for that principle. Being so open requires a commitment to certain kinds of claims that will count as reasons for that principle, specifically the kinds of reasons that bank on the three principles cited a couple of paragraphs ago.

We can see here, without extending the analysis any further, that adherence to the principle of respecting differences, if it is not to be merely a dogmatic stand, cannot be had in isolation from other principles. Such an adherence requires the embrace of an entire perspective, or—to revisit a term discussed in Chapter 1—a "discursive practice." This perspective must be called, unabashedly and against the wishes of many who contributed to it,[44] a moral one, involving as it does values and prescriptions for people's behavior regardless of their perceived self-interest.

Ratifying the principle of respect for difference, then, binds one to a larger moral outlook. This is not to say that it binds one to a full-blown internally coherent system of moral principles, but it need not say that. Rather, it directly binds one to several other principles and values, and, assuming that those principles receive some justification by appeal to still other principles,

43. I use the term "or" because I think that a commitment to any one of these principles justifies the principle of respect for differences, although the thinkers I refer to here seem to hold all of them.

44. Foucault, for instance, was reluctant to embrace any overarching moral principles, and Deleuze was positively disdainful of them.

it indirectly binds one to those latter principles and values as well.[45] (To be indirectly bound to a principle, we must understand, is not to be *less* bound to it. If, to appeal to a nonmoral example, I am committed to claiming that a certain book is brown, I am also committed to claiming that it is colored, and more indirectly to claiming that it is extended. But I am not less committed to claiming that it is extended than to claiming that it is colored.)

This bond is what creates the second horn of the dilemma. Let us recall that that horn notes that if we accept the differences of others on the basis of our own standards of tolerance (or some other value), then we covertly raise our own standards above those of others, and thus have not escaped from the first horn of the dilemma, that of identitarian fascism. What I want now to argue is that embrace of the principle—or of any other moral principle—indeed does involve one in a certain type of identitarianism, but that the embrace of this particular principle separates one's identitarianism from fascism.

As we have seen, the embrace of this moral principle is inseparable from the commitment to a network of moral principles and values. The network is one in which terms, values, principles, and the relationships among terms, values, and principles is given in a loose interrelated whole. It is thus a discursive practice. The practice is a loose one in two different ways. At the level of the individual who is committed to that practice, some of the implications of holding certain principles or values that may be (and, for most of us, undoubtedly are) unclear to that individual. There can be, in short, an internal inconsistency between the moral commitments that individual makes in a given situation and those he or she makes in another situation. That type of looseness is a fact about the way people stand relative to their moral commitments.

There is another kind of looseness as well, however, of the broadly logical sort. A moral discursive practice can be loose because it allows for the holding of competing moral views that are still recognizably within the practice. For example, two specific moral views can clash at points because of different weights those views accord to different values, yet both are still recognizably within a discursive practice that we would want to call "moral." One admittedly charitable way to read the conflict over academic multiculturalism is to ascribe to both multiculturalists and anti-multiculturalists the

45. I have been kicking around the terms "principles" and "values" here a bit loosely. For present purposes, let me define a principle as a claim that is meant to be action-guiding and a value as something to which people ought to have access. The principle of respect for differences is a principle. Autonomy is a value.

positive valuings of Western cultural heritage but differences regarding the values of other cultural heritages. Although they disagree, their disagreement is one that can be examined and perhaps even resolved, because it occurs within the context of a commitment to a network of values that allows reasonable discussion to occur. This type of network is an example of what Wittgenstein called a "language game." In the language game of morality, there seems to be no bar to holding several different moral views, each of them internally consistent and with some intuitive plausibility, that are mutually exclusive. I take it that, at a general theoretical level, that is what utilitarians and deontologists take themselves to be doing (although that may not be what each takes the other to be doing).

Think for a moment of the difficulty of holding a single moral principle, say, for instance, that it is wrong to torture small children just for fun. Surely one can utter the principle and claim to have no other moral principles, but can one *believe* just this one principle? It seems not. The reason is that believing it is going to involve, among other commitments, a commitment to the value of children and to the disvalue of torture. These commitments lead to other ones as well. Torture, for instance, is a causing of severe pain to another. If that is morally wrong, then one either has to be committed to the unacceptability of torturing other sentient beings or be prepared to say what the moral difference is between children and other sentient beings. Without extending the analysis, we can see that the holding of a moral principle is a holistic affair, not an atomistic one.

This holism implies something else. The language game of morality cannot itself be justified—at least not morally—since moral justification is something that occurs *within* the parameters of the network. Otherwise put, in order for a single moral principle or value to be justified, one has already to be within the set of commitments that would render it so justified. There is, then, no foundation for morality outside of morality—at least no moral justification, and what other kind of justification would matter here? And, since terms and principles are interrelated, there is no foundation for morality inside of morality either. Either one commits to the language game, or discursive practice, of morality, or one does not; but morality itself cannot be proved to one who refuses its terms.[46]

46. This is not to claim that within the discursive practice of morality there are no specific principles or values that go without justification. There must be those in order for justification to avoid embarking on an infinite regress. Those values and principles, the ones that at a given time or for given purposes cannot be justified, are the framework within which moral discussion takes place. To think of them as a framework, however, is not to think of them as a

Thus one can see the identitarian character of moral principles (although that identitarian character remains nonfoundationalist). The acceptance of a moral principle implies the endorsement of a more or less well-worked-out moral perspective—even if that perspective is limited—within which that principle falls; and, since that perspective is endorsed, competing perspectives are, for better or worse reasons, considered to be morally inferior. This is the reason that the second horn of the dilemma seemed to be thrown over to the first horn.

But if morality is necessarily identitarian in this way, why is it not necessarily fascist; that is, why does it not in principle refuse differences? Of course, a moral view can do that and still be recognizably moral. I take it that that is precisely what the anti-multiculturalist movement proposes, when it proposes anything coherent at all: Western culture is superior to other cultures, and thus it should be taught at the expense of attention to those other cultures. However, a moral view *need not* be both identitarian and fascist at the same time, and that is the crucial issue. How, then, to avoid the seeming necessity?

By embracing as one of its principles the principle of respect for differences. It is that principle specifically which drives a wedge between identitarianism and fascism and allows one to come to rest on the second horn of the dilemma without waking up later on the first. In order to show how, I want to look specifically at two kinds of situations in which one comes across different practices. The first kind of situation occurs when one is confronted with a competing moral discursive practice, say a set of radically different moral views from another culture. That is the more difficult test case for the principle. The second kind of situation, to which I want to turn more briefly, involves a confrontation with different nonmoral practices.

When confronted with a different moral practice, one is unavoidably confronted with at least some endorsements of activities that one finds morally reprehensible or with at least some prohibitions of activities one finds

---

bedrock. They are not something solid that guarantees the soundness of moral argumentation. (To think of them that way would be to reintroduce the idea of foundationalism that both holism and philosophies of difference seek to reject.) In fact, in their lack of justification they point to the contingency of the discursive practice. As Wittgenstein puts it, "[T]he *questions* that we raise and our *doubts* depend on the fact that some propositions are exempt from doubt, are as it were like hinges on which those turn" (*On Certainty,* ed. G.E.M. Anscombe and G. H. von Wright, trans. Denis Paul and G.E.M. Anscombe [New York: Harper & Row, 1969], 44), which is not exclusive of saying, "At the foundation of well-founded belief lies belief that is not founded" (33).

morally permissible. Without such confrontations, the practice cannot be characterized as markedly different from one's own. For most Westerners, ritual clitoridectomy would be an example of the first, and the proscription against women driving would be an example of the second. Our first reaction to such endorsements or prohibitions might very well be that they are wrong. And, if I am correct in my assessment of the identitarian character of moral principles, then that first reaction is not mistaken. It is an inevitable consequence of having moral principles in the first place.

Such a reaction, however, although not mistaken, need not be all there is to the story. It is perfectly coherent to say, on the one hand, that one or more of the endorsements of a different moral practice are wrong, and yet to hold, on the other hand, that it should be allowed to continue. That is because there is no clear path between saying that an endorsement is morally wrong and saying that that endorsement ought to be prohibited. The distinction at issue here, between the rightness or wrongness of a particular moral position and the rightness or wrongness of intervening to change that moral position, is in fact central to the idea of freedom of speech. There may be speech that is offensive and of which we would feel compelled to say—perhaps rightfully—that the speaker should not have said that. But to move from the claim that a speaker should not have said something to the claim that that speaker ought to be prohibited from saying requires much more justification. And for those of us that value free speech, it is hard to imagine that such justification will be forthcoming.

Now, the endorsement of free speech and the toleration of moral practices that one finds morally offensive can have very different bases. Free speech, for instance, can be defended on the ground of its cognitive value in leading toward the truth or, alternatively, on the ground that freedom to speak one's mind is part of one's autonomy and that one's autonomy ought to be protected. The toleration of practices that one finds morally offensive might have other bases. One of those might be an appeal to the consequences that seem to flow from intervention into cultures whose practices we do not approve of. On this argument, it might be claimed that although ritual clitoridectomy is bad, intervening to prohibit it in cultures that practice it might bring down consequences even worse than the practice. (I am not proposing such an argument, but rather showing how it would work.)

What might be worse? First, if clitoridectomy were an integral part of the culture, then its prohibition might lead to a more general cultural breakdown. Such a breakdown would force the people of that culture into lives that they would rather not live. (Recall the first justification for the principle of respect for differences, that power ought not to be exercised on people in ways they would not have it be exercised.) Moreover, when a culture breaks down, as when a species goes extinct, the world has lost forever the benefits of having that unique form of life. All these justifications for not intervening are, in fact, justifications for applying the principle of respect for differences to a particular situation, one in which a culture's moral practices are different from one's own.

This does not imply that the principle of respect for differences can always be applied, no matter what the moral differences are between another culture and one's own. That is why the principle carries with it a *ceteris paribus* clause. It is not difficult to imagine practices so morally offensive that they might justify intervening, especially when the general effects of an intervention upon the culture are minimal. A culture that allows its children to undergo great pain for no apparent reason is surely a culture that cries out for intervention. So too may be a culture that practices clitoridectomy, especially if the women of that culture find the practice offensive. Thus, the principle of respecting differences is one that, although always a player in moral deliberation, does not possess a trump card.

Given what has been said so far, that should not be surprising. The principle of respect for differences was justified on the basis of other principles and values that, it can be imagined, might counsel not respecting differences under certain conditions. If, for instance, one of the justifications for the principle is that power should not be exercised over people in ways that they would refuse, then, insofar as women would refuse clitoridectomy if given a choice, a reason has been given to support those women in their refusal.

To sum up, let me paint a brief general picture of how things might look from the perspective of someone, say myself, committed to the principle of respect for differences. I am committed to my own moral view, complete with its valuations, terms, principles, and relationships among them. Nevertheless, I realize that there are other views that differ from my own. The fact that I think that my own moral take on things is better than any competing take—or else, why not switch to the competitor?—does not commit me to saying that that other take should not exist, or that others should be converted to my own take. Why not? Because my own moral view also includes the principle of respect for differences. Thus, the principle of respect for differences allows both that I count my own moral view as best and that I can tolerate, promote, or perhaps even enjoy the views of others.

Here I want to pause to consider an objection that might be raised to the entire analysis I have given so far. It concerns an assumption I seem to be (nay, am) making regarding the status of moral principles: that they are universally binding. If moral principles can be held relative to a culture, then the assumption I am making about intervening might never arise, since what is right within the context of my culture might not be applicable to other cultures. (I should note that this move involves embracing the third horn of the trilemma.) I have defended the universality of moral principles elsewhere[47] and will not rehearse the argument for is here, most importantly because I do not need to. Here I have tried to show how, even with a commitment to universal moral principles, the principle of respect for differences would commend caution when approaching the moral commitments of other cultures. The case is even easier with moral relativism (assuming such a position to be coherent, which I am not convinced it is). For if our moral principles do not apply to other cultures, then there seems to be little motivation to make them live up to those principles. Differences are respected not because, as in the case with universal principles, there are moral reasons to do so, but instead because there are no moral reasons *not* to do so. Simply put, for relativism there is nothing morally questionable going on in a culture with a competing moral discursive network, and so no reason to intervene in order to restore moral order.

What I have been arguing so far is that one can embrace a moral view—and a universalist one at that—and still apply the principle of respect for differences to other moral views. In most cases, however, the practices to which respect is to be applied are nonmoral ones: cultural, aesthetic, or epistemic practices, for instance. Here the case is easier, since, inasmuch as such practices do not offend against deep moral principles or values, the principle of respect for differences counsels respect. The case is easier because, *ex hypothesi,* there are no moral issues involved in such cases, and thus no calls to intervene positively or negatively upon those practices.[48] But

---

47. *The Moral Theory of Poststructuralism.*

48. It is perhaps worth making a clarification here over a potential misunderstanding. Suppose another culture engages in practice that is morally relevant to me but not to the members of that culture. Have I not missed that possibility in the above argument by assuming that the conflict must be between two moral discursive networks? Actually, I have not missed it. The moral discursive networks I discuss can be seen as involving both permissions and obligations. Thus, the situation seemingly not covered by the other culture's competing moral discursive network can be seen as a permission by the network, making it no different—judged from the perspective of my culture—from a positive endorsement. For example, were clitoridectomy not addressed by the moral discursive network at all, one could assume that it would be considered a morally permissible practice; as such, the question of intervention would not be different in kind from that of a morally endorsed practice. (The only difference might lie in the fact that as a permitted, rather than an endorsed, practice, it might be easier to dispense of without more significant harm coming to that culture.) The upshot of all this is that, for the cases I am now discussing, we can assume that the practices in question do not have moral bearing for the person who is judging them from within a moral perspective that includes the principle of respect for differences.

if there are no moral issues involved, then basic considerations of tolerance and autonomy would seem to be enough to support a case for respect for differences. Such respect would at the very least require noninterference with practices that one does not recognize as possibilities for oneself. And it could involve more. Since disrespect for other practices often stems from ignorance about them, the principle of respect for differences might counsel that access to different practices be offered to people so that they might become familiar with them and therefore better able to respect them.

Thus the route to, say, multiculturalism in academics from the principle of respect for differences is well paved. If one is to respect the differences of other cultures, it helps to know what those differences are. And this implies, among other things, that a college education ought, other things being equal, to involve a multicultural component.

An important implication arises from the incorporation of the principle of respect for differences into a moral view. If the principle is embraced as part of a moral view, then the differences between, on the one hand, competing views within a specific moral network and, on the other hand, those views outside that particular moral network may begin to be effaced. This strikes me as a good thing, and for several reasons. First, it reflects the Davidsonian idea that ascriptions of radical incommensurability between conceptual schemes are incoherent because, roughly, if those schemes are incommensurable—in the sense of untranslatably different—then they would not strike us as conceptual schemes at all. Second, it allows points of contact between various practices and thus reinforces the principle of respect for differences. Finally, in allowing for points of contact with other moral practices, it offers possibilities for self-reflection from a variety of vantage points that, were different moral practices so radically divergent, would not be available.

The view I have been articulating here accomplishes much of what Levinas wanted to accomplish with his appeal to the ethical experience, and does so without any of the problems that beset Levinas's own view. Most important, it allows for a respect for others whose practices are not the same as my own, and whose take on things is different—even if describably different—from mine. That, I believe, is what Levinas is most concerned to accomplish, although he is unable to give it the normative force he sought. Moreover, it accomplishes something else, which is perhaps only of slightly less importance for Levinas.

In claiming that ethics (or metaphysics) precedes ontology, Levinas seems to want to give a status to ethics that in our scientifically oriented culture we often dismiss. It is not uncommon for those of us who teach for a living to hear that while science gives us facts, ethics or morality is merely a matter of subjective opinion. Such a view marginalizes ethical concerns by dismissing the status of ethical discourse. I have argued that Levinas, by allotting a pre-discursive role to ethics, in effect (although not in intention) reinforces this marginalization. If the positive account I have been giving in the last three chapters is correct, then the dismissal of ethics as a serious discursive prac-tice is misguided, and we should—both with and against Levinas—recog-nize ethics as a fundamental and serious discursive practice. Further, there is at least one sense in which ethics can lay claim to judgment upon all other practices. While Levinas argues that the majesty of ethics lies in its preced-ing all other discourses (as the saying precedes the said), I argue that its majesty lies in its ability to submit all other practices to judgments of moral scrutiny. Moreover, that scrutiny can yield answers that, inasmuch as they are justified, must be taken no less seriously than the answers of other dis-cursive practices. It is, then, in operating alongside and in intersection with other discursive practices, not beneath or beyond them, that ethics resists the marginalization that has been foisted upon it.[49]

By way of a conclusion, I want to offer two contrasting pictures of moral space within which respect for differences can be conceived, one that I have argued against and another that I have proposed. In the first, the traditional picture of an action being justified by an ultimate foundational stratum is rejected and replaced by a picture of judgment emerging from a subtending stratum, but one that no longer serves as a conceptually meaningful justifying foundation. Moral discourse, in other words, inasmuch as it exists, emerges from a nonorigin that offers justification in ambivalent and perhaps para-doxical ways. What this picture shares with the traditional one is a commit-ment to the idea that morality emerges from somewhere else; what it rejects is the idea that that emergence provides a straightforward moral justifica-tion for action.

The picture I have substituted shares with the one I have rejected a skep-ticism about foundations; but it does not share any skepticism about giving grounds or justifications. Rather than a nonoriginary space (or nonspace, if you prefer) from which moral conclusions are drawn, my picture involves

49. It should not be thought here, however, that ethics is itself immune from the judgments of other practices. To give a pedestrian example of how a scientific claim can affect a moral one: suppose that someone defending abortion, on the basis that the fetus has no rights until viability, were confronted with evidence that viability occurs (with the help of appropriate technology) at two weeks. This would certainly force a change in the moral position that per-son held, and that change would occur on the basis of a nonmoral judgment.

intersecting networks of practices, one of which is morality. Justification can occur within specific practices, and some practices can, from within the perspective they construct, judge others. But no practice, including that of morality, can be justified on the basis of some foundation that itself either needs no justifying or is self-justifying. To engage in moral discourse, then, to make claims or judge actions using categories that are recognizably moral, is to engage in a language game that is at once holistic, identitarian, and contingent.

My claim is that respect for differences is best preserved by embracing this second picture of moral space and including within it the principle of respect for differences. Summarily put, respect for differences is gained not by turning toward a constitutive analysis of difference as absence, but by embracing a holistic view of morality with a strong principle of respect for differences.

Now, some may feel a bit uneasy with the principle and the larger perspective I have outlined here. Its identitarian character may seem to be too heavily weighted. However, let me suggest, and I can only suggest it here, that the type of identitarianism I have outlined is the price of taking one's own morality seriously. To believe that incompatible moral views are just as good as one's own is, in the end, not to believe in one's own moral views, and in fact not to believe in morality. If we are really to respect the differences of others, we must take that respect—*our* respect—seriously. We do no favors to those who spend their lives being marginalized and oppressed for their differences—moral and otherwise—if we are willing to jettison our own commitment to the respect they so often deserve.

4

From Ontological Difference to Ontological Holism

Gilles Deleuze

The final study I want to undertake here concerns the ontological reflections on difference offered by Gilles Deleuze. In an important sense, Deleuze's considerations upon difference diverge from those of the previous three thinkers. As we have seen, for Nancy, Derrida, and Levinas, difference has been conceived in terms of absence, on the assumption that to conceive it otherwise is to reduce it to categories of the same. Deleuze, in contrast, wants to articulate a difference in terms other than those of absence. He wants to articulate a "positive" difference that, while similar to Nancy's and Derrida's in being both constitutive and internal to that which it constitutes, is conceived other than by means of the negativity of absence.[1]

Although this difference about difference exists between Deleuze and the other thinkers I have discussed, my argumentative strategy is characterized by sameness. I argue that difference cannot be conceived in the way Deleuze

---

1. It may be a bit misleading to characterize Levinas's thought of difference as negative, although not misleading to characterize it in terms of absence. In *Otherwise than Being or Beyond Essence,* 2d ed. (The Hague: Nijhoff, 1981; or. pub. 1978), he says, "Our inquiry concerned with the *otherwise than being* catches sight, in the very hypothesis of a subject, its subjectification, of an ex-ception, a null-site on the hither side of the negativity which is always speculatively recuperable, an *outside* of the absolute which can no longer be stated in terms of being" (17–18).

wants to do so—at least at certain points in his work—and that to accomplish the purposes Deleuze has in mind by so conceiving it, we need to embrace a contingent holism.

It is one of the ironies of Gilles Deleuze's thought that although it counts itself as a rigorous thought of difference, it often uses for its models philosophers whose own work has been considered tightly unitary or monistic. Deleuze's studies on Spinoza, Bergson, and even Kant, for instance, cannot be considered external to the heart of the Deleuzian project; indeed, it can be argued that those studies constitute its very heart. The thinker who wrote "difference is behind everything, but behind difference there is nothing"[2] is also the thinker who praises Scotus and Spinoza for discovering the univocity of being, and especially the latter for revealing it as "an object of pure affirmation."[3] How is it that the thinker of multiplicities, of haecceities, disjunctions, and irreducible intersecting series, is also the thinker of the univocity of being and untranscendable planes of immanence?

It is the argument of this chapter that such juxtapositions of unity and difference are not accidental, but are indeed the requirements of Deleuze's thought. Indeed, these juxtapositions are symptoms of a concomitance so necessary that it will not be overstating the case to claim that, in the end, Deleuze is not a thinker of difference at all, if by that is meant that he is a thinker who should be read as considering difference to be privileged over unity. The claim here is not that Deleuze understands himself as anything other than a thinker of difference; in fact, there are numerous instances in which he seems to consider himself exactly that. Instead, I try to make the case that he cannot coherently *be* a thinker of difference. In that sense, this chapter could even be called a "deconstruction," if by that term we mean that we are to find the suppressed term (unity) of a binary opposition internal to the possibility of privileging the other term (difference).[4] I also argue, though, that Deleuze need not be a thinker who privileges difference at the

2. Gilles Deleuze, *Différence et répétition* (Paris: Presses Universitaire de France, 1968), 80. Translations from this text and *Qu'est-ce que la philosophie?* are my own; all others are from the translations cited below.

3. Ibid., 58. See 52–61 for a discussion of Scotus and Spinoza on the univocity of being. Cf., on Spinoza, Gilles Deleuze, *Expressionism in Philosophy: Spinoza,* trans. Martin Joughin (New York: Zone Books, 1990), esp. chap. 3.

4. To claim that this is a deconstruction is not to embrace the wider claims I rejected in Chapter 2. Recall that in that chapter my beef was not with specific instances of deconstruction but with the general lessons Derrida draws regarding language and philosophy on the basis of those specific instances.

expense of unity. He can commend to us a way of thinking that values difference and that allows him to engage in the multifarious experiments into thinking with difference that have been his legacy, without having to go beyond what he can reasonably allow himself with respect to claims about the metaphysical or ontological status of difference.

In that sense, and in contrast to the previous three chapters, my argument does not see itself as going to the heart of Deleuze's project. If the arguments I have adduced in the previous chapters regarding Nancy, Derrida, and Levinas are correct, then there is something fundamentally misguided in their philosophical positions (although, as I have pointed out along the way, this does not mean that they have not brought important philosophical issues to our attention). In Deleuze's case, the privileging of difference is a misguided path that can be eliminated from his thought generally—and perhaps even from the ontology in which it is embedded—without substantial change to many of his fundamental commitments.

The attempt to assess Deleuze's ontological claims about difference cannot proceed in a traditional philosophical fashion. We cannot merely ask ourselves what his claims are, and then proceed to evaluate them. This is because Deleuze's conception of what it is to do philosophy, and thus what it is to make a philosophical claim, are hardly straightforward. When it seems in his texts that Deleuze is making a claim about the way things are, most often he is not—and he does not take himself to be—telling us about the way things are. Instead, he is offering us a way of looking at things. Thus, in order to begin to assess the Deleuzian claims of difference, it is necessary to understand what it is to be a Deleuzian claim; that is, it is necessary to understand what Deleuze is doing when he does philosophy. I hope to show that Foucault's suggestive remark that *Anti-Oedipus* is "a book of ethics" is in fact a fitting epigraph for the entirety of Deleuze's corpus.[5]

Only when we have understood Deleuze's conception of philosophy can we proceed to inquire about the place of the concept of difference in Deleuze's work, and from there proceed to an understanding of the necessary chiasm of difference and unity that urges itself upon, although never definitively establishes itself within, Deleuze's texts. Here the touchstone is Spinoza, the thinker of unity most often referred to—and referred to as such—in Deleuze's articulation of his position regarding unity. Finally, we can show

5. Gilles Deleuze and Felix Guattari, *Anti-Oedipus: Capitalism and Schizophrenia*, trans. Mark Seem, Robert Hurley, and Helen Lane (New York: Viking Press, 1977; or. pub. 1972), xiii.

what Deleuze can and cannot claim for difference within his own work, and indicate briefly why the strictures we set upon it should not be deeply troubling for his project, but only for certain realizations of it.

For Deleuze, the project of philosophy is one of creating, arranging, and rearranging perspectives; it is, as he puts it, "the discipline that consists in *creating* concepts."[6] To engage in philosophy is to develop a perspective, by means of concepts, within which or by means of which a world begins to appear to us. Such has been Deleuze's position from his first extended text, his book on Hume, in which he writes: "[A] philosophical theory is an elaborately developed question, and nothing else; by itself and in itself, it is not the resolution to a problem, but the elaboration, *to the very end,* of the necessary implications of a formulated question. It shows us what things are, or what things should be, on the assumption that the question is good and rigorous."[7]

This tells us much about what Deleuze thinks philosophy is not, but less about what he thinks it is. Philosophy is not the attempt, as Quine would have it, "to limn the world"; it is not the discipline that tries to "get things right," in the sense that it offers an account of how things are that attempts to replace numerous other accounts. To conceive philosophy as a project of truth is, in Deleuze's view, to misconceive it. "Philosophy does not consist in knowledge, and it is not truth that inspires philosophy, but rather categories like the interesting, the remarkable, or the important that decide its success or failure."[8] Although he does not tell us why philosophy ought not to be concerned with truth, his positive articulation of philosophy's task leaves little doubt that the reason is ethical and political rather than metaphysical or epistemological.[9] It is not because there is no truth that philosophy ought not to be concerned with truth (and it is a superficial reading that finds Deleuze engaged in a self-defeating denial of truth); rather, it is because philosophy ought to be about something else: specifically, about creating concepts.

---

6. Gilles Deleuze and Felix Guattari, *Qu'est-ce que la philosophie?* (Paris: Les Editions de Minuit, 1991), 10.

7. Gilles Deleuze, *Empiricism and Subjectivity: An Essay on Hume's Theory of Human Nature,* trans. Constantin Boundas (New York: Columbia University Press, 1991; or. pub. 1953), 106.

8. *Qu'est-ce que la philosophie?* 80.

9. Recall the discussion of Nancy in which the question was whether to interpret his claims normatively, that is, ethically and politically, or ontologically, that is, metaphysically. Unlike Nancy, I think Deleuze, perhaps against his will sometimes, lends himself straightforwardly to a more normative interpretation of the status of his claims, particularly in light of his recent metaphilosophical reflections.

In Deleuze's recent collaboration with Felix Guattari on the nature of philosophy, he articulates three central and intertwined characteristics that concepts possess. First, a concept is defined by its intersections with other concepts, both in its field and in surrounding fields. This is an idea that Deleuze speaks of elsewhere when he writes that "philosophical theory is itself a practice, as much as its objects. . . . It is a practice of concepts, and it must be judged in the light of other practices with which it interferes."[10] Second, a concept is defined by the unity it articulates among its constituent parts. This is called by Deleuze and Guattari the "consistance" of the concept.[11] It occurs when heterogeneous elements are brought together into a whole that is at once distinct and inseparable from those composing elements. Last, a concept is "an intensive trait, an intensive arrangement that must be taken as neither general nor particular but as a pure and simple singularity."[12] By this, we must understand the concept as a productive force that reverberates across a conceptual field, creating effects as it passes through and by the elements and other concepts of that field.

A concept, then, is not a representation in any classical sense. Rather, it is a point in a field—or, to use Deleuze's term, on a "plane"—that is at once logical, political, and aesthetic. It is evaluated not by the degree of its truth or the accuracy of its reference, but by the effects it creates within and outside of the plane on which it finds itself. The concept, write Deleuze and Guattari, "does not have *reference*: it is autoreferential, it poses itself and its object at the same time that it is created."[13] Thus philosophy, as the creation of concepts, is to be conceived less as articulation or demonstration than as operation. Philosophy brings together new points on, or introduces new points onto, the planes with which it is involved, and by this means either rearranges a plane, articulates a new plane, or forces an intersection of that plane with others. To evaluate a philosophy, then, is to gauge its operation, to understand the effects that it introduces, rather than to assess its truth.

There is another part to philosophy's operation to which I shall return later but which must be introduced now. "Philosophy is a constructivism, and its constructivism possesses two complementary aspects that differ in nature: creating concepts and tracing a plane."[14] As Deleuze and Guattari

10. Gilles Deleuze, *Cinema 2: The Time-Image*, trans. Hugh Tomlinson and Robert Galeta (Minneapolis: University of Minnesota Press, 1989; or. pub. 1985), 280.

11. *Qu'est-ce que la philosophie?* 25.

12. Ibid.

13. Ibid., 27.

14. Ibid., 38.

note, the plane traced by the concepts that create it is not reducible to those concepts. Rather, the concepts outline a plane that must be conceived as an open whole (which is not to say a totality): a whole in the sense that there is a relatedness among the concepts that exist on or within it, open in the sense that those concepts do not exhaust the plane but leave room for development and retracing. Deleuze calls the planes that are traced by philosophy "planes of immanence," in order to indicate that there is no source beneath or beyond the plane that can be considered its hidden principle. Unlike traditional views of philosophy, then, Deleuze's view rejects all forms of transcendence as descriptions of the nature or goal of philosophical work. In fact, first among the illusions that characterize philosophy's account of itself is "the illusion of transcendence." [15]

An illustration of the plane of immanence is offered in Spinoza's philosophy of the univocity of being. "What is involved," Deleuze writes, "is the laying out of a *common plane of immanence* on which all minds, all bodies, and all individuals are situated." [16] Spinoza's concepts do not exhaust the plane of immanence of which they seek to be the principles; nevertheless, taken together they constitute its geometry. In fact, for Deleuze the famous "geometrical method" of the *Ethics* is nothing other than the geometry of a plane of immanence.

Deleuze's term "plane of immanence" is akin to the term "discursive practice" as I have been using it throughout this book. Both of them are unities of concepts tied to specific practices in which those concepts receive their meaning. In what follows, I intend the idea of a discursive practice to be substitutable for that of a plane of immanence. It should be noted, however, that there are two significant differences between planes of immanence and discursive practices. The first difference is that, since planes are constituted by concepts, they are also constituted by the subtending differences that themselves constitute concepts. I argue below that the idea of a constitutive subtending difference, whether it be called "difference-in-itself," "singularities," or whatever, is incoherent and should be dropped. This difference, then, is one I hope to cancel out.

The second difference, which banks on the first one, appears in *Qu'est-ce que la philosophie?* In that work Deleuze and Guattari suggest that philosophy, which is the practice of creating concepts on planes of immanence, dif-

15. *Qu'est-ce que la philosophie?* 50.

16. Gilles Deleuze, *Spinoza: Practical Philosophy,* trans. Robert Hurley (San Francisco: City Lights Books, 1988; or. pub. 1981), 122.

fers from science in that the former does not refer, while the latter does. We can ignore the complexities of their discussion of science and concentrate on the reason that philosophical concepts do not refer. The concept "does not have *reference:* it is autoreferential, it poses itself and its object at the same time that it is created." [17] The reason for this is that concepts are "intensive," defined by the intensive qualities that compose them rather than by any extension. Extensional definition is referential, while intensive definition is not.

I have already noted that intensive qualities are singularities for Deleuze. They have nothing to do with the notion of intension that Anglo-American philosophers discuss, but are instead the subtending differences that constitute concepts. Thus, if the idea of subtending differences is incoherent, then the idea of contrasting philosophical concepts with scientific ones by means of an intensive/extensional or differential/referential distinction will not work. There is no bar to calling philosophical practice referential, while not denying that it is also creative. (I will not defend the idea that it is referential here, since that would involve a discussion of reference that is wide of my concerns. My point here is simply that we can think of philosophical and scientific practices as not being divided along this deep line that Deleuze wants to draw.) With that recognition, then the second difference between planes of immanence and discursive practices also falls away. If the argument against subtending differences is correct, then planes of immanence, when thought coherently, just are discursive practices.

Given this reading of the philosophical project, Deleuze's claim that it is a "practice," and in a sense very close to that I proposed in Chapter 1, becomes clear. Philosophy is a practice whose operations are to be evaluated by the effects that they give rise to. Thus we can see both that there is a place for truth in philosophy—although it is a secondary, derivative place—and that the primary task of philosophy is normative. The place of truth on this reading lies in the assessment of effects. If a philosophy is to be evaluated on the basis of its effects, there must be some truth to the matter of what those effects are.[18]

17. *Qu'est-ce que la philosophie?* 27.
18. Moreover, if we embrace a deflationist account of truth of the kind discussed in Chapter 2, then we need not posit a correspondence relationship between true claims and a world that transcends them. This is not to deny that some true claims must be true *of the world*, but rather to claim that truth can appear in many ways, which may depend upon many different discursive practices. In this way, the deflationist account, in addition to its other merits, can be marshaled in support of the principle of respect for differences articulated in the last chapter and is surely a motivation for Deleuze's own metaphysical reflections.

This does not mean that there is an objective factuality outside of all planes of discourse that dictates what claims those planes must make; what some analytic philosophers call "realism" is not a commitment of this approach. Rather, what this approach says, anecdotally, is that if two people are to agree on an evaluation, they must also agree on what effects a philosophy has had, that is, on what has happened as a result of the concepts it has created. In order to do that, they have to have recourse to a discursive practice in which an assessment can be made—one that, to all inspection and by the lights of that practice, appears to be a true assessment—as to what those effects are.

This assessment, however, is only a means to the end of evaluating a philosophical practice. As Deleuze and Guattari note, all such evaluation must itself be immanent in some sense: "We do not have the least reason to think that the modes of existence need transcendental values that would compare, select, and decide which among them is 'better' than another. On the contrary, there are only immanent criteria, and one possibility of life is valued in itself by the movements it traces and the intensities it creates on a plane of immanence." [19] This sense of immanence that Deleuze seeks for evaluation, however, remains ambiguous between two possibilities. The rejection of transcendental values can either be read as a rejection of all evaluation outside the specific plane of immanence on which the concepts are being created, or it can be read as a rejection of the idea that ethical evaluation is anchored in a moral reality divorced from all planes of immanence. The first rejection is wholesale; it denies the possibility that the concepts on a plane of immanence can be brought to bear in an evaluation of the concepts on another plane. The second rejection is more limited. It allows for cross-plane (or, in terms I used earlier, cross-discursive-practice) evaluation, and rejects only the idea that beyond all planes there is a transcendent moral reality that dictates truth to those planes.

It is important, although I believe unpalatable to Deleuze, that the rejection be of the second sort, that is, a more limited rejection. To reject the possibility of the evaluation of a philosophy outside of the plane it traces is to lapse into an aestheticism that allows for the possibility of a barbaric set of philosophical commitments that cannot be called such, because to do so would constitute an evaluation lying outside the plane of immanence on which those concepts are traced. To see how, let us recall the examples, adduced in the last chapter, regarding the limits of the principle of respect for

19. *Qu'est-ce que la philosophie?* 72.

differences. Suppose, for instance, that a culture had a practice of watching babies burn when they crawled into a fire. Not only would they watch them, they could offer an entire aesthetic evaluation of the burning process—quality of wailing, skin burn time, and so forth.[20] Now, if the concepts along one plane of immanence cannot be marshaled to criticize those along another, then moral criticism of this practice would be barred.

Moreover, and closer to Deleuze's concerns, the introduction of certain planes of immanence to counter the effects of others presupposes that some critical claims can be made on behalf of the former against the latter. If, for instance, the practice and claims of psychoanalysis cannot be criticized and schizoanalysis offered as an alternative, on the basis of concepts deriving from a plane of immanence exterior to that from which the concepts of psychoanalysis derive—a plane that contains more normative and political concepts than the psychoanalytic plane—then what is the point of such major works as *Anti-Oedipus*? Deleuze—and this goes for Foucault as well—counts on appealing, if not overtly then at least tacitly, to normative and political planes of immanence in his critique of oppressive discourses and indeed in the very idea of philosophy as a construction of concepts.

Although the more global rejection is barred to Deleuze, it is both coherent and plausible to claim that the very concept of barbarism does not lie outside all planes of immanence, that it lies on its own plane of immanence, without which we would be able neither to understand nor to use it. This latter possibility, a more or less anti-Platonic and nonfoundationalist one, although far more modest in scope, seems both necessary and undamaging for Deleuze's approach to philosophical evaluation. It is precisely this possibility for which I tried to provide the framework in the previous chapter.

That Deleuze himself is ambivalent between these two possibilities for rejection can be glimpsed by looking at his concept of "life." When he writes, for instance, that "[t]here is, then, a philosophy of 'life' in Spinoza; it consists precisely in denouncing all that separates us from life, all these transcendent values that are turned against life, these values that are tied to the conditions and illusions of consciousness"[21]—he uses the concept of life

---

20. Although such an example might seem repulsive to our sensibilities, I suspect it is not repulsive enough, as anyone who watched the citizenry, media, and political leaders react to the wholesale slaughter of Iraqi civilians in the Persian Gulf War can attest.

21. *Spinoza: Practical Philosophy*, 26. Cf. the continuation of the quote cited in the note 19 above: "A mode of existence is good or bad, noble or vulgar, full or empty, independent of the Good and the Evil, and of all transcendent values: there is never any other criteria than the tenor of existence, the intensification of life" (*Qu'est-ce que la philosophie?* 72).

both as a term, albeit nascent, within Spinoza's philosophy, through which it affirms itself, and as a value by which the entire philosophy is judged. It is both a term on the plane of immanence of Spinozist discourse and a term on the plane of the philosopher evaluating Spinozist discourse. The concept of life, then, is for Deleuze always partially transcendent to the plane to which it is being applied, although this does not mean that it is transcendent to all planes, but instead that it is irreducible to the plane of application. Thus, when Deleuze claims that, for Spinoza, "[e]thics, which is to say a typology of immanent modes of existence, replaces Morality, which always refers existence to transcendent values,"[22] we must understand the term "immanent" as referring broadly to all planes of discourse and "transcendent" as referring outside of all planes of discourse.[23]

Such a move—and I believe this may be what Deleuze dislikes about it so much—privileges normative planes in relation to other planes by making them the axes around which evaluation revolves. This, however, is precisely the Deleuzian view of philosophy, which sees philosophy as a creation rather than a reflection, and theory as a practice rather than a pure speculation.[24] If his concept of life brings evaluation closer to the planes that are being evaluated, it does not dispense altogether with a move outside those planes, as indeed it cannot without being endorsing many values that Deleuze's phi-

22. *Spinoza: Practical Philosophy*, 22. See also *Expressionism in Philosophy*, where he says of the *Ethics* that "*[a] method of explanation by immanent modes of existence* thus replaces the recourse to transcendent values. The question is in each case: Does, say, this feeling, increase our power of action or not? Does it help us come into full possession of that power?" (269). This assessment fails to address the question of which powers are to be increased and which diminished, a question that he answers by means of the concept of life.

23. This discussion has avoided the question whether we ought to consider Deleuze as holding that there is more than one plane of immanence at a given time. There is a tension in his thought around this question; for instance, in the Spinoza texts I discuss below, he seems to identify the univocity of being with the plane of immanence. However, in some later discussions, for example, *Qu'est-ce que la philosophie?* he seems to believe that there can be many at the same time. The truth may be, as he indicates on pages 51–52 of *Qu'est-ce que la philosophie?* that the answer is a matter of interpretation. In any case, nothing in the current discussion hinges on it; ethical evaluation can be another plane, or in another place on the same plane. Its importance remains central.

24. It is not entirely clear that Deleuze would always ratify the distinction that has been drawn here between the ethical and the metaphysical. In fact, in some of his passages regarding naturalism, it seems that his philosophy moves toward an effacing of this distinction. However, both the drift of his philosophy, especially in his last collaboration with Felix Guattari, and the incoherence of the alternative render this the most fruitful way to interpret Deleuze's conception of the philosophical project. The incoherence would devolve upon the attempt to engage in a metaphysics that posits a realm inaccessible to thought and proceeds to tell us what it is like.

losophy has ceaselessly struggled against. All of this, however, is not meant to claim that nonnormative planes are reducible in any sense to normative ones (a point whose importance becomes clear below), but rather to insist on the general importance of normative planes in Deleuze's view of philosophical practice.

Philosophy, then, is for Deleuze a project of creation, of bringing into being concepts that define new perspectives. It is primarily a normative endeavor, a discipline whose effects are to be judged normatively.[25] And it is within this context that we need to assess the role of Deleuze's concept of difference and the claims made for it in his work.

Deleuze, of course, privileges difference. The claims he makes on its behalf are both ethical and metaphysical, and in most cases the ethical and the metaphysical claims are entwined. Throughout his philosophy, he has tried to yoke a metaphysics of difference with an ethics of experimenting with difference, in a way that can leave one uncertain where the metaphysical claims leave off and the ethical ones begin. In *Différence et répetition,* for example, Deleuze claims that "[i]n its essence, difference is object of affirmation, affirmation itself. In its essence, affirmation is itself difference."[26] Here the nature of affirmation and difference is indistinguishable from their evaluation. One wants to ask here, is Deleuze claiming that we ought to affirm difference because that is what difference is—it is affirmation? Assuming we could make sense of this claim, it would seem to run perilously close to some sort of naturalist fallacy. On the other hand, is Deleuze simply claiming that when we affirm, we are always affirming difference? If so, then the normative force that Deleuze would seem to want for this claim is lost.

In fact, Deleuze is making neither of these claims. When Deleuze privileges difference, he is engaging in the practice he calls philosophy. He is creating a concept he hopes will help shape a perspective from which we see things in a new way. His metaphysical claims are not claims about the way things are; rather, they are the structure of a new perspective. And his ethical claims—which are indeed ethical claims—are the articulation of a framework for thinking about other practices when one has taken up the perspective created by the concepts of a given metaphysics. What we must ask,

---

25. Thus his focus upon values and evaluation in his text on Nietzsche: "Nietzsche's most general project is the introduction of the concepts of sense and value into philosophy" (Gilles Deleuze, *Nietzsche and Philosophy,* trans. Hugh Tomlinson [New York: Columbia University Press, 1983; or. pub. 1962], 1).

26. *Différence et répetition,* 74.

then, regarding the concept of difference, is not whether difference indeed does possess some sort of metaphysical priority, but how such a concept is meant to function, what effects it is designed to have. Concepts are like texts, we must treat them thus: "We will never ask what a book means, as a signi-fied or a signifier; we will not look for anything to understand in it. We will ask what it functions with, in connection with what other things it does or does not transmit intensities, in which other multiplicities its own are in-serted and metamorphosed, and with what bodies without organs it makes its own converge." [27]

The function of the concept of difference is at once to attack the unifying forces that have abounded in philosophical discourse and to substitute for such forces a new perspective by means of which one can continue to think philosophically. "It is necessary that a system be constituted on the basis of two or three series, each series being identified by the differences between the terms that compose it." [28] Systems should not be thought of as unities, but rather as compositions of series, each of which is itself defined on the basis of difference. Such differences, at the level of compositions of series, Deleuze calls "singularities." Thus, as Deleuze writes in *The Logic of Sense,* if we are to consider meaning as a product of sense (and whether we should do so Deleuze calls "an economic or strategic question"),[29] and if sense is composed by the two heterogeneous series of words and things, then words and things are composed of prepersonal, preindividual singularities: "What is neither individual nor personal are, on the contrary, emissions of singu-larities insofar as they occur on an unconscious surface and possess a mo-bile, immanent principle of auto-unification through a *nomadic distribu-tion,* radically distinct from fixed and sedentary distributions as conditions of the syntheses of consciousness. Singularities are the true transcendental events, and Ferlinghetti calls them 'the fourth person singular.'" [30] Thus De-leuze asks us to think of difference as constitutive all the way down, and of unity as a product of the play of difference.

But if difference is to be thought of as constitutive, this is in order to rid philosophy not of unities, but of unifying forces or principles that either pre-clude difference or relegate it to a negative phenomenon. After all, Deleuze

27. Gilles Deleuze and Felix Guattari, *A Thousand Plateaus: Capitalism and Schizophrenia,* trans. Brian Massumi (Minneapolis: University of Minnesota Press, 1987; or. pub. 1980), 4.

28. *Différence et répetition,* 154.

29. Gilles Deleuze, *The Logic of Sense* (New York: Columbia University Press, 1990; or. pub. 1969), 17.

30. Ibid., 102–3.

sees philosophical discourse, and indeed all discourse, as a process of *both* de-territorializing and re-territorializing, that is, as a process of both destroying previous thought and practices and generating new thought and practices. Therefore, it is not the fact of unities that fossilizes the creation of concepts, but the necessity that attaches to unifying principles, principles that dictate a necessary structure of concepts or an unsurpassable perspective. In this sense—as well as that in which difference is considered as a positive rather than the negativity of an absence—Deleuze's notion of difference is distinct from Derrida's notion of *differance*. The latter involves an inevitable play of presence and absence, a specific economy of the two that, although issuing in any number of philosophical possibilities, nevertheless governs them with a certain type of logic necessary to all discourse. Deleuze grants both that the intersection of different series may determine a specific structure and that neither the structure nor the intersecting series that produced it is subject to alteration by a being in virtue of that being's possessing a "free will." None of this implies, however, that there is a guiding principle that underlies structures and that would thus be a unifying force determining them. This is why Deleuze cites the Stoical distinction between destiny and necessity:[31] the former is subject to slippages of contingency of which the latter is incapable.

The concept of difference, then, is both positive and disruptive: positive in taking series (as well as singularities, desire, active forces, rhizomatic stems, etc.) as irreducible, contingent, constituting forces; disruptive in resisting all accounts of these constituting forces that would bring them under the sway of a unifying principle that would make them—or the phenomena they constitute—merely derivations from or reflections of one true world or source. These two characteristics converge on what may be called the essential, and essentially normative, role of the concept of difference: to resist transcendence in all of its forms.

As noted earlier, the "illusion of transcendence" is, for Deleuze, the primary philosophical illusion. That illusion consists in the idea that there is some unifying principle or small set of principles, outside the planes on which discourse and other practices take place, that gives them their order and their sense, and that the task of philosophy is to discover that principle or that set of principles. The history of philosophy is replete with such principles, from Forms to God to the cogito to language to *differance*. To recognize difference in its Deleuzian form is to reject the illusion of transcendence

31. Ibid., 6.

and to philosophize from the surfaces rather than from the depths or the height of transcendence. "The idea of positive distance belongs to topology and to the surface. It excludes all depth and all elevation, which would restore the negative and identity." [32] To think in terms of difference is to affirm surfaces, which can only occur when one ceases trying to take those surfaces as derivative from or secondary to something lying outside of them and begins to see them as the constitutions of series and the like that come to form them and that, in some sense, they are. And in this sense, the concept of difference is inextricable from the project of philosophy; for if philosophy is to remain a practice of creation, it cannot be bound to a transcendence that would stultify it. Philosophy is a practice of difference, which is at once an art of surfaces. "The philosopher is no longer the being of the caves, nor Plato's soul or bird, but rather the animal which is on a level with the surface—a tick or a louse." [33]

The question remains, however, of the relationship of surfaces to their constituting series, forces, desire, and so forth. If difference is taken as our sole guiding concept, then it seems difficult to understand how there could be planes or surfaces at all. By what principle or for what reason do we call one collocation of points a series, or one or several sets of series the articulation of a plane, if pure difference is our only guiding concept? On the other hand, how are surfaces to be introduced without their becoming a reduction of difference, without their becoming a new principle of transcendence? It would seem that any principle of unity that could be invoked to explain surfaces would have to be transcendent, at least to the difference it balances. It is at this level of questioning that Spinoza's thought of the univocity of being becomes crucial.

"The philosophy of immanence appears from all viewpoints as the theory of unitary Being, equal Being, common and univocal Being." [34] This claim, which applies equally to both Spinoza and Deleuze, must be understood if we are to see how a Deleuzian philosophy of surfaces and differences is to be coherent. What must be kept sight of is that Deleuze's concept of difference is essentially an antitranscendental one; he is trying to preserve the integrity of surfaces of difference from any reduction to a unifying principle lying outside all planes of immanence, a metadiscourse that would hold all other discursive practices under its sway.

The attraction of Spinoza for Deleuze lies precisely in the fact that, for Spinoza, there can be no transcendental principle of explanation precisely be-

32. Ibid., 173.
33. Ibid., 133.
34. *Expressionism in Philosophy*, 167.

cause there can be no transcendence. There is no outside from which a source (whether that source is a metaphysical one or merely an explanans)[35] could come to exercise sway. The philosophical problem Spinoza sets himself is one of developing a perspective within which the antitranscendental position can be coherently realized. For Deleuze, the central concept—concept in accordance with Deleuze's use of the term—is "expression." Expression is the relation among substance, attributes, essences, and modes that allows each to be conceived as distinct from, and yet part of, the others: "[T]he idea of expression accounts for the real activity of the participated, and for the possibility of participation. It is in the idea of expression that the new principle of immanence asserts itself. Expression appears as the unity of the multiple, as the complication of the multiple, and as the explication of the One."[36] Expression is Spinoza's concept, then, for characterizing the relationship among the traditional concepts of the philosophical discipline of his time. Although the term itself was introduced by Scotus, it achieves maturity only with Spinoza, for whom it is not merely a neutral description of being but at the same time revealing of being as an object of affirmation.[37] It is this concept that, by substituting itself for emanation and by displacing all forms of dualism, introduces into philosophy the antitranscendental notion of the univocity of being. "What is expressed has no existence outside its expressions; each expression is, as it were, the existence of what is expressed."[38]

The concept of expression comprises three related aspects: explication, involvement, and complication.[39] Explication is an evolution; attributes explicate substance in the sense of being evolutions of substance. By evolution, however, we must not understand a chronological development but rather a logical one. As Deleuze notes elsewhere in a discussion of the relationship of substance's production, "God in understanding his own essence produces an infinity of things, which result from it *as properties result from a definition*."[40] Attributes thus explicate substance; and in explicating it they necessarily involve it. Attributes, as logical rather than chronological evolutions

35. The difference here is immaterial because, as Spinoza notes throughout the *Ethics*, there is an indifference between being and being conceived. Cf., e.g., pt. 1, definitions 1–3 and 5.
36. *Expressionism in Philosophy*, 176.
37. For a brief history of the concept of the univocity of being, see *Différence et répetition*, 57–61. There, in fact, Deleuze cites Nietzsche as the crowning moment of the thought of the univocity of being, whose concept of the eternal return overcomes the problem that "the Spinozist substance appears to be independent of its modes, and the modes dependent on substance as if on another thing" (59)—in a word, a residual transcendence. Deleuze seems to have revised this assessment since then.
38. *Expressionism in Philosophy*, 42.
39. Cf. ibid., 15–16.
40. Ibid., 100.

of substance, involve substance roughly as the conclusion of a syllogism involves its premises. Given this relationship of evolution and involvement,
complication also follows. "Precisely because the two concepts are not opposed to one another, they imply a principle of synthesis: *complicatio*."[41]
There are distinctions to be drawn among the attributes of substance, and
those distinctions are real, but they are not numerical; the multiple is part
of—indeed, *is*—the one, as the one is part of the multiple.

Expression, then, is a concept that removes the possibility of transcendence from the philosophical field of Spinoza's time. Throughout all its expressions, being remains univocal. It must be seen at once, however, that
to be univocal is not to be identical: "The significance of Spinozism seems
to me this: it asserts immanence as a principle and frees expression from
any subordination to emanative or exemplary causality. *Expression itself
no longer emanates, no longer resembles anything.* And such a result can be
obtained only within a perspective of univocity."[42] What univocity implies
is not that everything is the same, or that there is a principle of the same underlying everything, but instead precisely the opposite. With univocity comes
difference, difference for the first time taken seriously in itself.

If there is nothing outside of the surface, if all there is, is surface, then what
characterizes the surface is inescapable, unsurpassable. There is no looking
elsewhere in order to discover or understand our world or our worlds.[43]
This thought, at once Spinozist and Nietzschean, returns us to the complexity and irreducibility that characterize surfaces, but does so with the affirmation that such complexity and such irreducibility are precisely *the characteristics of a surface*. Differences do not float ethereally as pure singularities,
in the manner that Deleuze would sometimes have it. In such a state they
would be nothing, not even differences. Deleuzian difference can arise as
such only in relationship to surfaces that are nontranscendable, only on the
basis of an ontological univocity. And it is in this way that difference can be
both posited and affirmed. It is posited as the result of a perspective—that
is, a creation of concepts—that denies transcendence and returns us to surfaces and their differences. It is affirmed because those surfaces and differ-

41. Ibid., 16.

42. Ibid., 180.

43. For a political development of this thought, see Antonio Negri's book—much admired
by Deleuze—*The Savage Anomaly: The Power of Spinoza's Metaphysics and Politics,* trans.
Michael Hardt (Minneapolis: University of Minnesota Press, 1991; or. pub. 1981). Although
Negri finds the crux of this thought in the third and fourth books of the *Ethics,* the development articulated here suggests that it is equally characteristic of the earlier books.

ences are no longer seen merely as derivative from or parasitical upon a unifying transcendent source or principle.[44]

Unity and difference, then, lie not at different levels, in good part because there are no different levels, some of Deleuze's claims to the contrary.[45] Such a recognition, however, although contrary to Deleuze's claims about the primacy of difference (as well as some of his resulting positions, as we shall see presently), is in keeping with Deleuze's view of the philosophical project as the normative endeavor of creating concepts. This is because the rejection of transcendence that motivates the contention that there are only surfaces still allows normative evaluation of those surfaces, determination of which concepts and planes ought to be promoted and which rejected. The normative evaluation itself arises from a certain plane, as was seen above; it does not arise from a transcendent space beyond all planes. Thus, thinking in terms of planes or surfaces, by rejecting the appeal to transcendence, encourages the recognition that those planes comprise created concepts, and underwrites reflective evaluation of those planes and their concepts as well as creation of new planes and concepts.

This position is also in keeping with the necessity of Deleuze's own philosophical creation. In order to develop the perspective that has been emerging here, Deleuze has had to create, not a number of distinct and unrelated philosophical concepts, but rather a surface composed of different but related concepts: concepts such as difference, expression, surface, and univocity. The perspective itself is at once the creation of concepts and the tracing of a plane of immanence that is distinct from the concepts populating that plane. The plane is the unity of different concepts, but not in the sense of being their product. Instead, it is a unity without which these concepts would not be the concepts they are; indeed, they would not be concepts at all. Alternatively, without the differential nature of the concepts, there would be no plane. At this level—and at all levels—a perspective is not the product of difference but the product coequally of unity and difference.

This dual necessity, the necessity of unity and difference in the formation

44. It should be noted that while Spinoza ties the univocity of being to a single plane of immanence—that of God—for Deleuze there can be many planes of immanence. Thus, while agreeing with Spinoza that it is all surface, Deleuze claims that there are many surfaces, although none of them are transcendentally anchored. Deleuze does not discuss this divergence from Spinoza, but it should be kept in mind in order to avoid confusing Spinoza's contribution to Deleuze's thought.

45. Technically, there are in fact different levels, or different planes, of immanence. These different planes, or levels, or discursive practices, interact with one another, but they do not found or transcend one another. What there are not, then, are subtending levels.

of any perspective, is the horizon within which Deleuze and Guattari's notion of the rhizome, discussed in Chapter 1, must be understood. The rhizome is testimony neither to pure difference nor to pure unity. The arboreal
perspective the authors eschew is the embodiment of the transcendental project of reduction to a unifying principle, but the rhizome is reducible neither
to some central point that forms its source or place of nourishment nor to
the stems that shoot out from it. The rhizome is a play of its stems' unity
and their difference, and it is only because of this play that it offers a view
of difference as positive, rather than negative, phenomenon. The rhizome, in
short, is the univocity of being, a univocity that, rightly understood, is the
affirmation neither of difference nor of unity, but of the surface that is the
intertwining of the two. In this sense, we must understand Deleuze himself
to be practicing the geometrical art inaugurated by Spinoza when he writes,
"Spinoza thinks that the definition of God as he gives it is a real definition.
By a proof of the reality of the definition must be understood a veritable
generation of the object defined. This is the sense of the first propositions of
the *Ethics: they are not hypothetical, but genetic.*"[46]

This necessity of Deleuze's thought means that we can no longer consider
him to be a thinker of difference, if by that we intend that he is a thinker
who privileges difference. Rather, we must come to consider Deleuze to be
a holist, in the Wittgensteinian sense.[47] By this, we mean that philosophical
perspectives, viewed in a Deleuzian fashion, must be considered neither as
realizations of a single driving principle by which our world can be explained
nor as a product of pure difference upon which unities are created as secondary phenomena. The antitranscendence path that Deleuze has trodden
requires him to reject the primacy of difference at the same moment that he
rejects the primacy of unity. As the latter reduces all difference to the tired

46. *Expressionism in Philosophy*, 79. We can see here the deep analogy between Spinoza's
geometrical art and inferentialism. They are both projects of defining discursive practices as
surfaces that are articulated by means of the connections of identity and difference among the
terms of that surface.

47. For Wittgensteinian holists—for example, Wilfrid Sellars, Robert Brandom, and at moments Richard Rorty—a linguistic or epistemic whole is characterized not by its closure but
rather by the fact that, for any element to have a meaning, there must be other elements to
which it refers. This does not imply that those elements form a closed totality. Rather, since
both language and knowledge are practices that are engaged with and by other practices, closure is impossible. This is the significance of Wittgenstein's claim that "the end [of epistemic
questioning] is not an ungrounded presupposition: it is an ungrounded way of acting" (*On
Certainty*, ed. G.E.M. Anscombe and G. H. von Wright, trans. Denis Paul and G.E.M.
Anscombe [New York: Harper & Row, 1969], 17e). For Wittgenstein's epistemic holism, see
On Certainty generally; his linguistic holism is contained in *Philosophical Investigations*.

repetition of a received pattern of discourse, the former renders all discourse impossible.

Deleuze, it seems, recognized this requirement on his thought in many places throughout his work. I have tried to show in Chapter 1 how a fundamental position of his can be interpreted along the lines of this requirement. However, he also wanted to circumvent it at crucial moments as well, in order to privilege difference. There is, then, at the core of his thought a tension he is never entirely able to move beyond. I want to turn in the next part of this chapter to that tension, in order to sketch out the limits of Deleuze's claims and to show where he falls prey to the temptation to surpass them. In doing so, I hope not only to call attention to certain, albeit local, failures in Deleuze's thought, but to deepen in a couple of spots the contingent holism that I have been articulating throughout this work.

There are three places in particular in Deleuze's thought where the tension between his recognition of the inseparability of unity and difference and his temptation to privilege difference raise questions that threaten the coherence of his thought. The first place is in his discussion of the idea of difference-in-itself, which appears primarily in *Différence et répetition* but whose underpinnings are worked out in several texts, most notably in his book on Bergson, entitled *Bergsonism*. The second place is in his critique of representation, which appears primarily in *The Logic of Sense* but is relied upon in many of the works of that period. The third—already briefly noted— is in his positing of singularities at the base of metaphysics. This third place appears throughout his work. I will address each of these in turn.

I have already referred to Deleuze's claim that Being is difference, and his related claim that behind everything lies difference and that behind difference lies nothing. The difference he is speaking of here is difference-in-itself. In order to understand both this claim about difference and the role difference-in-itself plays in his thought, I want to recall from an earlier discussion the dilemma with which I have confronted Deleuze. This dilemma, which I have argued precludes Deleuze from privileging difference, can be used here to force him (in absentia) to work out a number of concepts. So far as I know, Deleuze never explicitly confronts this dilemma; but it is surely there for him, and I think we can understand some of the moves he makes by starting from it. As we will see, the working out of these concepts does not save Deleuze from the dilemma, for much the same reasons I have been offering so far.

The dilemma, starkly put, is that it seems difficult to be committed both to the ontological privileging of difference-in-itself and to the denial of transcendence I have claimed as a central commitment of Deleuze's. The attempt to hold these two together, it can be argued, explains much of the complex conceptual apparatus Deleuze constructs during the period of *Différence et répetition* and *The Logic of Sense*.

Let me first motivate the dilemma specifically with reference to Being as difference-in-itself, and then explore its resolution. Traditionally, philosophy has located Being in a unity transcendent to experience. That unity has, of course, gone by different names. The One, God, and, of course, Being are examples of these unities. The problem with such views of Being is twofold. First, they denigrate concrete existence by allotting it a secondary, derivative status. Second, they tend toward reductionism, filing the edges off recalcitrant phenomena until they fit the categories appropriate to the privileged unity. This reductionism is both a philosophical betrayal of experience and a political invitation to totalitarianism. In place of Being as unity, then, Deleuze posits Being as difference. "Being is said in one and same sense of everything of which it is said, but that of which it is said differs: it is said of difference itself."[48]

If Being is in fact difference, this fact has eluded philosophers up until the moment of Deleuze's writings. In other words, in claiming that Being is difference, Deleuze is not giving utterance to a truism. He is making a controversial claim about the nature of Being, one that has gone unrecognized until now. (Let us bear in mind, however, that a Deleuzian ontological claim is normative rather than descriptive or explanatory.) Why has it gone so unrecognized? Because Being does not appear to us in the mode of difference. Rather, it appears to us in the mode of categories of the same, of unity. Indeed, the function of categories is to bring the disparate into a unity.

Thus, if Being is difference, it must be at least a difference transcendent to our current conscious experience. Moreover, inasmuch as our experience is categorically structured, it is transcendent to any direct experience we can have of it. At this moment, however, Being as difference threatens to go transcendent, to become a thing apart from our experience that structures it from the outside.

Now, the threat of transcendence is not damaging if Deleuze sees himself as offering a philosophy of the transcendent. However, as we have seen, he emphatically does not see himself as doing so. Deleuze sees all forms of transcendence, in good Nietzschean fashion, as at best misguided and at worst insidious. What transcendence brings—and it has been Deleuze's career to

48. *Différence et répetition*, 53.

struggle against this—is the devaluing of what is, by measuring it against a standard of what is not.

The idea that Deleuze abjures transcendence at all stages of his career, an idea I have argued motivates his entire philosophical project, may strike some as dubious, particularly when considering the period of writings in which *Différence et répetition* appeared. After all, did he not call his position of the time "transcendental empiricism"? While he did use this label, the transcendentality of transcendental empiricism is different from the concept of transcendence he criticizes. The only transcendence Deleuze seems committed to in his transcendental empiricism, if any, is some very weak form of transcendence to conscious experience. In an explicit denial of some deeper notion of transcendence, Deleuze writes, "In truth, empiricism becomes transcendental . . . when we apprehend directly in the sensible that which can only be sensed, the being *of* the sensible: difference, potential difference, and difference of intensity as the reason for diverse qualities."[49]

When Deleuze uses the term "transcendental," then, he is not referring to transcendence, but to something else. To see what else, recall that in Kant's transcendental idealism, transcendental refers not so much to transcendence as to conditions of possibility. What Kant seeks is to articulate the conditions of the possibility of experience, which necessitates (for him) the turn to consciousness. Deleuze's "transcendental empiricism" refers to conditions as well, but to what he calls "conditions of reality" rather than conditions of possibility. "We go beyond experience, toward the conditions of experience (but these are not, in the Kantian sense, the conditions of all possible experience: They are the conditions of real experience)."[50] (Going beyond experience here refers to a going beyond conscious experience, not a transcending of all experience.) For Deleuze, Being as difference provides the conditions of reality of all experience; and those conditions, as we shall see below, are immanent to reality.

Confusion may develop here for two reasons, the first being that the term "transcendental" seems to imply transcendence. I have indicated that it does not do so for Deleuze. The second reason is that "transcendental" may in fact refer to "transcendence" under some conditions. If the conditions of possibility or reality of experience were to be transcendent to experience— if, for instance, those conditions were to be found in a transcendent deity—

49. Ibid., 79–80.
50. Gilles Deleuze, *Bergsonism,* trans. Hugh Tomlinson and Barbara Habberjam. (New York: Zone Books, 1988; or. pub. 1966), 23. I am indebted to Patrick Hayden and Daniel Smith for helping me to get clear on the meaning of "transcendental empiricism" in Deleuze's work.

then the transcendental would also be transcendent. Again, Deleuze is not committed to transcendence in this sense. For him, transcendental empiricism refers to the conditions of reality, which themselves are immanent to reality.

For Deleuze, then, the task is to affirm Being as difference while denying himself access to any of the traditional transcendent approaches to Being. If Being as difference can be reconciled with immanence, then he needs to tell us a story about that reconciliation. And so he does.

The story he tells owes much to Henri Bergson's metaphysics of time. In Deleuze's study of Bergson, he notes that Bergson distinguishes two kinds of difference or multiplicity: "One is represented by space. . . . It is a multiplicity of exteriority, of simultaneity, of juxtaposition, of order, of quantitative differentiation, of *difference in degree;* it is a numerical multiplicity, *discontinuous and actual.* The other type of multiplicity appears in pure duration: It is an internal multiplicity of succession, of fusion, of organization, of heterogeneity, of qualitative discrimination, or of *difference in kind;* it is a *virtual and continuous* multiplicity that cannot be reduced to numbers." [51] This quotation ties together three themes that are of interest to us here: difference in kind, virtuality, and time.

When Deleuze speaks of Being as difference, or difference-in-itself, it is difference in kind, not difference in degree, to which he is referring. Difference in degree is a matter of distinctions among items that are fundamentally the same. Those differences are actual and susceptible of judgment. In another context, Deleuze writes that "judgment has precisely two essential functions, and only two: distribution, which it assures by the *division* of the concept, and hierarchization, which it assures by the *measure* of subjects. To the one corresponds the faculty of judgment that is called common sense; to the other, that which is called good sense (or first sense)." [52] Deleuze contrasts the difference that can be captured by good sense and common sense with difference-in-itself, difference in kind, which cannot be so captured, because it is not actual but virtual.

The distinction between the actual and the virtual is best approached through the distinction between the real and the possible, since Deleuze contrasts the two distinctions. The real is what is, what exists in the broadest sense of existing. (I will return to a narrower sense of existing below.) The possible is what does not exist, but might. The possible, then, is parasitical

51. Ibid., 38.
52. *Différence et répetition,* 50.

upon the real, in that the real provides the model for the possible. The possible is the real as it might be but is not.

For Deleuze, the virtual is rigorously distinguished from the possible. "The virtual is not opposed to the real but only to the actual. *The virtual possesses a full reality, insofar as it is virtual.*"[53] The virtual, then, has a place in the real; that place is, as we have seen, also the place of difference-in-itself, or what I will call in shorthand simply "difference." If the virtual—the mode of being of difference—can be conceived as real, not merely possible, then Deleuze can perhaps lay claim to having articulated Being as difference without having had recourse to transcendence in order to do so. Otherwise put, if the actual and the virtual are both part of the real, and if difference is virtual, then one need not step outside of reality in order to account for difference. Difference is immanent to reality.

Relying once again on Bergson, Deleuze articulates the distinction between the actual and the virtual to be a distinction between space and time, or, more exactly, between space as traditionally conceived and time as Bergson conceives it. "Everything is actual in a numerical multiplicity; everything is not 'realized,' but everything there is actual. . . . On the other hand, a non-numerical multiplicity by which duration or subjectivity is defined, plunges into another dimension, which is no longer spatial and is purely temporal: It moves from the virtual to its actualization."[54] For Bergson, of course, time has traditionally been conceived in a spatialized fashion; Bergson's contribution was to think time itself, not time as a succession of instants arrayed according to a spatial conception. For Deleuze, once we understand the Bergsonian conception of time, we will understand the reality of the virtual, and thus the immanence of difference.

In Bergson time exists as a thickness of which the present is an individual part, so that present is linked to past not merely externally but internally. The past, then, may be divided into two types of memory, one psychological and one ontological. Psychological memory is the conscious recollection of past events; it occurs when we reach back through time in order to locate an event. Now, when we locate an event in psychological memory, we do not merely isolate the event within the entirety of the past. An event that we remember is remembered within a double context: first, the context of the time in which the event took place; and second, the context of the entirety of our lived past, which forms the framework of both the memory and the remembering.

53. Ibid., 269.
54. *Bergsonism*, 43.

This larger framework implies that the past, for each individual, is the whole of the past. And moreover, each memory that occurs does so on the basis of this larger past, which forms the context within which psychological memory takes place. This larger past is ontological rather than psychological, since it concerns our constitution as temporal beings rather than our various psychological states. But there is more. For Bergson, this ontological memory is nonindividual. It is not that there are many different ontological memories corresponding to many different individuals. Rather, there is one memory, one past time, in which different people participate from different perspectives.

This last move is not difficult to see. Since the past in ontological memory is constituted not by any psychological process but rather by our ontological condition, there is no reason to reduce that memory to individuals. There is a past in which we participate and which constitutes who each of us is, but from a different perspective for each. Thus, there is only one time.[55] As Deleuze puts the point, "There is only one time (monism), although there is an infinity of actual fluxes (generalized pluralism), that necessarily participates in the same virtual whole (limited pluralism)."[56]

This ontological memory, or "pure recollection," exists in the mode of the virtual. "What Bergson calls 'pure recollection' has no psychological existence. This is why it is called *virtual*, inactive, and unconscious. . . . We must nevertheless be clear at this point that Bergson does not use the word 'unconscious' to denote a psychological reality outside consciousness, but to denote a nonpsychological reality—being as it is in itself."[57]

So far, we have implicated difference with the virtual and the virtual with time conceived as an ontological condition. To gain a full understanding of the work of the virtual, however, we must contrast it with the actual. And before we do that, we need to consider another characteristic of the ontological past: its conical form. Bergson argues that the past does not exist all in the same way, but rather in the mode of relative relaxation and contraction. More precisely put, the recent past carries with it all of the past, but in a more contracted state, while the distant past also carries with it all of the past, but in a more relaxed state. We can think of the difference this way. Between the more distant past and the recent past is a greater thickness of duration relative to the present. We do not want to think of this thickness of

55. Deleuze reads this idea of there only being one time as Bergson's rejoinder to Einstein's theory of the relativity of simultaneity. Cf. ibid., 81–86.
   56. Ibid., 82.
   57. Ibid., 55–56.

duration strictly as "more past," since that would be too spatialized a metaphor for Bergson's view; but it does capture something. In any case, if all of the past is contained at every point in the past, then the greater thickness of the more distant past allows the past to exist in a state of greater relaxation. Alternatively, the lesser thickness of the more recent past forces a greater contraction of the past. A bit crudely put: although the same amount of past has to fit into every part of the past, the more distant past has more room to fit it than the more recent past, so it exists in a less crowded state in the more distant past.

The image that Bergson uses in describing the nature of time is that of a cone, in which the present is the apex—point of greatest contraction—and the more distant the past, the more the cone expands toward its base. The image of the cone brings with it another characteristic of time to which Deleuze calls attention. The cone can be cross-sectioned, and in every section all of the past will exist in a state of greater or lesser contraction. But what is it that exists as past in greater or lesser contraction?

For Deleuze, it is difference: difference-in-itself or difference-in-kind. Deleuze does not provide an argument for this crucial move, but a broadly Deleuzian argument for it can be put forward. It cannot be identity that exists as past in greater or lesser contraction, because, if identity so existed, we would be forced to reintroduce a transcendence that he wants to reject. The reason is this: If what constitutes the being of the cross-sections of the past were identical, then all cross sections would be copies of the same model. In that sense, they would all be derivative. It would be as though there were a plan, model, or original of the past, of which all the sections of the past were so many mimetic instantiations. But if there were an original, and the sections were derived, then we would landed back in the kind of transcendence Deleuze abjures.

Recall that for Deleuze, transcendent (as opposed to transcendental) philosophy has two objectionable posits: an overarching unity and a removing of that unity from existence (broadly defined). If sections of the past were identical, they would exhibit that overarching unity Deleuze wants to avoid. And since every section of the past would be identical to every other, then it would be difficult to see any particular one as a model for the others. The model, then, would likely be found outside of the past in a transcendent unity.

The upshot of this argument is that difference constitutes the past, and that each section of the past contains all of difference at different levels of contraction. We are now prepared to distinguish the virtual from the actual.

Summarily, the past is virtual, while the present is actual. Putting it this way, however, requires clarification if it is not to be misunderstood.

We should note two points right off. First, the distinction between the present and the past is not the distinction between what is real and what is no longer real. The past is real—it is real as virtual rather than as actual. Second, the present, like each section of the past, contains all of the past, just in its most contracted state. *"While the past coexists with its own present, and while it coexists with itself on various levels of contraction, we must recognize that the present itself is only the most contracted level of the past."*[58] But if there are these deep affinities between past and present, what is the distinction? For Deleuze, the present is the actualization of the virtual; it is the bringing to presence of what exists in time.[59] That bringing to presence is fundamentally spatial. Thus, for Deleuze, space is linked to the present, and time to the past (but also to the past as contracted in the present). In that sense, we can experience directly what is actualized, but not what is virtual. And thus, to reaffirm what was said earlier, when Deleuze invokes the term "transcendental empiricism" to describe his work, the only sense of transcendence at work is transcendence to direct experience, not transcendence to reality.

There is, however, an ontological difference between the actual and the virtual. He marks this ontological difference by using the term "existence" when referring to what is actual, and "insistence" or "subsistence" when discussing the virtual.[60] This sense of existence as applying solely to the actual is existence in the narrow sense, as opposed to existence in the broad sense I have been using up until now to refer to what is real. If we construe existence narrowly, then Deleuze can be said to hold that the real comprises both existence and subsistence or insistence, that is, both the actual and the virtual. The actual contains both identities and differences of degree, while the virtual contains the differences in kind that form the ground of those identities and differences of degree. Being, then, is difference, difference-in-itself, which exists virtually in time and actually in space.

---

58. Ibid., 74.

59. When Deleuze distinguishes differenciation from differentiation in *Différence et répetition*, he is remarking the same distinction. "We call differentiation the determination of the virtual content of the idea; we call differenciation the actualization of this virtuality in kinds or species and in distinguished parts" (267).

60. For example, in *Cinema 2*, he writes of the cinematic time-image: "The virtual image (pure recollection) is not a psychological state or a consciousness: it exists outside of consciousness, in time, and we should have no more difficulty in admitting the virtual insistence of pure recollection in time than we do for the actual existence of non-perceived objects in space" (80).

Given this framework for Deleuze's conception of difference-in-itself, and in light of the previous discussion, the problems for seeing "difference without unity" as founding are manifest. Moreover, they appear in Deleuze's own discussion. The primary problem is that Deleuze posits unity at the point of positing difference-in-itself. In this case, the unity is that of time. The unity of time appears in two ways, both of which can be considered planes of immanence. The first way is in the unity of time as a whole, which constitutes an entire plane upon which difference is inscribed. The second way is in the cross sections of the cone of time. They, too, are planes of immanence. Difference exists (subsists, insists) *on* them, but each has its own unity. As in other cases of privileging difference, Deleuze here must construct his own thought in a way that, if he is to preserve immanence—to reject transcendence—forces him to invoke a concept of unity at every level of depth on which he invokes a concept of difference.

There is another question that may be put to Deleuze here. To pursue this question fully would take me far afield of my task, but it is worth calling attention to. In defending his claim that difference-in-itself is immanent to reality, Deleuze appeals to the concept of virtuality. He notes that virtuality, though real, has an ontological status different from that of actuality, a status he sometimes calls "subsistence" or "insistence." But he does little to clarity this different status. Such clarification is necessary to his project because on it hangs the question of what kind of immanence the virtual has. Merely to call it real is not very convincing, especially in light of the fact that the virtual is real in a very different way from the way the actual is real. And one cannot answer the question of these different realities merely by appeal to the difference between time and space, because it is the ontological status of time-as-virtual and space-as-actual that is in question. Without a clarification of the ontological status of the virtual, Deleuze runs the risk of offering, if the expression will be permitted, a distinction without a difference.

Now, one might want to defend Deleuze against this latter criticism by recalling the role of philosophy as that of creating concepts for normative ends. If the ontological privileging of difference is normatively justified, then what prohibits him from introducing the concept, even if it may strike one as a bit scholastic? This defense is questionable, however. The challenge I am proposing is that the concept of the virtual, or of subsistence or insistence, may be empty, particularly if we define concepts, as per Chapter 2, in terms of their inferential roles. If the virtual is introduced as an ontological concept but cannot be clarified ontologically, then it runs the risk of being a concept without meaning, which is no concept at all (not even a concept in the Deleuzian sense described at the outset of the chapter). And if the virtual cannot play the role of concept, then one must wonder what role it can play in saving Deleuze from the dilemma in which I have been situating his thought.[61]

Let me turn now, more briefly, to the latter two places in Deleuze's work where the tension between the recognition of the inseparability of unity and difference and the desire to privilege difference is great: the critique of representation and the positing of singularities. The critique of representation is bound to Deleuze's critique of resemblance and unifying principles. Representation is the practice in which the prejudices of the primacy of identity have become sedimented, where differences are either reduced, marginalized, or denied altogether. Moreover, in being the site upon which identity comes to dominate difference, it is as well the place where Nietzsche's "all the names of history" are frozen into a single one (itself called an "identity") and where the fluid and contingent nature of the philosophical project is forced to unify itself into a single and precise set of defensible claims oriented toward truth rather than remain a plane of concepts oriented toward creation. Thus the task of a philosophical project that would reassert the irreducibility of difference must also involve the subversion of the representationalist practice of language: "Representation allows the world of difference to escape. . . . infinite representation is inseparable from a law that renders it possible: the form of the concept as an identity-form, which sometimes constitutes the in-itself of representation (A is A), sometimes the for-itself of representation (I = I). The prefix 're-' in the word representation signifies this conceptual form of the identical that subordinates differences."[62] This subversion, although its effects appear throughout Deleuze's texts,[63] is performed in the most sustained fashion in *The Logic of Sense*.

The introduction of the concept of sense (an introduction that, as noted above, Deleuze made for reasons that are "economic or strategic" rather than epistemic) attempts to demonstrate that linguistic meaning is founded not

61. I do not want to suggest here that the concept of the virtual *cannot* be given clarification, just that it has not been given it by Deleuze, and I do not see how that clarification would run. Constantin Boundas, when faced with this criticism of the virtual, commented, "If the virtual is empty, then the DNA code that my cells carry with them is an empty verbiage." I am not sure where to take this suggestive remark, but it may point toward an answer to the worry I have raised.

62. *Différence et répetition*, 79.

63. Cf., e.g., *Anti-Oedipus* ("The whole of desiring-*production* is crushed, subjected to the requirements of *representation*, and to the dreary games of what is representative and represented in representation" [54]).

upon a representationalist relationship between words and the world, but rather upon a play of words and world that itself escapes representation. Sense "is exactly the boundary between propositions and things." It is thus incorporeal, escaping the possibility of being brought into representation by virtue of escaping the very categories of being upon which representation is founded. In fact, "we cannot say that sense exists, but rather that it inheres or subsists." Meaning is founded on this sense, this happening or event of sense, rather than upon any correspondence between words and the world. "What renders language possible is the event insofar as the event is confused neither with the proposition which expresses it, nor with the state of the one who pronounces it, nor with the state of affairs denoted by the proposition. . . . The event occurring in a state of affairs and the sense inhering in a proposition are the same entity."[64] Moreover, sense itself is founded on nonsense, which, as Deleuze notes, is not an absence of sense but rather a play of different series of singularities.

Such an analysis of sense reflects the tension in Deleuze's thought between a desire to give primacy to difference, here embodied in the event of sense, and a recognition of the inseparability of unity and difference as reflected in the effort to preserve unity—but as a second-order phenomenon composed of differences. Here, however, as elsewhere, where the primacy is given to difference, the thought becomes incoherent. When the identity of representationalist theories of language is rejected in favor of its opposite, difference embodied in the concept of sense, then discourse itself is abandoned. If meaning were merely the product of difference, there would be no meaning, but merely noises unrelated to each other. In order for meaning to occur, identity must exist within difference, or better, each must exist each within the other. To speak with Saussure, if language is a system of differences, it is not only difference but system as well; and system carries within it the thought of identity. Putting the matter baldly, a thought of pure difference is not a thought at all.

Deleuze's problem here is that he has cast the issue in terms of a binary opposition between the primacy of identity and that of difference. However, as the concept of the plane of immanence testifies, unity is not equivalent to a transcendent reducibility. Here the unity—that of linguistic identity—can occur on the plane of immanence, as long as the conception of language as a correspondence between words and world is abandoned. Such an abandonment, which is the abandonment of transcendence at the level of linguis-

64. *Logic of Sense*, 22, 21, 182.

tic meaning, does not imply the rejection of identity but rather a rejection of its subsumption under a principle of transcendence. The project of an account of meaning, then, would be to construct a narrative about meaning that relied neither upon a principle of identity nor upon the subversion of such a principle.

The account of linguistic meaning I sketched in Chapter 2 attempts to do just that. In particular, by jettisoning the idea that truth involves word-world relationships, it rejects the idea that the truth of a claim need be guaranteed by a certain type of connection that claim has to a language-transcendent reality. Now, some may worry here that an implication of this view is that it promotes the idea that there is no connection between language and the world, so that one can say just about anything and consider it to be true. I need to pause a bit to say why that is not the case. There is a rock and a hard place in this neighborhood, and I want at least to point a way between them. To do so is essential if the promotion of difference to which Deleuze is committed is to be preserved without a fall into epistemic arbitrariness.

On the one hand, the rock: if there is a transcendence that guarantees the truth of some discourse and the falsity of all others, then the Deleuzian philosophical project of creating concepts may come to be seen as misguided. This is because those planes of immanence, those discursive practices, that are not guaranteed by some metaphysical transcendence would come to be false. Now, falseness is no guarantee of misguidedness; as Nietzsche noted, it is an open question whether we should embrace truth as opposed to falsity. However, as I noted above, any evaluation of whether to do so will bank on the evaluation of consequences, which itself will bank on the truth of such an evaluation. Moreover, and at a more pedestrian level, many people are loath to embrace beliefs they think are false, and so the motivation for the creation of concepts and planes of immanence would become unappealing if we were to know in advance that those concepts and planes were false.

The hard place appears when one tries to steer too far clear of the rock. If, in rejecting transcendent guarantees, one allows that any discursive practice can generate truth, then there seems no constraint on the types of discourses that can be considered serious competitors for our epistemic assent. For example, there is nothing in that position that allows us to preclude the teaching of creationism—that is, the doctrine that species were created individually by God and did not evolve—alongside evolution in our biology classes. Although Deleuze champions difference, I suspect that it would be doing him no service to saddle him with a philosophical position that endorses the teaching of Christian fundamentalism in schools.

The trick, then, is to recognize epistemic constraints on belief without resorting to a transcendent guarantee that would endorse a particular discourse or small set of discourses and reject all others. Otherwise put, the trick is to embrace a nonfoundationalism that does not lapse into complete arbitrariness.

The position I have been articulating throughout this book does allow for such a recognition. There are indeed epistemic constraints on belief, and yet those constraints do not have the straitjacket effect that would undercut the Deleuzian project. Fundamentally, the constraints are three. The first involves intralinguistic justification. If the view presented in the previous chapters is correct, then when one endorses a claim, one is doing so within a particular discursive practice—a language game. That is, one commits oneself not only to an individual claim but to an entire discursive practice (which, as discussed in the last chapter, does not entail that one commit oneself to all the same claims as others engaged in that practice). Doing so, however, introduces constraints on what can and cannot be said. The constraints are those involving what can and cannot be justified within the inferential network of that discursive practice.

If, for instance, I claim that running roughshod over practices that differ from my own is morally permissible, I will be unable—if the argument of the previous chapter is right—to justify that claim within the discursive practice of morality. Thus I will not be justified in believing that claim. This does not mean, of course, that I am incapable of believing that claim. I am capable of doing lots of things that are unjustified. But the worry the hard place introduces is not a worry about what I am capable of believing, but about what I am justified in believing.

The second constraint on belief is interlinguistic rather than intralinguistic. It concerns what happens between discursive practices rather than within them. People, of course, do not commit themselves to just a single discursive practice any more than they hold to a single claim divorced from all linguistic practices. To recall Deleuze's terminology here, people operate along several planes of immanence. The relationship among those planes, or practices, is not one of founding, but of intersection. Above, I noted that moral planes intersect with other planes when one is evaluating those other planes for the moral acceptability of the effects of operating on them. That kind of intersection is common. To cite an example, biological questions about fetal brain function intersect with moral questions about the permissibility of abortion. In that case, what is going on along one plane acts as a constraint to what is going on—or to what can justifiably be said to be going on—along another.[65]

Recognizing this point also involves the recognition that, while people can endorse divergent discursive practices, a single person can justifiably be held to the criterion of consistency with regard to his or her specific choices of what practices to endorse. One cannot, for instance, justifiably endorse a discursive practice—or, alternatively put, operate on a plane of immanence—that commits one to beliefs that conflict with the commitments of another, competing discursive practice. (This in spite of the prattle about the hegemony of consistency that periodically surfaces in the nether regions of Continental thinking.) It is this constraint of interlinguistic fit that provides the answer to the question why, for instance, creationism ought not to be taught as a serious epistemic competitor to evolution. It is not that an integrally consistent creationism cannot be articulated; there seems no bar to that. Rather, it is that creationism is inconsistent with other discursive practices we embrace in microbiology, geology, archaeology, and physics. And if one argues that it is possible to reject all these discursive practices and become Christian fundamentalist across the board, then I cannot argue with that. I can only point out that if the practices of science are worth teaching to our children and worthy of our epistemic assent, then creationism is not.

The third constraint in one sense is, and in another sense is not, about the relation between language and the world. In order to make the point, let me say something and then, in a particular way, take it back. What I want to say is that the world constrains the formation of discursive practices of belief. In forming our discursive practices, particularly those that concern the structure of (parts of) the world, we bump up against reality. And that bumping prohibits us from forming certain kinds of beliefs, or at least certain systematic relationships among beliefs. If, for instance, I believe that I can walk through solid objects, like my front door, and if my other beliefs are more or less what they are (except for the revisions that need to be made to make them consistent with that one), then I am very likely to bump up against a reality recalcitrant to my beliefs. And in that way, the extralinguistic world is a constraint on my discursive practices.

Before I take back what needs to be taken back, let me emphasize that

65. This point is the same one I made, in another context, in my discussion of how works like those of Foucault can be brought to bear in asking how to evaluate the concepts used in one discursive practice by means of another.

such a constraint does not operate as the kind of transcendent guarantee Deleuze wants to balk at. This is because, as Quine points out in his famous article "Two Dogmas of Empiricism," beliefs face reality as a whole. If a particular belief faces a recalcitrant experience, there are many places in the whole—in the network of discursive practices a person endorses—where modification can occur. That modification must occur is the constraint the world imposes; but it cannot dictate where. Thus, there are many different possible networks of discursive practices that can face reality, as long as those practices are both internally and externally consistent. In that sense, extralinguistic reality constrains but does not found or guarantee particular discursive practices. The project of creating concepts and planes of immanence remains intact.

Now for the retraction. As I have put the point, it runs headlong into objections that both Derrideans and nonfoundationalists of the kind I described in Chapter 2 would raise. How can the relationship between language and what is outside of it be talked about? Does that not assume that one can get outside one's own linguistic practices in order to assess that outside? And would that not be to reintroduce, in a slightly different form, the foundationalism this entire book has been rejecting?

In some sense, the answer to these questions is yes. What needs to be pointed out, in order to secure the point I am trying to make, is that my talk about language-world relationships is happening *within* the context of a certain set of epistemic commitments. I am talking about what the world is like, or rather how it constrains language, not from above language but from within it. It is a commitment to a certain view of how language and reality interact from the point of view of certain discursive practices: practices that involve commitments about physics, biology, sociology, and so forth. Many discursive practices, we must recognize, are not talking about themselves but about the world. Inasmuch as we endorse those practices, we endorse whatever can justifiably be said about the world from within their inferential structure. Thus, it is not a leap outside of language or linguistic practice that underlies that discussion of the third constraint upon belief; rather, it is a taking seriously of the claims of certain linguistic practices. And that taking seriously involves no more than a taking to be true, in the sense of true outlined in Chapter 2.[66]

---

66. In defending the articulation of the third constraint in this way, I see myself as endorsing what Hilary Putnam defends under the rubric "internal realism" in his book *The Many Faces of Realism* (LaSalle, Ill.: Open Court, 1987).

As I have tried to emphasize in the course of discussing these three constraints, they are both holistic and, relatedly, tolerant with respect to different kinds of belief formation (or, otherwise put, conceptual creation of the kind Deleuze proposes). The first constraint is holistic because the internal consistency that it requires can be had in many ways; there is no one-to-one correspondence of concepts and the world that a transcendent guarantee of the kind Deleuze rejects would promise. There is no single arrangement of, for instance, moral discourse that guarantees consistency, and thus many ways moral discourse can be articulated.[67] (This is a reiteration of the point I made in a different context in the previous chapter.) Ditto for the second constraint; many different arrangements of discursive practices preserve consistency. Finally, as discussed, the language-world constraint is also holistic. There are many different ways of articulating how one is bumping up against things; world-bumping occurs in an epistemically nonauthoritarian manner.

This last discussion has been intended to bring out one of the virtues of the approach to discursive practices I have been promoting, specifically its ability to navigate between the Scylla of transcendence and the Charybdis of complete arbitrariness. I have tried to show how this virtue preserves what Deleuze wants in an analysis of language, without having to introduce the incoherent notion of "sense" that Deleuze resorts to. In the course of his discussion of meaning, however, another set of terms arises that constitutes a second tension of Deleuze's thought regarding unity and difference. These are terms that vary throughout Deleuze's corpus, but occupy similar roles in each case. The term used above is "singularities," but "haecceities"[68] and perhaps "constituents"[69] perform the same functions. For Deleuze, these concepts are invoked in order to name the primary differential components whose collocation traces a plane of immanence.

It is by means of these concepts, then, that the primacy of difference emerges in Deleuzian philosophy. These concepts, which are, strictly speaking, placeholders for what lie beneath all qualities, which compose them but do not themselves have qualities, are the positive differences that subtend all unities. For Deleuze, they exist—or, again, subsist—beneath language,

67. As the specific commitments within a discursive practice become increasingly fleshed out, this constraint becomes more restrictive. But this is not a problem, since the creation of concepts Deleuze proposes does not preclude the increasingly fine-grained development of a particular plane of immanence within which those concepts appear.

68. Cf., e.g., *A Thousand Plateaus*, 260–65, and *Dialogues*, trans. Hugh Tomlinson and Barabara Habberjam (New York: Columbia University Press, 1987; or. pub. 1977), 92–93.

69. This is the term—*composantes*—Deleuze uses in discussing the parts that make up a concept in *Qu'est-ce que la philosophie?* e.g., 25–26.

concepts, bodies, consciousness: in short, beneath all phenomena of experience. They are unexplained explainers, in that they must be brought into play if we are to offer an account of the world that gives primacy to difference, but precisely because there is a primacy of difference that lies beneath linguistic practice, they themselves escape all accounting.

It should be clear at this point that such a strategic move is bound to fail. To posit a concept whose function is to give primacy to difference is to violate the necessary chiasmic relationship between unity and difference. Such a positing betrays the univocity of being by merely inverting the picture of a philosophy that would give primacy to identity; in doing so it renders incomprehensible the concept of surfaces without which transcendence cannot coherently be denied. Only a philosophy that finds difference on the surface rather than in a source beneath or beyond it—even when that source eventually becomes the constitution of the surface—can articulate a role for difference that possesses both coherence and normative power. In allowing a place, often a constitutive place, for positive differences that are not themselves already differences of a surface, Deleuze allows his thought to lean exclusively on one half of the intertwining that is necessary in order to prevent his fragile project from collapsing.[70]

It may be asked, then, If Deleuze's metaphysical conceptualizations in this area are inadequate, how would the contingent holism I am proposing reconceptualize ontological difference more adequately? The short answer is that it would not reconceptualize it at all. The metaphysics—or perhaps a better word here is "ontology"—of contingent holism is austere. The question of what there is above and beyond the positings of specific discursive practices is, to a contingent holist, an impossible and perhaps even senseless question. The reason for this has to do with the nonfoundationalist character of the position I am proposing.

To ask for an ontology above and beyond the regional ontologies of specific discursive practices is to request a discursive practice that says either "Here are the commitments of all the specific discursive practices summed together" or "Regardless of what specific discursive practices say, here is the fundamental ontological character of the world." The first statement is impossible because of the holistic character of commitment to discursive

---

70. On the interpretation of Deleuze offered here, one might wonder what becomes of his notion of "intensities." Intensities should not be thought of as transcendent constitutive singularities, but as both produced and producing. Intensities arise when two or more planes of immanence come into contact, and often either force changes on those planes or become part of the site of a new emerging plane.

practices. As the second constraint upon epistemic belief discussed above indicates, beliefs in one area may conflict with beliefs in another, but that does not tell anyone which belief should be abandoned. It is open to the person whose beliefs are in question to choose which belief (or discursive practice that founds that belief) to abandon. Thus, there can be no "sum" of ontological commitments of discursive practices, because there are conflicting ontological commitments among (but, one hopes, not within) discursive practices.

This does not entail, of course, that for any one person there cannot be a sum of ontological commitments. Quite the contrary. Assuming someone's beliefs to be coherent, there is no reason to suspect that the sum of their ontological commitments cannot be given. For that person, the world comprises those things to which the discursive practices he or she endorses are committed to there being. In denying that there can be a sum of the ontological commitments of all discursive practices, one denies that the commitments of the sum total of discursive practices can fit neatly together into a seamless whole.

The second way to interpret the request for a general ontology, that it give us a view of what is, regardless of what specific discursive practices say there is, is the traditional project of metaphysics. It is the project that Derrida criticizes throughout his work, and rightfully so, since such a project is necessarily foundationalist. It is the attempt to discover, beneath or above all the specific discursive practices that articulate the world, the One True Discourse that will subsume all the others. To put it in Deleuzian terms, it is the illusion of transcendence at its most illusory. (It is ironic, then, that Deleuze, of all people, periodically posits something—difference—constitutive of planes of immanence.) I will not spend time here arguing against this project. I have recalled in Chapter 2 some of the arguments against it, and believe that I can safely say that the bulk of recent philosophical thought—both Continental and Anglo-American—can be read both as an assault on this project and as an attempt to conceive, in the wake of its demise, a new philosophical project.

By way of conclusion, let me reiterate that neither of the tensions I have treated in the last part of this chapter—Deleuze's semantic antirepresentationalism or his privileging of differential elements—is a necessary or inextricable aspect of his thought. What Deleuze's reliance on Spinoza—and, I believe, his equally important reliance on Bergson—demonstrate is a recognition (if at times a concealed one) that a thought of difference cannot give primacy to difference. The fact that Deleuze sees himself as creating concepts rather than offering metaphysical truth-claims does not exempt him from the problem of the primacy of difference, because the dilemma of such a primacy is that it either renders the thought incoherent or returns to the transcendence it sought to avoid. The Deleuze we must bear in mind when we read him is the rhizomatic Deleuze, the Spinozist Deleuze, the Deleuze of surfaces of difference, and not the Deleuze of singularities or haecceities. Any thought that takes difference seriously—and indeed we live in an age that desperately needs a thought that does so—cannot avoid the unity that attaches itself to the project of such thought.

Conclusion

From Difference to Holism

At the outset, I said that although the criticisms of the philosophers whose work I discuss here is intended to be conclusive, the program outlined by my positive rearticulations is not. I have said all that I have to say regarding the critical work in the previous chapters. Let me add a few final words on the positive rearticulations. That I could not, in a single volume, carry through a thoroughgoing positive rearticulation in any chapter should be obvious enough. In each of the areas I discuss—community, language, ethics, and ontology—there are volumes of substantive issues that connect with my remarks and that still need to be grappled with. There are three virtues I hope attach to my positive rearticulations. If any of these is lacking, then I have not done my job in rearticulating the phenomena addressed by Nancy, Derrida, Levinas, and Deleuze.

The first is a requirement on any philosophical thought: consistency. In the present case, the consistency has to run in two directions. There has to be consistency within the positive rearticulations and across them. Over the course of the previous chapters, I have tried to develop a philosophical view, and with it a program for research, that hangs together at least in the minimal sense that one can commit oneself to all parts of it without contradiction. Of course, lots of different and largely implausible philosophical positions can do that. On top of that minimal consistency, I have tried to sketch what might be called a consistent "picture" of philosophical work. The consistency of the picture may be a little more difficult to articulate, but it involves sketching the outlines of a philosophical vision that, while jettisoning the traditional philosophical program of foundationalism, remains philosophically viable. (For those who balk at my switch from picture to vision, let me refer them to Merleau-Ponty's pregnant remark about painting: "It is more accurate to say that I see according to it, or with it, than that I see it.")[1] I am hardly the first to embrace this vision. As I pointed out in my introductory remarks, it is embraced explicitly by many recent pragmatists and at least implicitly by Michel Foucault. What I hope this work adds to theirs is both a breadth of vision across many areas and an account of its applicability to recent French thought.

The second virtue the positive rearticulations need to possess lies somewhere between plausibility and compellingness. A breezy plausibility is not enough; I hope there is more here to motivate the general perspective than what might be offered in a few allusive epigraphs. Compellingness, however, would be too much to ask. Especially if what I have said is right, then there is much more to be worked out before the program can be compelling. Some parts of that program have been worked out. Especially in the area of language, Robert Brandom's *Making It Explicit* and Mark Lance and John Hawthorne's *Grammar of Norms*[2] not only do justice to the view offered here, but go much further than I could ever hope to. What I hope to have accomplished here, then, is the articulation of a view that, in addition to possessing internal consistency as a philosophical picture, points in promising directions for further work.

The third required virtue is that the rearticulations address the problems that have motivated the research programs I have rejected. I take it that the problems of totalitarianism, nonfoundationalism, and respect for the other are central to the perspectives that have helped define recent French thought. Moreover, I take it that my positive rearticulations have addressed those problems. If they have not, or if there are important problems that the rejected perspectives address that my own fails to address, then either the perspective I have articulated or one of the perspectives I have rejected needs to be revisited. Recent French philosophical work concerning difference, even

1. Maurice Merleau-Ponty, "Eye and Mind," in *The Primacy of Perception,* trans. James Edie (Evanston, Ill.: Northwestern University Press, 1964), 164.
2. Cambridge: Cambridge University Press, forthcoming.

when it has gone wrong, has nevertheless done so in ways that often merit further reflection. The point of my positive rearticulations has been to sketch the form such reflection ought to take. Thus, if my positive rearticulations—and the general perspective they delineate—can lay claim to offering a genuine alternative to the work of those philosophers I have rejected, they must capture the problems and the insights to which that work has called our attention.

The perspective defined by those positive rearticulations is broadly pragmatist, in the sense that it takes practices as the entry point for philosophical reflection. It is nonfoundationalist; it rejects absolutism in favor of a recognition of the contingency of the practices in which we are engaged. It is holist; it claims that one cannot commit to one part of a practice at a time, whether that part is semantic, ethical, or ontological. It is normative, recognizing the inevitable normativity of our reflections on community, language, and ontology (as well as the obvious normative practice, morality) and also the politically charged nature of our practices that Michel Foucault has pointed out. It is also philosophically modest, although in a way very different from the philosophical modesty of the French philosophers of difference discussed here. While the latter claimed modesty for philosophy on the basis of broadly transcendental arguments about the limits of philosophical (and other) theories, my perspective effaces any strict boundaries between philosophy and empirical research. Although, as I argued in Chapter 2, philosophy is more nearly conceptual than many sciences, both science and philosophy must have recourse to conceptual as well as empirical reflection and research. Philosophy loses some of its traditional pretensions to being the first science, because it stands alongside, rather than beneath, the sciences and other discursive practices. (It also stands within them, and they within it.)

Such a philosophical perspective points, I believe, toward a resolution of philosophical problems whose significance has been made manifest for us by recent French philosophy. It does so in a way that avoids the weaknesses of some of that philosophy. And it has the added benefit that it allows room for fruitful dialogue between Anglo-Americans and Continentalists in addressing those problems, since many of the positive rearticulations I construct here borrow from trends in both traditions.

The paths constructed for us by those whose work I have argued against must be abandoned in favor of better ones; the rejected paths lead us either into dead ends or culs-de-sac. Whether the path whose outlines I have traced will mark any progress depends not only on whether it meets the three virtues I have said it requires, but also on whether the future clearing of that path will bring us any closer to the places we want to go. (And, of course, whether we want to go there may be something we do not learn until we arrive.) Which makes this as good a place to close as any, since much of that clearing will have to be made by hands more capable than mine.

Index

Todd May is the author of three other books published by Penn State Press: *Between Genealogy and Epistemology: Psychology, Politics, and Knowledge in the Thought of Michel Foucault* (1993); *The Political Philosophy of Poststructuralist Anarchism* (1994); and *The Moral Theory of Poststructuralism* (1995).